MY CHINA YEARS

BY HELEN FOSTER SNOW

My China Years
Totemism, the *T'ao-t'ieh* and the Chinese Ritual Bronzes
The Chinese Communists: Sketches and Autobiographies
     of the Old Guard
Women in Modern China
Historical Notes on China
     The Beginnings of the Industrial Cooperatives in China
     The Chinese Student Movement, 1935–1936
     The Sian Incident, 1936
     My Yenan Notebooks
     Korea and the Life of Kim San
     The Left-Wing Painters and Modern Art in China
Red Dust
Fables and Parables
The Chinese Labor Movement
Song of Ariran
China Builds for Democracy, a Story of Cooperative Industry
Inside Red China

LOCAL HISTORY

The Land Beyond the Kuttawoo: The Madison Story
The Guilford Story, or Menuncatuck Plantation
The Saybrook Story
The History of Damariscove Island in Maine:
     With the First Englishmen in America

MY CHINA YEARS

A MEMOIR BY

Helen Foster Snow

William Morrow and Company, Inc.

New York   1984

Library of Congress Cataloging in Publication Data

Wales, Nym, 1907–
  My China years.

  Includes index.
  1. China—History—Republic, 1912–1949.   2. Communism
—China—History.   3. Wales, Nym, 1907–
I. Title.
DS774.W243   1984   951.04   83-13477
ISBN 0-688-00786-4

Printed in the United States of America

First Edition

1 2 3 4 5 6 7 8 9 10

BOOK DESIGN BY ANN GOLD

To

G. L. and Sheril Foster Bischoff

ACKNOWLEDGMENTS

My thanks go to the Hoover Institution at Stanford University in California, custodian of my files on the years I spent in China, a controversial period in the history of that great nation for which my historical notes constitute often the only contemporary written record; and to G. L. and Sheril Foster Bischoff of Costa Mesa, California, who handle my Literary Trust.

Most particularly, I am grateful to Betsy Boyd Cenedella, who undertook the difficult task of editing the manuscript of *My China Years*, and accomplished it expertly.

AUTHOR'S NOTE

This book, like my other books on China, uses the Wade-Giles system for spelling Chinese terms and places. Wade-Giles was in general use from the nineteenth century until 1979, when the Chinese government introduced a new system of romanization called *pinyin*, which is in process of being adopted in foreign countries. For example, my favorite province of Shensi (in Wade-Giles spelling) is spelled Shaanxi in *pinyin*, while the neighboring province of Shansi is spelled Shanxi. A key to *pinyin* will be found in the back of the book.

The dialogue in this volume is based on memory—mine was known as phenomenal until recently—and I jotted down many of these conversations years ago. I have also drawn on six volumes of notes culled from my 1930s files before I sent the Nym Wales Collection to the Hoover Institution at Stanford University, California (Nym Wales was my pen name). It has turned out that my historical collection is a unique source, even to the Chinese, for the details of various incidents and situations. If for no other reason, I'm glad I dragged those forty boxes halfway around the world.

CONTENTS

PART ONE: SHANGHAI

PART TWO: PEKING

MY CHINA YEARS

PART ONE

SHANGHAI

CHAPTER 1

Arrival in
Shanghai, 1931

As the S.S. *President Lincoln* steamed with empty buoyancy up the filthy Whangpoo River, twenty-one young Americans on deck leaned forward eagerly for the first glimpse of the skyline on the Shanghai bund—the river bank. The men wore starched white tropicals; an Annapolis lieutenant carried my golf bag, a Virginia cavalier (very starchy) my tennis racket.

It was August of 1931, three weeks from home, 5,065 miles away. I intended to stay at most one year. I did not leave Asia until December of 1940, glad to escape a year before Pearl Harbor.

Not one of us was a tourist. The twelve bound for Manila were all Army or Navy, mostly married couples. The six "BAT boys," under contract to the British-American Tobacco Company, were on their way to a place they dreaded named Ershilupu. Of the Shanghai arrivals, I was one of two women. Pat Murphey and I planned to share a hotel apartment while her husband was up the Yangtze River as lieutenant on a gunboat of the Yangtze Patrol.

No one on the passenger list had been in the East before. I was the only "expert" on China. Had I not read Pearl Buck's *The Good Earth*, which had just come out? And I was studying *China Yesterday and Today* by E. T. Williams. At home I had read a typed report written by J. B. Powell, lent me by an Old China Hand, telling of Powell's kidnaping from the Blue Express by bandits in 1923 along with over twenty others, including American women. I had also been trying, without success, to understand a big tome I had brought aboard ship entitled *Chinese Currency* by E. Kann. One of the jobs I had lined up in Shanghai, in addition to my primary post as clerk in the American Consulate General, was to report back to the Silver Lobby, as it was ungraciously called, on the advantages of using silver instead of gold as the currency standard.

In 1929, along with the Wall Street collapse, a sudden rise in the gold exchange and the depreciation of silver had all but ruined the silver-mining interests in the United States, and China's foreign colony was living like royalty on very little, due to the favorable rate of exchange. I had saved much of my high salary as assistant to the secretary of the American Mining Congress—spearhead of the Silver Lobby—so that I might travel abroad and write. I passed the foreign-service test for clerks and looked for an overseas diplomatic post where my Spanish, French, or Italian might be useful. The only strings I could pull were silver ones, and now, with the goodwill of the Silver Lobby's Senator Reed Smoot and some of my father's Stanford University fellow alumni who had been or knew some Old China Hands—like then President Herbert Hoover—I had arrived in the land of silver.

The third job I had lined up also had a tenuous connection to the economic situation. At home the Great Depression was reaching its depth, and the American Mail Line steamship company out of Seattle was almost bankrupt for want of tourists. Because of this, I had a string assignment with the Scripps-Canfield League of newspapers based in Seattle—but strictly for articles calculated to revive the dead tourist trade to the "golden, glamorous Orient."

As we entered the fifth busiest port in the world, our living standards were about to be raised many times. With every American dollar worth four to five Chinese dollars, we were joining the 3,808 other Americans in Shanghai, among a total of some 7,000 throughout China, all living in princely style as the rest of the world was being "crucified upon a cross of gold." I was self-confident and eager to learn, but eventually I had to give up trying to master the currency intricacies. (And I never did quite accept the idea that the Great Depression was largely caused by the gold standard.)

Never again would the foreign-owned Shanghai bund glitter with prosperity as it did in those five prime months before Japan attacked the Chinese part of the city in 1932. The tallest building on the bund had just been completed by the British-Arabian Sassoons, who were moving capital into Shanghai. This was the Cathay Hotel, where rich big-business taipans entertained each other in rented suites going begging for want of tourist trade.

It was the heyday of the Whangpoo harbor, with naval and merchant ships anchored majestically among the lowly batwinged junks and rocking sampans. The Union Jack predominated, Japanese and American flags dipping respectfully in the sultry calm. As the S.S.

President Lincoln passed, we waved to every ship. Even the dour, clean Japanese waved back, though they always seemed to reserve one hand for hanging up the laundry on deck.

Along the miles of wharves and godowns, nearly all cargo was handled by human labor, and every laborer was a Chinese. No non-Chinese, then or since, was allowed to take a job away from a Chinese, except for a very few jobs of noncompetitive type and nonmanual labor. (No missionary ever took one copper away from any kind of Chinese; all mission salaries and expenses were paid from home, or they would not have been allowed to stay in China at all.) The waterfront was controlled by gangster *pongs*. No one trifled with them, not even the Japanese.

There had been a time in the first half of the nineteenth century when Americans dominated the trade in the East, chiefly by way of Russell & Company of Connecticut, founded in 1818. Along the warehouse side of the Shanghai bund for several blocks their ancient red brick godowns still stood, built like—and as—fortresses. Part of the American tradition was even older: The first American ship to China was sent on George Washington's birthday in 1784.

On the S.S. *President Lincoln* we felt ourselves part of this old tradition. I stood in the prow, facing the future like the figurehead on an old clipper ship, bursting with health and ambition. Getting to China had been a federal case for me, and I meant to make the most of it, not to waste one minute. My foot was on the rail, ready to step out on the soil of China as soon as the tender drew up to the jetty.

Though we had all been warned that foreigners had to travel first-class for "face"—and had accordingly paid $500 for our first-class steamship tickets—it was in the American tradition to go not to the expensive new Cathay Hotel, but to the ancient Astor House. Built by an American clipper-ship captain and ship's carpenters, the Astor had once been the finest hostel in the East. I prevailed on our whole group to register in a body.

How did I know about the Astor House? It was the seat of a dynasty in journalism, that of the three exports of the University of Missouri School of Journalism, the Millard-Powell-Snow succession. I had letters of introduction from my father's Stanford alumni friends to Thomas F. Millard, dean of all newspapermen in the East, who had lived there after arriving in 1900 to cover the Boxer Rebellion for the *New York Herald,* and to his protégé J. B. Powell, who had taken up quarters there in 1917 when he was sent for by Millard to help found the *China Weekly Review*, the most influential American publication in the Far East. (I was taken on immediately as a book reviewer for the *Review*—job number four—and was later its Peking correspondent.)

I did not have a letter to their protégé Edgar Snow, who had arrived at the Astor House in 1928 to become assistant editor at the age of twenty-two. But I had a folder labeled with his name, full of his articles, including some I had clipped from the *New York Herald Tribune Magazine*. One of my duties for the American Mining Congress had been to clip pertinent material from that newspaper, and as I had sat at my desk with scissors at the ready, I had thought, *Why can't I travel and write articles like that?* I even imagined (how wrong I was!) that the feminist owner, Mrs. Ogden Reid, and the feminist editor, Mrs. William Brown Meloney, might prefer articles by a woman to those of Edgar Snow.

The Astor House was within walking distance of the landing place, but we were advised to take rickshas anyway. We thought we were being attacked by a mob—they turned out to be competing rickshamen—and then had to thread our way through filthy, ragged beggars in all stages of disease. The agent from the American Mail Line steamship company, who met the ship, stood up in his ricksha and waved back to us. "Nobody dares hurt a foreigner in China now," he called. "It just looks dangerous. Don't pay any attention to them."

In front of the Astor House our twenty-odd rickshas stopped on both sides of the narrow street and we got out, paying ransomlike *cumsha* tips, as all new arrivals did, glad to be put down in a safe harbor. We were in the bend of the river, and on the embankment just opposite the Astor House was a massive, fortresslike old building with palatial window trim. As my rickshaman let me off by its heavy door, I shuddered a little at the desolate, empty-looking place.

"What is this spooky building?" I wanted to know.

"It's the old Czarist consulate," I was told. "We had a little gunfire here three years ago." Apparently, the Soviet consul had barricaded his staff inside, and 150 former Cossack officers in Czarist uniform tried to seize the building. They wanted to set up their own émigré government-in-exile in Shanghai. The police did not interfere, but the Soviets fired through the door and the Cossacks marched away. That may have been the last act in the civil war. In Canton some of the Soviet consular people were murdered by Nationalist Chinese in 1927. Diplomatic relations were, of course, broken off. (When I returned to Shanghai in 1973, more than thirty years since I had left it, I found both the American and Soviet buildings looking older but no wiser. The hotel was used for overseas Chinese. The consulate was boarded up. Neither nation had a consulate in Shanghai, and the Soviets had placed a million hostile troops on the northern Chinese border.)

In the Astor House lobby we were not kept waiting to register. Each of us had a white-coated, obsequious, smiling roomboy as escort to our rooms, where they took up posts in the corridor, alert to our slightest wish.

Just a brief ricksha ride from the jetty had raised all of us from the ranks of the common people into a mandarin-Brahmin caste, nobility with the dollar sign on our foreheads, in a strange land of cheap coolie labor.

I well remember the moment I caught the treaty-port mystique. I stood in the middle of my big, lofty room (costing about U.S. $2 a day with food) and sniffed the dampish, gray-mildewed mosquito net covering the whole of the huge Victorian four-poster bed. Then I struggled to open a few heavy mahogany or teakwood bureau drawers. They were lined with camphorwood or sandalwood, some with cassia wood, and their perfume mingled with the musty air. Whenever I chance upon that scent, I feel nostalgic for the East. Some of my old papers and manuscripts still smell of storage in camphorwood.

When I read *Anna and the King of Siam*, I wept with nostalgia and lighted some sandalwood incense. Anna Leonowens had arrived to take a job in the East about fifty years before I did, but I identified with her comic-opera confrontations and culture shock. As I write this manuscript, with sandalwood burning, it seems unbelievable that another fifty years have gone by. The things that seemed so desperately important to that American ingenue of twenty-three in her room at the Astor House seem to have been transformed into scenes for a musical comedy.

CHAPTER 2

Ming at the
Chocolate Shop

We were much too excited and eager to see the city to unpack. I could hardly wait to have a look at the American Consulate General, where I had been promised a job at a high salary. That would be my main job—I knew my other projects would not make any money. The nine arrivals for Shanghai, including Lieutenant Murphey and his wife, accompanied me in rickshas to register.

We hardly noticed the heat, though it was almost unbearable; the hotel manager had said it would reach 104°F, which was not uncommon. Nor did it occur to us that a bad typhoon might be blowing up from the far South, and that we were in the low pressure before a storm. No Old China Hands were out in the midday sun, nor even any mad dogs or Englishmen. After tiffin—lunch—they took long siestas.

We stopped on the Garden Bridge to look over Soochow Creek, only a few yards from the Astor House in this special corner of Shanghai. On the other side of the bridge, dominating the bund proper, was the British Consulate General, the Union Jack wilting on its imperial mast. As our rickshamen walked slowly along the bund, I looked out across the harbor beyond and thought of the big taipans and tycoons seated on the benches watching for the tall sails of their ships to come in.

I did slightly resent the fact that the ancient, rambling red brick American Consulate General was not on the bund, which the British monopolized, though it *was* only a block inland. As we lined up at the passport counter to register, I noticed that the floor sagged and creaked.

I asked the thin, tall, friendly vice-consul if Edgar Snow was in Shanghai now, and was told that he was just back from India. "Do you want to see him?"

"I have it in mind," I replied, a little guardedly.

"I'll phone him for you."

Phone conversations were anything but confidential. Everyone was amused at a shouted conversation that, on the consulate end, went something like this: "Snow? There's a Miss Foster here who wants to

24

see you. Just in from Seattle today . . . Fat? Oh, yes, fat and fifty but well-preserved . . . Rich? Dripping with diamonds. She's got body-guards. . . . Armed? Yes, each one has two of 'em. . . . I wouldn't bother if I were you, Snow. I'll take care of her for you. . . . Well, then, let me introduce you. . . . Let me ask."

He put his hand over the mouthpiece and in a stage whisper said, "He's invited us to tea at the Chocolate Shop—right away. It's close by."

"Can do." I could hardly contain any more excitement my first day.

The whole group, full of fun, chorused their readiness to join us. "She can't be without her bodyguards, not with all those diamonds," said one of the BAT boys.

"This is an interview—business," I informed them with dignity. "My first for Scripps-Canfield."

The vice-consul explained that the Chocolate Shop was the only place in Shanghai where you could get ice cream. "But the first thing you need, Miss Foster, is your own private rickshaman, guaranteed as a bodyguard by our Number One boy here at the consulate, cost about five dollars a month your money, all day long. You wantchee, no wantchee?"

Pidgin English was the lingua franca of the whole China coast then. Newcomers loved it.

"Wantchee," I agreed.

The gray-haired, dignified Number 1 boy appeared with a rickshaman of about forty. He had an honest, weatherbeaten face, a wide smile, and a shiny new black ricksha lined with sparkling white embroidered cushions.

"Melican missy likee, no likee?" the Number 1 boy inquired with a mandarin bow.

"Likee!" I climbed into the vehicle—which I used until I left Shanghai a year and a half later.

At the new, modern American-style Chocolate Shop, we sat at a small table with the Murpheys, limp in the dreadful humid heat.

"Snow's always late," the vice-consul said, fanning my flushed face. He explained that Snow had gotten sick in the tropics on his Indian trip, and had come back to Shanghai for treatment and to write a book. Snow did things in his own way, he said, never in a hurry. Just at that time, he said, Snow was in the doghouse because of an article he had written denigrating "The Americans in Shanghai." In afterthought he added, "He's not married. . . . Neither am I, in case you want to know."

I ignored that lead.

"Here he comes now." My escort stood up, waiting to shake hands.

I looked up to see a thin but well-built figure in a white suit. Edgar Snow was so pale that his freckles showed through. I hoped he did not notice my disappointment—I had pictured him as a brave, strong, and healthy world traveler. I was not used to sick-looking people but to athletic types, being myself something of a physical culturist, off and on. Was this the price you had to pay to be a real traveler in the East?

Just the same, he's handsome and attractive, I decided, struggling to overcome my unworthy first impressions. He had wavy brown hair and beautiful, long-lashed, warm brown eyes that sometimes misted over as we talked. In later years I thought he looked like Laurence Olivier. *How can I get him out of that shapeless suit and into Harris tweeds with padded shoulders?* I wondered, disregarding the 104-degree season. I could tell his ego was sound. So was his male ego; it was not dependent on tailoring or on making a good first impression. I liked him for that, and realized it was much more grown-up than my own wish always to make a good impression, to be attractive, to be liked.

Just the same, I was not sorry when he appeared to be captivated at first glance. He was stumbling over chair legs, looking steadily at my face as he walked toward me.

"Dr. Livingstone, I presume." I giggled as he pulled out a chair to sit down, barely acknowledging introductions, always staring straight into my eyes.

"Miss Stanley. Miss America, I mean. I haven't seen anything like this since I left Kansas City in 1927." It was an unusually pleasant masculine voice. "You remind me of the girl next door. I'd forgotten what girls like you even look like. And I don't see any diamonds, rich fat lady of fifty."

In the late 1920s and early 1930s, the youth code was always to make fun of each other. It was a kind of college-humor Chinese guessing game. Like the Chinese, we never broke the surface but looked archly inscrutable. You could say anything—as long as you didn't say it. It was non sequitur, but it could make a point—as long as there was no point. Ed and I always talked in this good-humored, bantering, light Ping-Pong fashion, even in the dreariest times. The Chinese loved it. They were trained to hide behind a smooth surface and witty riposte.

(I swear that this exchange actually took place one time at the Chocolate Shop: "Bring me a strawberry ice cream soda without any strawberry," I asked the waiter.

He bowed and discussed this with his peers in a corner, then came back and, with a blank, inscrutable face, said: "Missy, stlawberry no have got. You must have without chocolate.")

The American style was to achieve humor by repetition. It was a new invention, perfected by J. P. MacEvoy and Ogden Nash, but in our case it also went back to Mark Twain, making a point by sharpening it to a contradiction.

"I don't like diamonds." I held out my bare fourth finger. I told Ed I had read just about everything he'd ever published, and asked him to be my first interview for Scripps-Canfield. "They won't take anything but 'golden, glamorous Orient' stuff to revive the tourist trade—Richard Halliburton type. Did you go swimming at the Taj Mahal?"

He said I was a bit late—he'd been out of the Halliburton stage for some time. He'd had dysentery ever since he got to the Taj Mahal and was deathly sick with malaria when he got to the Shwedagon Pagoda.

"There goes my first newspaper job," I sighed. "Can't you arrange to be a Halliburton just for one interview? I thought there was something known as the 'call of the East.'"

"That's what I was told before I got here," he said. "The call of the East is 'Boy!' 'Boy, draw my bath.' 'Boy, untie my shoes.' 'Boy, lift my little finger for me.' Most 'boys' have gray hair."

I persisted. He must have discovered *some* wonderful things.

Yes, he had: Someone he referred to as a little man in white diapers running a spinning wheel. He told me about Gandhi and about his "ugliest but wittiest" disciple, the chief anti-purdah feminist of India, Sarojini Naidu. And Nehru. And, he said, "Choosing between *pukka sahib* white tie and white diapers, I prefer Gandhi."

Ed was natural, casual, easy to be with, obviously well-bred, even civilized. He was self-assured in a special way and not afraid to be himself, with his own ideas. I liked that. But, oh, I did wish he wasn't wearing a suit that looked as if one of Gandhi's tailors had made it.

I pushed the ice cream soda out of the way and put my briefcase on my lap. Both of us forgot our sodas as the others ordered one after another.

I handed my Edgar Snow folder to the original. I told him that part of my job for the American Mining Congress had been to clip articles on China and silver, and that on my own I had clipped everything I could find by Edgar Snow.

As he looked up from riffling through the folder, tears came into his brown eyes. His voice was a little liquid: "I'd have written better if I'd had a photograph of you doing all that industrious clipping. I'm beginning to forget about the people I'm supposed to be writing for—all those wonderful homeside Americans like you. Why, you're the first person who ever asked me for an interview, Miss Scripps-Canfield."

I moved to the edge of my chair and leaned forward in my most diplomatic and constructive manner—already building him up. "Don't you realize you're the most famous American writer on the Far East except for that missionary, Pearl Buck?" *The Good Earth* was already a classic, like *Kristin Lavransdatter*. "She certainly killed the golden, glamorous Orient myth—if it is a myth; I'm not admitting that yet."

Then I told him that I was a partisan of *silver*, not gold. "I'm the unofficial plenipotentiary extraordinary without portfolio—no, I have the portfolio—of the Silver Lobby. We like the Chinese because they have the good sense to base their currency on silver instead of gold. We have lots of surplus silver to sell."

Ed was never slow to seize any opportunity to make good-natured fun of me or anyone else: "Doesn't like diamonds, doesn't like gold—now you're getting down to my currency level, Miss Silver of 1931. This is *ming*, manifest *ming*, solid-silver *ming*, pure and unalloyed. Man, who stands alone between Heaven and Earth, as the Chinese say, deserves a little *ming* once in a lifetime. When I was on the edge of Tibet, I was inspired to buy a silver saddle-ring, though I didn't know one girl who would like it—not even my sister, Mildred."

"What on earth—or in heaven—is *ming*?" I wanted to know. "I didn't come all the way to China to wear anybody's silver saddle-ring. I came here for exactly the same reason you did. I intend to become a Great Author—and to travel. I've been saving money a long time. And reading all the books."

"Oh, I see, Miss Kipling Lowell-Thomas, you've been reading *Beyond the Khyber Pass* and *With Lawrence in Arabia*—just as I did in

Kansas City. Well, Mrs. Great Author, with the compliments of the future Mr. Great Author, here's the dope: *Ming* is the Chinese word for fate, for destiny. That's what brought you here to the Chocolate Shop. Put it with another little word and you have a big idea—*ke ming* is the term for revolution. It means 'the changing of fate.' That's what's happening to me here in the Chocolate Shop between heaven and earth."

"You'll wear that ring," the vice-consul declared, feigning jealousy. "I never saw this much *ming* at any small table before."

I was meeting Ed at a crossroads in his career, "the low point of my life so far," he said. He was permanently affected by his Yunnan-Indochina-Burma-India experience, not only depressed by recurring physical illness but by the hopelessness, fanaticism, and poverty everywhere. Then, arrived in Shanghai, he found a solid hostile front of Americans, irate because of his satirical article about them in *The American Mercury*—even Millard and Powell were angry. Also the British police had paid a White Russian informer to write a fictional dossier on him as a radical, and he was put on the Japanese blacklist in 1931. The happy-go-lucky, irresponsible, iconoclastic, and irreverent child of fortune of the 1920s had to face adult problems for the first time in his life—in confrontation with a dangerous world where such trifles as published articles were no longer looked upon as harmless.

At that first meeting in the Chocolate Shop, Ed picked up my clipping of his article on "The Americans in Shanghai," and his face turned grim. "This is the first time in my life I ever felt rejected," he said. He was being ostracized, even attacked in print. He said he now knew how J. B. Powell must have felt when he was voted out of the American Chamber of Commerce in 1927 for supporting the Kuomintang. "I really don't know why I came back to Shanghai," he said.

"Had to be the silver saddle-ring." The vice-consul came up for air from the depths of his ice cream soda.

"Why *did* you come back?" I asked, my pencil and notebook professionally poised.

"I was on my way around the world. I got as far as India when I learned my mother had died. That took the heart out of my travels home. I decided to backtrack and write my travel book in Shanghai where it's so cheap now—thanks to Miss Silver Lobby. Also I needed Dr. Gardiner." (Dr. W. H. Gardiner was an American institution in Shanghai, much beloved by everyone.) Ed went on: "Something strange is happening to me. I'm just not the type to be depressed. I don't seem to be able to write. Even the paper looks black to me now. I actually feel chilly in all this heat. Maybe that's the malaria coming back again."

I told him he sounded like an Old China Hand Ancient Mariner with an albatross around his neck. "Just think, you've done all the things I'd like to do—but no female can ever travel like that. Oh, how I love to travel—but I'll probably never even see the Mekong River. If I were you, I wouldn't be whining and complaining. I'd be writing a best seller. I like books. I believe in books. I'm not trying to be a foreign correspondent. That's just for fun." All my natural scolding enthusiasms rose to the occasion.

"Well, Miss Pollyanna of all time, you've got as far as the Chocolate Shop on Nanking Road." Ed came back to life again. "What are *you* complaining about? As for writing your book, you have to do it the first year in China or you lose the outside perspective. I'm tired and sick and stale and out of touch with my readers. Who would want to read a dismal, complicated book? It would be too negative, too hopeless."

He was homesick, too, he said. He'd been away three years. He had left the United States in 1928 at the peak of prosperity before the Depression. His brother, Howard, and Buddy Rogers had shared an apartment with him in New York, where Ed was a junior partner in the Scovil advertising agency. (Buddy soon married Mary Pickford, who was still beautiful when I visited them in 1941. Howard became New England manager of the National Association of Manufacturers—after once being the famous Arrow Collar model. Both the Snow boys lost interest in inheriting their father's Snow Printing Company, which put out the *Kansas City Star*, where Ed got his first newspaper experience while still at the University of Missouri.) "I intended to spend only one year on a trip around the world," Ed said, "and here I am back in this dreary vacuum. I can't even write here."

"Don't give up your travel book," I scolded. "I can't wait to read it. Don't you realize all the bright young people in America want to travel and can't? You're their vicarious substitute. Imagine traveling with a *National Geographic* trip by caravan! Do you have a good title?"

"Yes, *South of the Clouds*. But the minute it's finished, I'll be on my way home by train through Europe—Siberia and all that."

"You can't imagine how hard it was for me just to get to Shanghai," I said. "I wouldn't have been allowed to come except for being promised a job at the American Consulate General. I had to mobilize my father's Stanford University alumni from President Hoover on down . . . and the chairman of the Senate Finance Committee . . . and the top Republican moguls west of the Mississippi . . . and the big tycoons of the American Mining Congress, where I gave up a good job—for a lowly secretary, I mean—"

Ed was laughing out loud by this time. It was obvious I was already taking the place of his trip home, supplying the fresh American audience he needed.

That was the last time I ever saw him depressed and unhappy, though he insisted he was when he left China in 1941. Until then he never worried, and seldom did anything he did not want to do. "Except for you, I would have left China in 1932," he summed it up later. "You gave me a whole new lease on life in China—nine years or more."

"Let's go to the French Club for *thé dansant*," the lively bachelor vice-consul proposed. There, he said, was the real Shanghai, where every nationality might be found, the most popular place in town.

The shining big dance floor of the Parisian-type building was by no means empty, as the White Russian orchestra played "April in Paris"—which sounded more like "Winter Near Moscow," a dark Dostoyevskian chant with wolves chasing the droshkies in the snow.

I could tell by looking at him that Ed was not a good dancer—and also that he saw no reason why he should be. He was limping slightly as he walked over to ask the orchestra to play his favorite hesitation waltz, called "Wonderful One."

He'd been kicked in the knee by a packhorse, he explained. "But it will go away. I haven't danced much since I left New York." More often he spent his evenings in J. B. Powell's office while Powell got out the *Chicago Tribune* late cables. That was the chief American intellectual center in the Far East, where the correspondents collected at all hours. "But both Millard and Powell are miffed at me now for that article."

We new arrivals looked critically at specimens of the 2,554 French and 9,603 British in Shanghai, along with various other types. After we had danced awhile in all that dreadful heat, Navy wife Pat Murphey decided that the place was dismal. Everyone looked pale and sickly. She wanted to go where people were having fun.

"You're all going to look like that a year from now," the vice-consul observed. "That's the price you have to pay." He suggested that we might like to look at the Columbia Country Club, if it wasn't too far to go in the heat.

"There's no fun in China or anywhere else I've been in the East." Ed spoke in his best Ancient Mariner tone. "The White Russian places have the best food, if you can stand the dismal émigré vodka-drowned expressions."

At the Russian restaurant, the waiters and orchestra wore sashed satin Russian blouses and real Cossack boots, and they rolled as they stepped, like cavalrymen. A mournful balalaika filled the spaces between Viennese waltzes. (Oh, how I loved to dance Viennese waltzes!)

This was a haven. The women acted like princesses—some of them said they were—and the men like Peter the Great, as they sipped tall glasses of tea sweetened with strawberry jam. There were about 150,000 White Russians in all China, the vice-consul told us. About 40,000 armed forces had arrived here in 1927.

"J. B. Powell says there are *three* hundred and fifty thousand in Manchuria alone," Ed put in. "No statistics are worth anything in China. I spend most of my time just trying to check on the facts."

I supplied a remembered statistic: that out of 13 million Allied soldiers killed in the war, 8 million were Russians. "I'm for the Kellogg Peace Pact, like President Hoover," I added. "Hoover fed ten million children and adults in the Soviet Union after the civil war."

"Oh, you've got to keep the Yangtze Patrol going," Lieutenant Murphey said. He was arriving to take command of a gunboat on that river. "We had to land a thousand Marines here in 1927."

"I never even heard of the Yangtze Patrol till I met you," I said.

I had never heard of Admiral Kolchak, the émigré leader, either, and I had never read Lenin. But I had read Tolstoy, Gorky, Chekhov, even Dostoyevsky—and I could play "The Volga Boatman" on the piano! As for Marx, I thought first of the brothers, not of Karl, whom I had not read—but I had been told he had dangerous thoughts.

Ed and I were enjoying the beef Stroganoff, but the Murpheys detested the chicken Kiev.

"You remind me of my mother," Ed offered.

"You're my first foreign correspondent," I countered. "But don't say things like that. I'm clad in Athenian armor. I have made a resolution not to be married till I've done some traveling, written a book, and reached at least twenty-five."

"I had the same idea," Ed said, "and now I'm writing my first book—trying to, anyway."

"I'll be starting my first book any minute," I said.

"Let's go back to the Astor House," Pat Murphey said, ending the evening. "I think I have malaria already. Never have I been this tired before."

The weather was cooler now and the streets were much more crowded with trolleys, taxis, human carriers, bicycles, and an army of rickshas jamming the intersections, where big turbaned Sikhs from the Punjab cracked their *lathis* to move the traffic.

My high heels were killing me. But I had not noticed it till I pulled off my shoes in the big hotel room. I opened every bureau drawer wide, releasing their aromas of sandalwood, camphorwood, and cassia. I was almost too tired to think as I climbed the two steps into the high old bed, carefully closing the mildewed net against malarial mosquitoes.

Inside my Shanghai mosquito net, I resolved not to stay long enough in China to look pale and sickly. I valued my health. Sports were part of the new liberation of women, especially for Americans. The A students hid behind the persiflage of the twenties and played mixed doubles. I thought of my handsome, athletic, West Point army flyer, Russell Emery, who had filled my stateroom with American beauty roses and plans to get himself transferred to Manila or Tientsin. We used to ride horseback on Sundays, and he had been a football star, a friend of Red Grange, and a sportswriter intending to be a Great Author.

Emery's ideas about maximum development in every direction were not uncommon then, except for girls. One of these ideas was to raise the level of marriage to a new dimension—a vital working partnership instead of a domestic arrangement. I had more than one swain with the same plan—not to get married before the age of twenty-five, not before studying abroad, or at least traveling, and not before establishing oneself a little in one's "own work."

Even though the Great Depression was coming on black and ominous, American youth in those days was bursting at the seams. We were all in love with life, with each other, with the human potential. And the future was ours—not British or Japanese. For Edgar Snow to challenge the British and Japanese in China was implicit in his arrival in Shanghai in 1928.

In 1931, meeting your first foreign correspondent was no trifling matter. I already knew that Edgar Snow had his mind on his work and made fun of "Greek Goddesses," as he used to call me, downgrading athletics. He did not think about himself at all. He was already living in the new world—a world I had hardly even guessed at. How did I know he was *right?* How did I know (as he did) that "this thing is bigger than we are"? We met at a third point—and that point happened to be the fulcrum of the lever that moves the world. We were in league with the future, and we both knew it—yes, the first day.

Filtered through an old gray mosquito net five thousand miles from home, the youthful American me-Tarzan you-Jane image began to fade. Reality began to superimpose itself.

As I write now, I think back to December of 1940 and the President liner steaming out of the Whangpoo River for Honolulu and San Francisco. A thin, pale, sickly American female weighing about one hundred pounds huddles at the rail, freezing in her old fur coat. The tide is retreating, running out. Japanese warships own the harbor and Japanese planes are already poised for Pearl Harbor the next year. We have "lost China." I have lost nearly ten years, so it seems, as I realize none of my own work has been finished. Yes, I look like a dowdy missionary who has given up material things for higher purposes. In my old blue steamer trunk are the same clothes I packed in the States in 1931, wrinkled symbols of the lost Greek Goddess days.

In the winter wind of 1940, I remember the healthy, self-confident, all-American Girl Scout ingenue of 1931 whom Edgar Snow made fun of in the Chocolate Shop. I remember how hard she worked at any job, how much effort she put into being liked and attractive, how diplomatic, careful, and constructive she was, how often an unpaid civic or social worker.

This girl gave up material things and never counted the cost. What did she receive in exchange? In 1931, I intended maximum development of the individual in all ways, but I was torn away from my goals by the typhoons of history. The individual was sacrificed for the common good. Or was I? I liked the principle of individual development. I didn't lose my sense of humor, though this was rare for those who lived in the East. I could still smile with Benjamin Franklin: She lived much and suffered much, most of which never happened—the rest of which happened to other people.

EXCERPT FROM A LETTER

AUGUST 30, 1931

This is the first time since I left that I have actually had five minutes to call my own. . . . I am sitting proudly in my joint overlooking the rooftops of the most fascinating city in the world.

The business district of the International Settlement is all clustered about the bund; the Bank of China, for instance, is directly across the street from the river. This is the Whangpoo River, very dirty and yellow, but I haven't seen any bodies floating around in it. Since the terrible floods in Hankow, however, it is said the Yangtze, some distance away, is at this time very likely to have such things. Every day several hundred refugees arrive from Hankow and are put in tents and cared for. They have had a siege of cholera and most of us sissies are intending to have shots of serum against it as soon as possible.

There is always noise in China, everywhere, and you never know whether it's mourning or feasting or peanut vending. It's all the same sound. . . .

I've been living across the hall with a naval officer's wife. For my place I pay $210 mex., which is at the exchange rate of 4.52 at the local money shops. For this I get four meals a day in the most approved fashion and have no further expenses, except tips to the "boys." [Except for *cumsha*, no cash contaminated the paper tiger paws of Shanghailanders. "Chits" were signed and nobody ever looked at the figure—nor did anybody refuse to pay up. The code was strict, imported from the *pukka sahibs* of India—the "plopper" master or missy, as the Chinese called them.]

The place I live in is one of the nicest buildings in Shanghai. It is called the China United Apartments, and it is only five years old. . . . An apartment here is operated on the all-American plan. . . .

I have a roomboy who answers the buzzer and runs any errands, at all hours of day or night. Then there is a "coolie," who keeps my room in apple-pie order.

35

The Chinese are neat and most orderly. At the Astor House, I left my thousands of funny bracelets strung from Gehenna to breakfast on the dresser, and when I came back, the coolie, who was a rough laboring type, had made a little design with them along the ledge; everything was sitting soldierly in place otherwise, too. One is afraid to touch anything.

I am supposed to tip the boy $5 a month and the coolie $3 (mex., of course). I have an amah also, a missy amah. A missy amah is a personal maid. My amah is named Anu. She is pretty and young and married and shy and sweet. She comes once a week and stays all day for $1.40 mex. She takes complete charge of my wardrobe—darns my hose, washes everything that looks the least bit eligible, presses everything in the place, and keeps the drawers of my furniture most orderly. I haven't yet learned her filing system, which is a bit distressing in case of having to dress—which occurs three or four times a day.

Then I have a massage amah who gives a massage all over for one hour for $1.50. I have her come almost every night, because I am so tired and nervous that she helps a lot. Her name is Mei and she is a famous personage in Shanghai. She is sixty years old and looks only thirty. She has marvelously pretty hands and tiny (at one time bound) feet. Mei told me she had had a most unhappy life because her father threw her mother out into the street a few weeks after their marriage, because she had large feet. No man is obligated, it seems, to keep a woman in marriage if she has pockmarks or unbound feet that were not mentioned in the marriage contract. (That is, in the "good" old days.) They lived in poverty until Mei was sixteen, when she was married. Her husband was unkind to her, too, and ran away and left her with a baby daughter, which she brought up. Mei has a very decided dislike for men and marriage and has made me swear solemnly never to permit myself the sacrifice. . . .

In the dining room, we have a headwaiter with one or two subordinates and two boys for each table. The serving is very formal and unbelievably attentive. If you show the slightest preference for anything, they never forget it. Mrs. Murphey and I have a penchant for tea toast, made very thin, so we are fairly swamped with it. The chef here is Swiss and the desserts are simply wonderful.

About what one does or does not eat: I went to the doctor the first day or so in town and he told me not to worry but to eat everything that has been cooked very recently and nothing cold—and added that few people get through the summer without difficulty. In the summer all food here is Chinese, from the truck gardens up the Yangtze Valley and from Tsingtao, but in winter many of the vegetables are imported. The local advisers say to eat anything at all at any of the good places in town, and then remark as though it had no pertinence that they or their friend or friend's friend have just been back from the hospital where they have spent the past month or so, as though it were a sort of summer resort. I eat all the hot soups, no fish because it is from the river, all kinds of hot meat orders, all kinds of hot vegetable orders, no cold meats or salads, and no fruit whatever, excepting stewed and bananas (which are small and green-colored) and pomelos, which are very good. The dishes are quite cosmopolitan. I never know what I'm getting but am learning fast. This is the principal use I've made of my foreign languages so far—deciphering menus. My only indiscretion is ice cream and cakes. I am always hungry and sleepy here and feel very well—getting a little fatter, as a matter of fact, in spite of how rushed I am. . . .

About my position [while waiting for my consulate job to come through, I was working for a firm of industrial bankers]: I've never been in such a place before. We are busy every minute. I don't do much stenographic work, but open all the mail that comes in and distribute it, and otherwise do such work as the general manager's office would handle. There is a Portuguese named da Silva who works with me. I am sort of the personal secretary and do the outside enterprises principally. Well—I'm only in the last day or two able to gather what it's all about. This da Silva is a genius. He usually stands up at his desk with the telephone in one hand, talking alternately with the person on the line and someone in the office (you can do this, incidentally, because every once in a while the connection is broken for a few minutes) while he figures up something on an envelope and buzzes for the office boy with one toe—then he will leap over and do something fivefold somewhere else. The leisurely Orient, my eye! It is an American firm, federally incorporated, but there are only three Americans in the place, of which I am one. . . . There are fifty-two or fifty-three members of the staff in all, and most of them are Eurasians or Portuguese, some French and Russian and Chinese, etc. etc. etc.

The general manager is only thirty-two years of age and considered the smartest businessman in town. . . . He is giving me an increasing amount of responsibility. This week I am writing advertising copy for some of his more or less personal enterprises and have several things to do that require a little plain and fancy arranging. I can see no end of opportunity here in every line, but it requires, as all things worthwhile do, a great deal of energy and struggle.

The manager's office is quite nice really. The furniture has possibilities and I found myself the other day quite unable to keep my housewifely digits off it, so I conceived the brilliant thought of having certain cigarette stands and a fireplace, which looked as if they might have metal under them, polished. I called in the Number 1 Chinese boy and told him to have it done. Well, it seems this was against all tradition. They'd never been touched since the Ming dynasty and I finally had to get some metal polisher and show the coolies how to do it. They went to the Chinese manager and told him, "Plenty trouble, plenty trouble. Missy want clean—no can do."

Well, anyway, after two or three days, it looks like the shiningest place you ever saw, and the Chinese are much more respectful to me. I guess I made "face" with them instead of losing it. When they go by my desk, they turn and stare at me in the most fascinated way. I suppose they're speculating about just how far the renovations are to be carried.

I can't keep my hands off the filing system, and am now negotiating most diplomatically to change it a bit. You can't imagine how diplomatic I've learned to be. You see, in China you don't demand things. You have to be strategic. And everybody's hair bristles at the mere mention of the word "change." . . . But it is interesting, and I am slowly learning how the town works in a business way.

I must tell you about the telephones. It takes at least half an hour to get any number (only one exchange) and when you get it, you are always in imminent danger of being cut off, and you can't hear a thing, the lines are so busy. Everybody shouts at the top of his or her voice and swears furiously at the operators. I think my first impression of Shanghai business was the terrifying way people here answer and talk over the phone—but I'm very sympathetic now. . . .

CHAPTER 3

Foreign Correspondent

My career as a foreign correspondent was a brief one. As stringer for the Scripps-Canfield League, I was supposed to supply features glorifying the glamorous Orient.

My first photograph to horrify Scripps-Canfield was of water above hubcaps and first floors flooded even though sandbagged—the aftermath of the worst typhoon in years. It had been clocked in Hong Kong at 136 miles per hour, and on August 10, a gunboat figured it at 175 mph. Shanghai didn't even keep records, so common were typhoons, but the closest I had been to one before was reading Joseph Conrad. On the morning after the storm, I was soaked by my rickshaman, who enjoyed taking me along streets where the water came up almost to the seat of the ricksha. Everywhere the rickshamen were laughing and splashing each other as we passed by. Most of the basements near the bund were flooded up to the ground floors, and the big buildings seemed to sway on their piles in the mire, but the Chinese appeared to take it as a joke. The foreigners all looked apprehensive, especially those with any knowledge of construction engineering.

My next unglamorous photograph was of some of the 120,000 refugees pouring into the city from the worst flood in recorded history, along 900 miles of the Yangtze River, which was near Shanghai. In three weeks over 600,000 people had perished and 12 million homes were destroyed.

In September, Edgar Snow had gone up the Yangtze in a launch chartered by the press corps to see the flood. He let me read his graphic dispatches for the Consolidated Press Association and *New York Sun*— of corpses piled high on junks, of hordes of starving people stealing from the dead and ravaging the living.

Ed was basically a humanitarian. He had already been permanently affected by witnessing the ghastly famine in 1929 in the Northwest, where cannibalism was not uncommon and human flesh was sold in shops in a few places, as well as the misery of India and other places he had traveled. (One of the astonishments of his life came in 1960 when he found that all the multiple millions of China were actually being fed—no one was starving, he wrote me.)

Floods and drought and famine were not the worst thing, he told me that September. The worst thing was the helplessness of the 350 million Chinese. China had had fourteen major civil wars recently and, Ed said, "Chiang Kai-shek can't think of anything better than to press on with the civil war against the Reds and to increase taxes on the peasants—some of them are collected seventy years in advance."

"None of this fits in with my Pollyanna psychology," I said. "I may decide to leave China sooner than I expected."

On September 19, Colonel and Mrs. Charles Lindbergh were scheduled to arrive by plane and we expected them to land in Shanghai. But no, they photographed the flood from the air and came down in the middle of it—in Nanking, the capital city of Chiang Kai-shek. Lindbergh had been the chief inspiration for the wave of Innocents Abroad—we had all identified with him in 1927.

"I hope you notice that Lindbergh takes his wife with him," I reminded Ed.

On the Lindbergh day came news that was world-shaking, at least for that bowl of jelly called the League of Nations. The Japanese had attacked in Manchuria on September 18, and were taking over the 30 million Chinese and Koreans who lived there, their first step in the occupation of much of China which was not rolled back until 1945, after World War II.

This news galvanized every foreign correspondent in China and Japan. They found themselves on the only real war front in the world since 1919. All excitement, they were busy planning the trip to Manchuria.

Ed did find a few fidgety minutes to bid farewell to me as he bought woolens for the frigid Northeast, his head bent forward in the bird-dog Lindbergh look, his brown eyes sparkling at the opportunity to see a *real* war.

He left me several books on advertising he had brought from New York. I was studying the subject, and had been writing a little copy for a few American companies. "If you run across anything golden and glamorous for me, I'll pay by the inch," were my last words to him.

I wrote a pitiful letter to Scripps-Canfield, which was read, as were all my letters, by the American Mail Line tourist bureau and the

Silver Lobby as well. It may have precipitated a mass resignation in the tourist bureau. I touched lightly on the dangers of cholera, typhus, typhoid, and other perils in the refugee camps, and estimated that the number of corpses in the streets of the International Settlement alone would far exceed the figure of 28,000 for 1930.

I said I couldn't find one other "tourist" in Shanghai except myself so far; that just as soon as possible and passable, I intended to go to the cities near Shanghai—Hangchow, Soochow, and Wusih—in search of the golden, glamorous Orient. I told them that foreigners in China were afraid to travel because of the danger of all kinds of disease everywhere, and the only method of travel was by train, where the crowding Chinese expectorated freely, especially those with tubercular coughs. I said I was willing to risk my young life for Scripps-Canfield but I couldn't go alone—I had to find a group to go with me.

Rustling up traveling companions was not easy. Shanghai was a foreign treaty port, and I did not set foot on the "real" China for some weeks after reaching the Shanghai bund. Few Shanghai foreigners ever left the city, except sometimes on houseboats or for the tour up the Yangtze Gorges, or sometimes to Peking by coastal steamer. Tourist facilities were in their infancy, though the China Travel Service had guest houses in a few cities. Foreign travelers were not allowed to stay elsewhere, and the police were held responsible for their safety and good behavior. Neither the travel service nor I could come up with a group for my grand tour, except a few newcomers, one of them a National City Bank youth in knickers who never smiled the whole time.

As soon as Ed came back from Manchuria, I pounced on him to join the group. At every point of the compass, it seemed as if Ed was the indispensable person—the only one who shared my ideas. He had written the first tourist guide to the national railways of China—but he had no special wish to retrace any of these travels, especially in the wake of the diseases rampant since the big flood. He had got enough disease in India and Burma.

I was warned that my smallpox vaccination would not be effective against the "black smallpox" then common among Chinese, so before traveling I was vaccinated with this terrible virus. I was deathly sick with all the symptoms of the disease and in bed for about ten days. Dr. Gardiner said it was similar to a light case—a real case was likely to be fatal to a foreigner.

Ed was impressed when I arranged to visit and photograph a big

Chinese home and scheduled a pair of guides who spoke the local dialects (Chinese always seemed to come in pairs). Even for one-day train trips, all these cumbersome plans had to be made.

In the days of Marco Polo, Hangchow and Soochow were reported by him to be the most beautiful cities in the world. I began with Hangchow and its big lake, where we had to pay for a sightseeing boat at a rate twenty times higher than any Chinese would be asked.

I discovered that Ed not only hated to be photographed, but usually refused to take any pictures of me. "Why waste the money?" was his explanation. I am now looking through an old album for the first photograph we ever had taken together—in a grove of tall bamboos near the Laughing Buddha—snapped by the knickered National City Bank man. We both look like canaries that have swallowed the cat—the expression we used to exchange with each other after our various successes in China.

In Soochow the stench from the street canals was so overpowering I could hardly focus on the ancient quaint bridges of this walled city. Soochow had been founded in A.D. 484 by Ho Lu-wang, whose grave mound is still there, never excavated. This filthy, crowded city of 500,000 was still back in the time of Chaucer, I figured, and showed no sign of emerging.

Everywhere we were surrounded by good-natured, staring crowds in all stages of refugee rags and disease, some dying on the street corners. And the two Chinese guides and interpreters detested their job. These treaty-port Chinese were more afraid of the crowds than the foreigners were. Most of all, they didn't want foreigners to see the horrors and poverty of inland China. Such Chinese were themselves refugees from the turmoil and civil war of the interior; their survival, in the protection of the foreign concessions, was paid for in capital squeezed out of starving tenants far away.

We talked about *The Good Earth*. They violently hated it and the author too. (In her old age Pearl Buck was refused a visa to China because the Communists also detested her later writing, but for opposite reasons.) Finally, I realized that these so-called nationalists were not patriots in the least—actually they were hostile, because they were what the left-wing students called "running dogs of imperialism."

The idea of the treaty-port Chinese hangers-on of foreign power was to "save" China by wearing foreign-style suits, speaking good English, and begging for foreign aid. This idea was popular later in Taiwan, Seoul, Saigon, Phnom Penh, Bangkok, where else? Their minds were still back in the medieval ages, yet their hands were on modern weapons. They were charming and clever enough to make fools of Americans and to collect billions upon billions of dollars from them just by announcing themselves to be anti-Communist while doing little work in that line.

Handing out money, weapons, and jobs does not change the old type of *thinking* of such puppets. That revolution usually can occur only as part of participating in a change in the mode of production, of being involved in new relations in social production—Marx was correct about this. The Soviet Union (like J. B. Powell) always foolishly imagined Chiang Kai-shek to be a "bourgeois nationalist," whereas the Chinese Communists refer to him as a feudal comprador.

The Chinese puzzle was and is difficult in any language, and when Marxist terminology became the fashion, confusion was compounded. In China the terms might mean just the opposite of the English words. This was partly semantic warfare. Chiang Kai-shek often referred to the Communists as counterrevolutionaries.

It rather amazes me that even in 1931 I realized how empty, tenth-rate, and useless such treaty-port-type Chinese were. They were not even worth trying to talk to. Ed, always good-natured and tolerant, found them silly. They were men without a country—without even minds of their own.

As I look back now, I realize that Shanghai had only one golden-glamorous thing beyond compare. It was the brave and beautiful and lonely widow of Dr. Sun Yat-sen, Soong Ching-ling, who lived there most of the time until her death in 1982, and was vice-chairman of the People's Republic from 1949. Of course she refused to be interviewed when I was finally able to meet her through Ed, after reading his article about her. (He may be the only journalist to whom she ever granted an interview about her personal life—just as he was the only person Mao Tse-Tung ever told about his life for publication.) Ed had already been influenced by Madame Sun, and before I left Shanghai I understood why.

One thing in China truly appalled me: foot-binding. I had seen the practice in Shanghai, but the real shock came in the old cities when I realized that peasant women refugees were actually dying because they could hardly *walk*. Their feet were stumps. They were crippled, victims of mass mutilation, a phenomenon as grisly as any ever known anywhere on this globe. In 1931, most women over thirty had bound feet because the practice had not been outlawed until the 1911 Revolution of Sun Yat-sen. It was a measure of the pathological condition of society in China and had existed for a thousand years, since Neo-Confucianism thought up this new concept for the degradation of women.

I actually cringed, my skin crawled, and my stomach turned over when an emaciated dying woman in Soochow tried to beg from me, hardly able to stand on her stumps, her face drawn with pain and stained with tears in the dusty hollows of her eyes. When I asked my guide to hand her some money, she toddled forward a little and then fell down, pointing to her stumps to explain why she could not rise respectfully.

I decided to make a study of the whole situation of women, and in China I never failed to gather information on this subject. *

Despite such evidence of the subjugation of women, no true cult of machismo exists in China, and Chinese men are the opposite of aggressive in sex matters. And where Western women are concerned, most Chinese consider them unattractive, even repulsive. Therefore, it was a particularly telling incident that occurred in Hangchow. Only an Old China Hand would see the significance of it, as Ed did. He was so impressed that he even included it in his memoirs twenty-five years later.

"That was when I decided you were going to be a big success with the Chinese," Ed informed me, "and that I couldn't live without you. I wanted to stay around to see what happened."

We were riding in sedan chairs around a hilly bend, when a muscular coolie appeared carrying a teetering load of heavy lumber on his shoulder. With sweat dripping, he glanced up at me in astonishment, burst into a wide smile, turned up his thumb, and called out to Ed as one woman-owner to another: *"Ding hao!"*

That, roughly translated into the vernacular, meant "Wow!"

"All right, Miss America, hold still," Ed said as he climbed out of his sedan chair. "I'm going to take your picture. This probably never happened in China before." This is almost the only time I remember his volunteering to take my picture. Usually he made fun of my photographic requests, even when I stood pitifully waiting before some famous landmark.

---

* My book *Women in Modern China* was published in 1967 at the Hague by Mouton and Company. *Women in Traditional China*, a controversial study, is yet to be published.

I wondered what the coolie liked about me. Perhaps my slightly Oriental eyes? My grade-school admirers used to call me Squint.

It wasn't only my eyes, Ed explained, but my round baby face, which he characterized as "adorable in any language."

"It's going to be your fortune in China," he said. "You can make the grade without even trying."

The important result of the incident was that I *expected* the Chinese to admire and like me from then on. Half the battle was won by that psychology alone.

Such moments of rapport with the people of China seemed big events to me then—and seem even bigger now. I really loved them, and in my mind I multiplied them by millions of the *lao pai hsing* ("old hundred names" or clans), as the common people were called then. It was not so hard to overlook the stench, the poverty, the disease, the danger, the discomfort, when you felt you had a special Chinese-American relationship with millions of people, and one of them let you know it existed on his side, too.

EXCERPTS FROM LETTERS

OCTOBER 18, 1931

I am just returned from a trip through the Chinese city, tired,
bewildered, and feeling leprous. You would never believe so many
people could congregate in so small a space. You see, Shanghai is
divided into the International Settlement, the Chinese city, and the
French Concession. Before the war, the Germans also had a
concession, but they forfeited it. The Chinese city is "over the
bridge," and not many foreigners go into it. I went with my friend
Edgar Snow, and we tramped about for hours around the narrow
streets. Small crowds gathered whenever we stopped and stared very
hard. My companion understands Chinese quite well and it is
interesting to go around with him. He says the Chinese call me
"Moon-face" and make all sorts of remarks about the size of my
feet. . . .

It was fun in Soochow. The city has a leaning pagoda twelve
hundred years old and is surrounded by a wall some thirty feet high
and five or six feet wide. . . .

West Garden was beautiful. It had a sign: "See these fine fish.
In the pond on purpose to preserve the lives of fish of West
Garden."

(The Chinese and Japanese are delightfully sure of their
English. A famous sign in Shanghai at a tailor shop says, "Ladies
have fits upstairs.")

We saw temples and temples. It was thrilling at dusk to invade
an old Buddhist temple of "Five Hundred Gods," full of incense
and winding halls. Our foreign shoes made an irreverent clatter that
echoed in these dark, quiet vaults. The priests were preparing for
the funeral of a very important man. They made marvelous paper
models of an automobile, phonograph, complete furnishings of a
house, a horse, etc. to be burned at the funeral. . . .

There were many posters up in Shanghai today on the subject
of the Japanese invasion of Manchuria. It is an exciting time. We

are expecting serious trouble in Shanghai every day. The Japanese shops are all closed under the boycott and they have landed two transports of marines. No doubt you are reading about it in the papers. . . .

I am doing advertising for several people—the leading nightclub, the leading insurance company, the largest automobile concern, and my own company. How it all happened is this: Our advertising manager was out of town for a month when I first arrived, and I suggested once that our publicity man was not doing such hot work, so the manager declared that if I could do any better to proceed. I did, with the result that I am now advertising manager of the corporation in addition to my other duties, and have a publicity director to distribute the stuff. . . . I write a new ad each week for each of the four papers here, and also for each issue of the magazines, so you can see I have no time to twiddle my thumbs at night.

Shanghai is a marvelous place for an enterprising young person with ideas. It is a total loss for many things, but I see so many opportunities that I can hardly decide what to do. . . .

NOVEMBER 1931

So great is the business development here now that real estate has not kept up with it. Two enormous eight-story hotels are opening in a month. I have moved from my old apartment upstairs to the top story where I command a view of the city. The room is fitted up like a studio, with lovely carved blackwood furniture they had in storage—a desk, bookcase, tables, etc. I have converted my bathroom into a dressing room. I am sitting at my own personal typewriter—model of 1849—and before me are eight books on advertising, all the Republic of China could produce.

In addition to my advertising I am writing book reviews for the *China Weekly Review,* and I edit a page in the *Spectator,* a local small-talk magazine, neither of which are lucrative but lots of fun. . . . Then I take French lessons and Mandarin. . . .

CHAPTER 4

My First War

In early January 1932, the imminence of war with Japan was beginning to penetrate the International Settlement of Shanghai. There had been rumors of evacuation, and my long-awaited call to start work at the American Consulate General had come.

The night life of Shanghai was in full swing; parties were scheduled weeks ahead in the usual tradition. There were no alarming headlines in the newspapers. But we were aware that something was happening. We noticed signs, "Sale, Cheap Sale," in stores dealing in Japanese goods, and we knew that the Yokohama Nursery where we bought dwarf trees and fresh-cut roses had suddenly changed its name to plain "Flower Shop." And a Japanese transport of marines had steamed into our quiet port.

On the nineteenth and twentieth, there were riots between groups of Japanese and Chinese, and Japanese warships in the harbor were put on alert. Ultimata began passing between the Japanese consul general and Mayor Wu Teh-chen, and barricades went up in the streets.

By January 27, war nerves were taut in Shanghai. We were expecting a Japanese attack at any moment, and anytime a door banged or a ricksha tire blew out, we had to be dragged out from under our desks at the Consulate General.

I wrote home:

If you only knew how tragic and strange it is to be here now! I never thought I'd be in the middle of war, and especially such a war. It seems almost incredible that such a thing could happen in the twentieth century. China is absolutely helpless. It is simply torn from one end to the other. Flood, famine, disease epidemics, the Reds and bandits tearing up the interior, and the government officials cutting each other's throats in Nanking. There is no government, and if there were, it is absolutely bankrupt. They have issued bonds until the country is knee-deep in them. . . . Government schoolteachers haven't been paid salaries for six

48

months. And the most pathetic thing of all is the army. What an army! In Hangchow last month I saw boys from fifteen up, wearing tennis shoes and with the most harmless faces. I actually saw in the rear lines, the boys holding each other's hands, like Chinese schoolboys do in the streets. On the train coming back, there were a troop of them, and as they fell asleep one would hold the other's head. And no navy, no air corps, no ammunition.

Today the Chinese are building trenches and barbed-wire barricades and there are supposed to be about sixty thousand soldiers here to guard the Chinese city. It is as if the R.O.T.C. at home were sent out with their measly little twenty-twos to fire at machine guns. . . .

If the coolies and farmers of China lay down their rickshas and tools to fight even one day, their families and they themselves must starve, so close is the struggle for existence. . . . It would take a coolie ten years to save enough money to buy a gun, and he could never buy ammunition. And the government couldn't even supply one round.

General Feng Yu-hsiang (incidentally, this is the famous "Christian General" who one time baptized a whole regiment with a fire hose and distributed Bibles among them for compulsory reading) was in Shanghai recently, decrying the militarists and imperialists who for twenty years have used China as a playground for personal glory, and trying to rouse the "masses" to a realization of what's happening. They don't even know. They can't read, and the means of communication, even roads, are so bad that people in certain villages twenty miles from each other have never seen each other and scarcely know the name of the neighboring town. A soldier in China is just a poor boy trying to earn a living, and he doesn't even know what or why he fights.

The young students in China are simply wild. They realize the critical position of the country and the absolute hopelessness of it. The famous student movement of China, with their strikes and struggles to get a spirit of nationalism abroad, is one of the most pitiful things I have ever heard of. And so terribly heroic. The girls are very delicate and entirely unaccustomed to any outdoor activity, and the boys in their silk gowns and thin soft shoes look like girls. It is the price of four thousand years of silk cushions, I guess.

The general opinion here is that Japan has this all planned nicely with pins on maps so that no hitch can possibly occur. Also, it is assumed that Chiang Kai-shek is so thoroughly convinced of this that he has only one hope, that of preserving himself as nominal head of China under Japanese control, at least economically. What a wonderful little country of sixty-five million people this Land of the Rising Sun is! She actually is laughing up her sleeve at everyone in the world, and just playing with the League of Nations with diplomatic fabrications to stall them off. But isn't it a wonderful time to spring all this: Russia pledged to a five-year plan, England holding India by the skin of her teeth, China absolutely a crippled beggar, every country engrossed with its own very serious problems—and by the time they find breathing space to see what's happening in the Orient, Japan will be sitting on the top of the world.

Right now the Japanese are treating China exactly as a subject country. . . .

On January 28, 1932, the Chinese part of Shanghai was plunged into a real war between the invading Japanese and the defending Chinese Nineteenth Route Army. I had a grandstand position on the tower of the China United Apartments, along with my Navy-wife friends who also lived there.

For thirty-four days we could hear the whining of shells and mortars, the artillery duel, and some bombing. At night we watched the flashes of gunfire and the flames spreading among straw huts not far away. "Facing Danger in Shanghai" was the caption under my photograph in the homeside newspapers.

In my old letters and newspaper clippings I find some of my dispatches.

"The Japanese planes flew over the city and bombed the main railway station. The Chinese city is raging with fire, and there is no hope of controlling it. Japanese marines have taken complete possession of Chapei district."

One article quoted my description of ten thousand evacuees moving into the International Settlement from Chapei: "They turned around occasionally to see the flames rising hundreds of feet in the air. They snatched what they could of their household belongings and fled . . . into the Settlement, which already is densely populated with 1,000,000 people. . . . Hospitals and places of refuge were overflowing. . . . We don't know what is going to happen here. The 31st Infantry is here and 17 of the soldiers are bivouacked on the eighth floor of this building, so I think foreigners are safe."

Ed was in high spirits, rushing around to be on the spot for hostilities. The first night, January 28, a group had been watching for hours from our tower when Ed arrived to get an overview of the war terrain. He was grimy, exhausted, hoarse with excitement—but his brown eyes sparkled with exhilaration. He had been under fire for the first time in his life!

"The Chinese are resisting," he announced with partisan triumph, but the English officers obviously did not believe him. Ed told us he had gotten to the North Station by 11:35 and warned the Chinese railwaymen the Japanese would attack about midnight. Then he started back through Hongkew and confronted lines of Japanese blue-jackets firing along both sides of the street. He ducked into an alley and escaped to the boundary of the Settlement. From the gate there, he'd been watching the Japanese occupy the area with machine guns, armored cars, and armed motorcycles, "killing as they go," he said. "But they've got wounded now coming back in groups."

"In other words, you walked right into the Japanese advance." My tone was not entirely approving.

"It has never happened before and it will never happen again," Ed said, "that anybody could be so close to a war and watch it safely— all because we're foreigners."

That was an opportunity I longed to grasp. "Do you realize I could be the only woman war correspondent in the whole wide world," I said, "if you got a press card for me? The only one since 1918—if any existed even then."

"The Settlement gates are guarded. No woman would be allowed to do anything."

"I could peek," I argued. "Only one little teensy-weensy bit of cardboard. In my whole life, I'll never again have this opportunity. I need it for my book even more than you do. I only want the credentials. I only want to be able to *say* I was a war correspondent for a day. How could I get into any danger?"

"I see what you mean." Ed was dubious. "But I'll look like a fool if you get into any trouble." He did allow that I could look into "the Red Cross stuff, refugee women and children, all that."

In the end he took me to the Settlement police headquarters, where the British chief was struck dumb by the request. We emerged with press card No. 206 for the *New York Sun* with my photograph stamped on it and a pass "to enter and leave the Settlement during a state of emergency." I also got curfew pass No. 2663. These are the only proofs in my scrapbook that I ever was a war correspondent, even for one day.

One of my letters home reads in part:

Yesterday I went out to the battlefield—or near it. Edgar Snow took me to the North Station of Shanghai, where the big casualties were. From an observation post, I could look around. Down the street before me was a Chinese dugout. Half a small block away were Japanese marines. Their machine-gun nests were pointed out to me. On the pavement lay a figure draped in white—the first casualty of the war, a Chinese bugler. . . .

In the dugout we could see two young Chinese soldiers—about seventeen—romping with a woolly black pup, who was enjoying it hugely. They were laughing and saluted us when we attracted their attention. Not so the Japanese. When we went to the next corner, the street dividing the International Settlement territory, guarded by the 31st Infantry of Americans, and Japanese terrain, we stepped out into the street about three steps to look up. Immediately two Japanese leveled their bayonets at our respective breasts and there was no trifling with them. The wartime language of a salute and a smile was not in their vocabulary; they were all duty. Yet they look so much alike—these cousins of the Flowery Kingdom and the Land of the Rising Sun. The Chinese sentries around were quite uncovered and casually smoking cigarettes, but the Japanese kept well-hidden.

In some archive there may still be a newsreel of me interviewing Mayor Wu Teh-chen and inspecting refugee camps full of cholera, typhoid, and dysentery. This was filmed by Ed's good friend H. S. "Newsreel" Wong, who was with Paramount News.

Newsreel Wong made an appointment for me to interview the Chinese commander, General Tsai Ting-k'ai. Nothing could be better for Chinese morale, he figured, not to speak of getting a best-seller newsreel of an American girl in such a setting. I put on my riding outfit and boots, with my foreign-correspondent trenchcoat. In his special press car with driver, we got past the Settlement guards and circled to the rear of the Chinese lines. A few hundred yards ahead, an explosion rent the air.

"That's General Tsai's headquarters," exclaimed Newsreel. "I thought it was safe here." His driver started back without waiting for permission, hitting every pothole.

I was too surprised to be afraid. Besides, no foreigner showed fear to the Chinese.

"Don't mention this to Ed," I warned. "He'll take away my press card."

"But I thought you were his official assistant and that he wanted a good story!"

Ed was furious when he learned about my close shave. After that nobody would do anything to help me, but the Chinese heard about this event and it did nothing to harm American prestige. My subsequent photographs were chiefly of barbed-wire barricades, sandbags, and nonaction civilian affairs.

However, the instant the war stopped and the Japanese withdrew, a young American lieutenant in Intelligence took me with one or two others to Woosung Forts, which had been under siege from the Japanese naval guns in the harbor. My press card got me in. The forts were still smoking and bodies still lay in the shelters. In one of them, two young soldiers had died of percussion.

We took our photographs standing by the big artillery. That was a scoop on Ed, who examined my photographs respectfully. During this war Ed was under fire and bombing several times, as he had hoped to be—always in the middle of events. (Evans Carlson, who was later under fire with him in 1937, subsequently told me that Ed was one of the bravest men he had ever known in a life of soldiering.)

In Japan the premier, Inukai, was assassinated for ordering the retreat. The Chinese Nineteenth Route Army lost about fourteen thousand casualties, and some twenty thousand civilians.

This was the first time Chinese soldiers had ever stood up to a modern army; they had done so against the wishes of Chiang Kai-shek, who had advocated nonresistance. Since 1927, Chiang had been in a bind, with the Japanese threat on the coast and civil war in the rear. He preferred to fight the civil war, against his own people; the Japanese seemed less of a threat to his position. But the students of China preferred revolution, and resistance to Japan.

EXCERPT FROM A LETTER

WINTER 1932

I've a boyfriend now whom I like enormously. He's a writer, quite a
famous one, and only 27 years old. But we both in a way hate to
give up our careers. I like him better than anyone else I have ever
known, I believe, and he really does seem to have a good deal of
talent, and a wonderful adventuring spirit. Went all through the
bandit country of Yunnan, an outlying province of China, near
Tibet, into Indo-China and the interior of India *alone* with his own
caravan. He is a correspondent for the Consolidated Press here. But
I am very wary of any entangling alliances for some reason. . . .

CHAPTER 5

Nowhere Else
on Earth

Confucius Say: Superior Woman Talk About Self:
Smart Woman Talk About Superior Man.

It was always said that Shanghai was like nowhere else on earth, especially for the few foreign women there. With men ten to one or
thereabouts, even the most ordinary female was queen for a day, particularly the few Americans. Consequent male attention was not particularly flattering, though it could be fun, but I had a demanding job
and kept, by Shanghai standards, pretty much out of circulation. Half
a dozen wealthy and powerful young taipans were looking for wives,
but I did not like the Shanghai Mind.

Most Americans stayed at the few apartment-hotels with modern
plumbing and foreign-style meals. My tiny room at the China United
cost less than U.S. $50 a month with food, roomboy, and service for a
pukka memsahib. A masseuse came every day for about U.S. thirty
cents. A part-time "wash amah" kept my appearance immaculate, but
wore out my white kid gloves and satin evening shoes with her
attentions.

Every morning my roomboy escorted me down in the elevator.
My U.S. $5-a-month rickshaman was waiting in the most-favored-
nation stand, his proud smile lighting up the whole day for me, the
ricksha cushions as clean as my wash-amah-tended clothing.

As I wrote home, "I sometimes think the lure of the Orient is
simply the extremely low cost of everything. One lives like an empress
for less than nothing."

Just across the street was the big Race Course, a shady green park
for promenading dressed to the nines, as in London. Chiefly the British played polo and rode their race ponies here, it was so exclusive.

I never tired of the scene on the crowded main thoroughfare—
Bubbling Well merged into Nanking Road. The Chocolate Shop was

at a point jutting out into Nanking Road, across from Kelley & Walsh's Bookstore. Here Ed and I held our state occasions barricaded behind ice cream sodas—nice, clean Young America against the corrupt Old World. We felt ourselves to be heirs to The Future, while the British drank Scotch at the longest bar in the world in the Shanghai Club on the bund, and the Japanese drilled in their barracks. (In 1973, I looked for the Chocolate Shop. After 1949, Nanking Road was widened, and this outpost of American civilization tumbled into oblivion, along with much, but not all, American civilization.)

Madame Sun Yat-sen also made appointments at the Chocolate Shop and loved it. It was the most American spot in all China, with nostalgia in every scoop of clean, safe ice cream. It was new and the only place where foreigners could feel secure drinking milk.

The opening of Henningson's Dairy meant that foreign babies born in China could be assured of a sanitary supply of cow's milk. But there were still few foreign families who risked having babies in China. Their servants lived at home, and from there might carry all their constant and varied family diseases to their employers. Chinese babies never had anything but human milk, and had plenty of antibodies in their blood against diseases that killed a foreign child within days.

Foreign women were of two minds about living in China. Good family men, like J. B. Powell, sent wife and babies home to be safe. But the Navy wives at the China United held court in a group and would talk about the China days to the end of their lives. Most of them were trained in southern charm, like Wallis Warfield, who was known to them already.

This was the era of "glorifying the American girl" and of the Duchess of Windsor. Wallis had been a Navy wife at the Palace Hotel in Shanghai and in Peking for a year in 1924. Almost fifty years later she said, "It was one of the best, most exciting times of my life. Can you imagine a place where there are ten men for every woman?" *

Wallis had got her first training in how to become queen of England in China, where she learned to handle a train of admirers and how to hold court. In England women were not yet allowed real freedom, so Americans were already trying to take over the British Empire—Consuelo Vanderbilt (the Duchess of Marlborough), Lady Cunard, Lady Furness, Lady Astor.

It was déclassé for British-born women to try to be charming,

* R. G. Martin, *The Woman He Loved* (New York: Simon & Schuster, 1974).

attractive, and liked, especially in outposts of Empire. They had to be respected. The secret American weapon was not very secret: Both sexes tried to be attractive and liked, not only by their peers but by the natives abroad, whom we suspected of being human if properly approached. The big object was to make a good impression—high style, high standards of conduct, and high *cumsha*. American women were allowed some freedom but at a constant high price—they had to be charming at any cost, no matter how much their feet hurt. Abroad they had to set the example—from the YWCA to the Standard Oil wives far in the interior.

Only a few were beautiful outside (Wallis Warfield was no beauty); the others had to learn how to be charming inside out (an art Wallis perfected as no other woman, though Annapolis southern Navy wives knew all her ancestral secrets).

I worked hard and overtime at everything I tried, much harder than other girls—a kind of Girl Scout ingenue. Everything was important to me. Everything had meaning. I kept all my options open, one of which was to hold more than one difficult top job for a young girl.

I loved my job. At first, I was only a clerk at the American Consulate General, among four other women, older and long experienced. They ran the show for the half-dozen consuls and vice-consuls and were by no means subordinate. Soon I was made private secretary to the consul general, and social secretary. An older clerk took the dictation. I figured this was the best job in the East for a secretary. Our salaries were astronomical when you translated the sums into purchasing power. I was saving as much as I could to travel and write my book, just as I had in the States.

I had my own impressive office and even an office coolie to put in my carbon paper. During my tenure, Edwin S. Cunningham, the "Czar of Shanghai," was at the height of his career as chairman of the Joint Committee for the Sino-Japanese Agreement. He was senior consul in Shanghai, and no other consular officer in the world had such real authority. I was right at the fulcrum of power, the point at which the British were giving it up and the Americans taking over. When official British or Japanese callers arrived, I kept them waiting a suitable period of time for purposes of American "face." Admirals and generals were given to understand that civil power came first.

Seated behind my desk, with gardenias or tuberoses on it, I was something of a personage as I handled diplomatic appointments with a high hand. The Japanese and Chinese were cautious of lese majesty.

The French and Italians were chivalry incarnate. My first Fascist was Count Galleazo Ciano, married to Edda, daughter of Mussolini. He was minister to China, and I practiced my infantile Italian on him on social occasions.

Young unmarried foreign women were almost nonexistent in China. Bachelors came early and made appointments with the consul general just before lunch, with a view toward inviting me. But I was so bound up in proper protocol that I seldom accepted and then only after consulting my social mentors.

This devotion to duty paid off handsomely. I became a kind of American mascot. Mr. Cunningham's wife, Rhoda, was too sick to manage social activities, so I was given responsibility for—and a free hand with—the entertainment and social affairs of the consular body, as well as the American Consulate General and the whole American community. For foreigners the Shanghai war was all spit-and-polish, gold braid and festivity, intoxication with esprit de corps, but no action beyond tea dances. The Wallis Warfields of the time never had more fun. Army wives in Manila were sent for; I met them at the ship with gardenias. They knew all about my activities and said Army had never before been so handsomely treated by any diplomatic arm of the government.

How proud I was when the 15th Infantry arrived from the Philippines with two of the handsomest officers ever exhibited in the East— Colonel Lorenzo Gasser and Major L. T. Gerow. Navy had always been socially acceptable but not Army—not without West Point credentials, anyway—but I changed things. Colonel Gasser and Major Gerow held a formal dinner in my honor at the French Club in appreciation.

Not to be outdone, the Admiral of the Fleet gave a tea dance in my honor aboard the flagship. The armed services were all dressed up with nowhere to go except the functions I arranged at the expense of the Consulate General. The top officers detailed their aides to be at my command at all times.

Ordinarily, the only American armed force on land in Shanghai was the Fourth Marines under Colonel Richard Hooker, which stayed mobilized to guard the Settlement. Probably there was one man in the American armed forces in China for every two American civilians.

Beyond the call of duty, I arranged receptions, dinners, even bridge parties to make the American presence felt in style, always seeing to it that local news photographers were invited. I hoped to intimidate both the British and Japanese.

The idea of a USO was unheard of then. There were no precedents to go by, as this was the first real "war" since World War I. Every man there was desperate to be under fire—it would be for the first time, except for a few at the top. In the back of my mind were two ideas: (1) These men are willing to risk their lives for us, and (2) Japan will probably not withdraw without the threat implied by the presence of these foreign armed forces. And then there was (3): Doesn't every one of them look knockout in his uniform?

I made a point of introducing different nationalities to each other at big receptions, and also invited officers to civilian diplomatic affairs where they weren't supposed to be—with the consent of my mentors, of course.

The climax of my hostess career was as "Secretary of the American Community Committee for the 4th of July, 1932"—which was how I signed my letters. I had to organize the celebration on the grass of the Race Course, with bands, uniforms, flag-raising, and a big reception. It was to be in no way inferior to the King's Birthday Garden Party, for which women dressed as at Buckingham Palace, with big hats and long gowns that preferably dragged on the grass. I had already designed my own dress for formal garden parties—pale blue eyelet embroidery with black velvet sash—but, alas, it didn't drag on the grass. From a Virginia Navy wife of Wallis Warfield punctilio, I bought her *proper* gown—long, trailing pink lace with a bertha collar and black velvet sash, worn with a wide-brimmed, dippy leghorn hat trailing a black velvet streamer. (I wore this for years on such occasions, as she had worn it before me.)

While officiating in all that dreadful heat, holding up my long skirt with one hand, I caught a glimpse of Ed watching me with enamored wistfulness from the sidelines. I waved at him regally. He saluted with a wonderful smile.

International top society was not represented in Shanghai then, except by the Sassoons, friends of the Prince of Wales. When they entertained at their own Cathay Hotel for Willy Vanderbilt, I was asked to be his partner for dinner and dancing.

Before summer, the Lytton Commission of the League of Nations arrived on its way to Manchuria to study the Japanese occupation. I had to arrange their interviews. They—especially William Biddle,

General McCoy's aide—wanted me to join their staff, not only in China but in Geneva. Only a few months before, I would have fainted with delight at being offered such an opportunity. Now I had grown wings for any wind. I didn't want to waste any more of my time on other people's work. It was time to do my own. I was collecting materials for a book—the book I never wrote—learning as I went along. Edgar Snow was rushing out the manuscript of his first book, *Far Eastern Front*, and not allowing outside distractions. I liked him for that.

One senior consul, Paul Houston, undertook to educate me when I confided to him that I had come to the East to write a book. He was ill with kidney problems (and died a few months later), but he picked me as the heir to his Old China Hand experience and loaned me books to read from his extensive library. In strict confidence, he also handed me his long consular report on the Canton Commune of 1927, when he had saved the lives of some Soviet consular people at a time when the Kuomintang was murdering others. He was the first person I met who knew anything firsthand about the Communists in China. This was no doubt the first objective and factual report to the State Department on this controversial subject—the kind which later caused the Old China Hands to be pushed out of the State Department by the China Lobby McCarthyists. Houston was very proud of this report, even emotional. It was ammunition for the liberal Kellogg-Johnson noninterventionists. He was a kind of watchdog over the Shanghai-minded Cunningham, and he asked me never to mention anything to Cunningham about him.

"There is nothing you can't do," Houston said to me in last-testament tones. "You really are unusual." He felt that I asked the right questions, that I was constructive and thought like a leader: "Always wanting to know what is to be done—not blaming others."

"I'm a typical American, only more so," I said. "Why not do the impossible?"

"Maybe," he said, but typical Americans never came to China. He felt that was what was wrong with most writing about China. "We only get the peculiar ones—or they wouldn't have come here in the first place." To him, a sinologist was synonymous with the medieval mind, and he advised me against the study of the Chinese language. "It will damage your brain cells," he said.

I also inherited the China experience of an Alsatian-German-French man named Dr. Victor Frêne, the only teacher of China studies that I could find. He had been buried in Shansi for twenty-five years as a sinologist trying to learn about the "real" China. His finding was totally negative. Nothing could be done to modernize China except to remove the children from their families when they were taken off mother's milk and to put them in completely Western boarding schools, hermetically sealed from all Chinese influences. A proof of the efficacy of this program existed in the famous Soong sisters. Their parents had forced them as children to live at the Bridgman boarding school in Shanghai, to become Westernized years ahead of other Chinese. Then they had been pushed to graduate from college in America. The result was that two sisters became First Ladies of China, Ching-ling marrying Sun Yat-sen, and Mei-ling marrying Chiang Kai-shek. The other sister, Eling, married Dr. H. H. Kung, premier of China, and was the mentor of the "Soong dynasty," which was the liaison for American aid to China after 1927.

"But you're missing the main point," I informed Dr. Frêne: Nothing would have happened had these sisters been educated in France or Germany. They were trained in strict puritanism—the foundation stone of American civilization. It built the British Empire, too. "It's the principle of the steam engine—percussion is power," I said. "You should read Emerson, instead of Kant and Freud."

Dr. Frêne was so astonished, he actually kowtowed three times, head to floor: "You are the teacher. I am the humble pupil." He felt I had the secret of what he called "sense power." What was wrong with the Chinese, in his opinion, was that they had brainpower but no sense power—their nervous systems were atrophied, degenerate, hopeless. "You have what the Chinese lack," he said. "You must be superintendent of my schools."

"It's nothing but self-discipline," I said. "But it's not negative. You have to generate power first. It's no use putting the lid on an empty kettle. You have to get up steam. It has to be productive, creative, electrical."

EXCERPT FROM A LETTER

SPRING 1932

Most of the foreigners complain that Shanghai is a hermetically sealed collection of buildings and that you can't get away for a weekend. I don't understand that. There is everywhere to go, close and far, by river, canal, rail, although there are no motor roads. . . .

I organized an expedition to Wusih, about five hours away from Shanghai by rail ordinarily, and now, on account of disturbed conditions, about eight hours.

Next to Shanghai, Wusih is the most important industrial center of China because of the textile mills. I heard it was dirty and not worth the trip, but I was anxious to see it anyway. Moreover, it was said to be infested with bandits, pirates (on the lake), and soldiers, and considered dangerous, which is a lot of tommyrot. I am not afraid of any Chinese in China. It's only a matter of common politeness and they wouldn't conceivably do any traveler any harm, except, of course, a case of kidnaping.

We left on the Shanghai-Nanking Railway. . . . The train was to leave about 3:00 P.M. . . . We got there at 2:30 and could hardly get into the first-class coach, much less sit down. After squirming around for five minutes, I squirmed a suitcase down and plunked myself upon it. The Chinese don't pay any more attention to white women with burdens than to white women without burdens, which is quite fitting and proper but not much assistance in the matter of luggage.

The seats near the windows were mostly occupied by officers going to the interior for duty. They all wear dark blue cotton uniforms and puttees, and usually tennis shoes on their feet, with caps like the French. The uniforms are a sort of greenish-blue color and awfully faded-looking, due to sun, rain, and legitimate washing. They wear identification on their sleeves in the form of bands painted with Chinese characters, and their rank insignia on their shoulders, and they actually pin them on with safety pins—

great healthy ones—as if they were perfectly good military ornaments. They don't look martial and trim, but they are all good-humored and friendly and I like them very much. . . .

We went into Wusih. One of my friends had a card to Mr. Yung, whom he knew slightly, so we went to see him at the Sung Sing Cotton Mill No. 3, which looked like a summer palace beside a canal. It was painted white with ivy growing on the smokestack and a garden in front with trees and benches.

We first met Mr. Yung's secretary and the Assistant Manager of the mills. . . . Finally, Mr. Yung came out himself and we exchanged the social amenities by bowing and introducing each other as in a prizefight ring, with hands clasped together. This Mr. Yung was most charming. He spoke no English. . . . We talked for a while about this and that across a Chinese polished table.

I didn't know that it was possible to have such a three-cornered conversation before. We asked questions of the secretary and he immediately interpreted into Chinese and Mr. Yung answered. . . .

Mr. Yung spoke the most beautiful Mandarin. This is spoken in "tones" or certain cadences and rhythms that is difficult to explain but nice to listen to. It is said that Chinese well spoken is far the most beautiful language in the world. That is why poetry has so flourished in China. . . .

We then went through a cotton mill and a textile plant. They were using Massachusetts machinery. It was entirely modern. Hundreds of small boys and girls worked there, however. It was depressing in that respect. . . .

Wusih was impressive, particularly because no foreigner has had anything to do with its development. It is an all-Chinese community, and there is no doubt but that it is evidence that China only needs a little capital to progress right along with any other country.

CHAPTER 6

The Shanghai Mind

"Don't associate with Snow or Powell. They're *pro-Chinese*." The tone of voice of one of my social arbiters was frightening, an icy warning from some arctic region I did not understand. "But Powell's sisters are nice friends for you. They're the loveliest girls who ever came to Shanghai. Mrs. Powell had common sense enough to take the children back to the States."

This was not my first encounter with what was called the Shanghai Mind, but it was the first time I recognized it. I had to start growing up. I was self-confident, but I was new and cautious. I did not want to be contaminated by anything that sounded as dreadful as being *pro-Chinese,* or to come into conflict with the local Establishment, which was receiving me not only with open arms but with every kindness and helpfulness. My parents were solid civic leaders, and I was the type who liked to be popular and proper and admired, the type elected to school offices every year. Yet even so, I had always had an independent mind scholastically, with my own ideas. I had never before been exposed to any dangerous thoughts.

The Powell family had all but adopted Ed when he first arrived in Shanghai. Aged around forty in 1931, J.B. was and looked like a night owl behind his glasses; he had to be up late to get cables off to his newspaper, the *Chicago Tribune.* J.B. had sprue of the liver and never drank anything but tea. Devoted to his wife and children back in the States, he saved his money to send to them.

While Shanghailanders were ostracizing Powell and Snow as *pro-Chinese,* the Japanese in 1931 made a blacklist of correspondents with those two names at the top. Both were watched on their travels, and we never knew how far the Japanese would dare to go. Powell always said, "I prefer Chinese bandits to any Japanese."

I took my Snow-Powell problem to Ed, telephoning him to meet me at the Chocolate Shop. "A disaster threatens," I told him. "Our

Great Love may have to be nipped in the bud."

"Oh, I can still associate with you, but only on overcast days," Ed said, smiling over his ice cream soda. He explained that to be pro-Chinese meant you were for the independence of China and against foreign intervention. It meant you were for giving up the unequal treaties and the treaty ports.

"You don't mean the end of extraterritoriality?" I was alarmed. "No foreigner could live here without that." Under extraterritoriality, people living abroad enjoy freedom from the jurisdiction of the country in which they reside, and are responsible only to the laws and courts of their native country. Because of extraterritoriality and "gunboat diplomacy," foreigners were sacrosanct in China; foreign women were strictly sacrosanct. No Chinese ever touched a foreign woman—it was taboo.

Now I reminded Ed that it had been only thirty-one years since the Empress Dowager had ordered all foreigners and all Christians in China to be massacred. And in 1927, I said, "Chiang Kai-shek was cutting off the heads of girls just because they had short hair—he thought it proved they were Communists. That's what Hallett Abend told me." (Hallett Abend, one of my father's Stanford University fellow alumni, had arrived in China just in time for the 1926–1927 revolution, and his 1930 book, *Tortured China*, influenced my thinking.)

"Oh, well, you don't have short hair." Ed always made light of things. On a more serious note, he told me that the Germans, Russians, and Austrians had no extraterritoriality. Only twelve nations did. Giving up unequal treaties and the like would certainly mean the end of British and Japanese imperialism in China, but Millard and Powell figured Americans could build up friendship with the Chinese. They trusted the Chinese of the Chiang Kai-shek variety to learn Westernized ideas.

Ed explained that imperialism comes in stages, and recommended that I read Lenin in order to understand it, as he had in India. Millard supported Sun Yat-sen and the 1911 Revolution. Powell supported the 1925–1927 Kuomintang revolution and was ostracized for it in Shanghai, but Madame Sun Yat-sen now thought Chiang Kai-shek counterrevolutionary. As for Ed, he agreed with Madame Sun that China needed more revolution—lots more.

I subscribed to Powell's *China Weekly Review*, and did book reviews for it; my first article for J.B. was on "The Shanghai Mind." (He said it was brilliant!) I read all of Millard's dull books. At teatime I listened to Ed read his work aloud, and contributed "homeside" comments and criticisms. I couldn't see anything wrong with their points of view; only Ed took his anti-imperialism a step beyond that of the older men.

Only Americans could have done the things any of us did. No one else was in a position to carry out such activities. I still feel strongly the natural and historic friendship between Chinese and Americans— we can both be self-contained and need feel no mortal enmities. As for political affairs, these are as changing as the seasons.

There were times in Shanghai when I actually felt *alone*—a tiny kernel of wheat between two huge millstones. I never felt crushed, though—only in danger of it. The nether millstone supported the case for anti-imperialism. The upper millstone was made up of the "imperialist" diehards of the Shanghai Mind, headed by my boss, since 1919 the "Czar of Shanghai," American Consul General Edwin S. Cunningham, who dated back to 1914 in China. He defended the big-business taipans of the treaty ports.

By 1927, foreigners were being evacuated from the interior to the treaty ports, and many escaped elsewhere and never returned. The Nationalist Kuomintang armies from Canton reached Hankow and Nanking on the Yangtze River within about six months. In Hankow, Madame Sun Yat-sen was in the left-wing government, which negotiated with the government in London for the return of the British Concession, but which collapsed when it split with Chiang Kai-shek's right wing.

In Nanking several, perhaps half a dozen, foreigners, it was said, were killed by Nationalist troops, and "Reds" were blamed. (I could never find any evidence or reason why the Reds should be so idiotic, but Powell believed the story.) Chiang Kai-shek soon set up his government in this city, making a deal with the terrified foreign interests in Shanghai.

Powell was in Shanghai when labor unions took over the Chinese section of the city, where more industry was concentrated than in any area of equal size in East Asia. They were led by Chou En-lai, but intended to cede control to the Kuomintang. Gangsters massacred about five thousand workers near the railway station, providing a reason for Chiang Kai-shek and his troops to take over.

Meantime, 40,000 foreign troops had arrived to protect Shanghai and its 75,000 or so foreigners. (The American troops were under the

Quaker general Smedley Butler, who had orders not to fire on Chinese troops—and reported later that his forces had not fired a single hostile shot while stationed in China.) Powell's *China Weekly Review* took a lone, valiant stand against armed intervention, backed from Washington by the policies of President Coolidge and Secretary of State Kellogg. The American Chamber of Commerce passed resolutions demanding armed intervention by the powers and attacking Powell.

· Neither Powell nor Millard ever learned to pronounce the name of Chiang Kai-shek, but they were not stampeded by these 1927 events. Powell would never use such terms as *bourgeois nationalist*, but that was what he believed Chiang Kai-shek represented, or might if coddled and manipulated by friendly Americans.

It took me a long time to decide what Chiang did represent. It was really "compradorism," which is what the Chinese call capitalism, and which was the other side of the coin of "imperialism." Fortunately, I was not caught in the fog of Sinitic-Marxist semantic warfare. I was in the middle of reality and had to learn from the facts, not from imaginary categories, each one caught in a contradiction. When the Chinese use the term *feudalism*, they actually mean the old *prefeudal* Confucian system of the tribal and patriarchal clan-commune. The Chinese Communists now call Chiang Kai-shek a feudal comprador, which was what I figured he was in 1935–1937 when it was hardly the fashion, and the Soviets, along with Powell, were still anxiously trying to whitewash him as a "bourgeois nationalist."

In 1932, I was too busy to think all this through, but nothing was ever wasted on me. Edgar Snow was almost the only person in Shanghai willing to talk to me about the Chinese and their problems.

Anti-imperialism might have few representatives in China, but they had the power of the press and public opinion at home, not only the Millard-Powell-Snow press but the voice of important missionaries who were "sinicizing" their investment. These watchdogs against foreign intervention had the White House and State Department behind them—the Quaker Hoover, and Kellogg of the Peace Pact of 1928, whose Quaker emissary was the minister, Nelson Trusler Johnson, so anti-interventionist, so anxious to run away from *any* involvement that even Powell called his legation budget "running expenses."

It is no accident that I joined this side—I was a protégée of the Stanford-Hoover isolationists. Yet I had to decide for myself, under daily pressure from both millstones, which viewpoint I would adopt. I had arrived in Shanghai with letters of introduction that were not social notes but commands for the Old China Hands to take care of Young America out to inspect the outposts of Empire. Both Cunningham and his enemies Millard and Powell so interpreted them. I was the surrogate for American youth in my small way and I knew it. And from the first I identified with the cause of youth in China, which was to build a whole new world.

I was not an expert except in generalities. I had never excelled in any one thing; I was always the runner-up. Yet by way of this broad, varied study in many fields, I acquired a kind of perspective by trying to see things both steadily and whole. I admired Ed for being ostracized and not afraid to stand alone. By myself, I was not big enough or strong enough or talented enough or with resources enough to do the things I subsequently did in China, nor could I have done them except as part of a team with my husband.

It is only at the point of maximum contradiction that the individual can have an active role in history. This is a parable of one small individual, on the edge of nowhere, yet reaching out to steal the Promethean fire that lights the future.

About the political situation: Chiang Kai-shek is dominating the scene as usual and the militarists in North China are doing battle as usual. The Left Wing (Wang Ching-wei and the boys) from Canton are doing a little talking and nothing else. Wang has vacillated so much that the country has entirely lost faith in him, and no one has any prestige but Chiang by virtue of his airplanes and guns. Everyone predicts the fall of the Nanking government every minute but they're still going strong. Chiang has directed all his forces against communism in the interior.

I think there are some 70,000,000 "souls" under the Communist regime in Kiangsi and the near vicinity. They call it the Soviet Republic of China and have put out paper money, stamps, and have a highly organized government apparently. They have adopted Russian Sovietism and have given the land back to the peasants. The peasants give them fullest support, and many of the soldiers of the militarists are turning Red.

It is said that every other peasant in the Yangtze Valley is a Red spy and that the Nanking troops have great difficulty getting about because of it. The peasants are oppressed more than ever before in history, it is said, and are getting restive under it. Taxes have been collected *seventy* years in advance in Szechuan, and the militarists are commandeering whole villages in their wars. The Nanking government has done nothing that was in the original reconstruction scheme of the Kuomintang. It is all they can do to keep in power by buying bullets and guns for their armies, much less build roads and industry. Every province is completely subjugated by a warlord, and he squeezes the people to the nth degree in order to keep his neighboring warlord from stealing any of his income.

I was at dinner with Dr. Joseph Rock (the famous explorer for the *National Geographic*), who is back from Yunnan, and he says the peasants are forced to plant opium instead of food for

69

themselves, in order to provide revenue for the provincial government. They have completely exterminated the Reds, he says, by the simple process of decapitating all suspects, and otherwise, on the least provocation.

The campaign against communism has reached fantastic proportions. Every day one reads in the paper of dozens of students found with copies of Karl Marx in their pockets or on their study tables, who are taken into custody by a military court and never heard from again. Shanghai is rather a nucleus in a way for this sort of activity, it is said, and "tons" of literature are perpetually being found by the Settlement and Chinese police. The unfortunate owners are summarily executed. The Shanghai factory workers have learned to strike in no uncertain fashion, and it is a bad month that one or another public utility is not on strike—the bus company, the telephone company, factories and such. Wages have been cut since the war and prices are rising. But there are no particular disturbances in the Settlement—they're too carefully nipped in the bud.

The Communist element in China is said to be the student class who can see no way out but by the forcible overthrow of the militarists, for no one has any faith left in their good intentions. The Kuomintang is an entirely different institution since good old Dr. Sun died in the middle of his humanitarian labors, and it is denounced on every hand. There is no leadership in China whatsoever.

General Sutton is said to be back in China to consider a kind of Fascist regime, which together with the threat of foreign intervention and the Japanese menace makes life here rather uncertain, and most interesting. . . .

CHAPTER 7

When I Married
Mr. Snow

On my twenty-fifth birthday, Ed appeared early—the only time he was not late—with gardenias. The celebration was to include tea at the Chocolate Shop and beef Stroganoff for dinner, in honor of our first introduction.

Over American ice cream sodas, Ed looked down shyly as he noted the passing of my twenty-fifth milestone. I could write my book better in Peking, he suggested hopefully. Peking was cheap and quiet. And if I really wanted to travel, where did I want to go?

"Borneo," I announced instantly. "That's the least explored place still—unless Osa Johnson has got there first. And Formosa. And the Celebes. And Java. And Bali. And Singapore. And every treaty port on the China coast."

"Maybe we could work something out," he said. "I don't have much to offer—but try this. It's adjustable. You may never get closer to Tibet than that."

I took the Tibetan silver saddle-ring and tried it on the wrong finger. I put him off: "I'll keep it in my purse for now. Books come first. You hurry up with yours and I'll hurry up with mine."

"This thing is bigger than we are, to coin a phrase." Ed looked trapped. "I've known that since the first minute we sat at this same table a year ago. It's not only the real McCoy *yin-yang*. It's *pa-kua* destiny.* Don't you realize yet that this marriage was not only made in heaven, it was made in a Celestial Heaven, the Number One *ding-hao* kind? Together, anything is possible. What a team we'd make!"

Yin-yang means female-male in Chinese, a concept underlying everything in the universe. It is symbolized by a circle containing two equal halves divided by a curved line to imply motion. *Pa-kua* means the Eight Principles or diagrams for fortune-telling.

"The *yin-yang* can wait." I had to keep the situation under control, as usual. "As for *pa-kua*, let's get our fortunes told and walk in Jessfield Park on my second birthday in China."

We took a taxi to the temple on Bubbling Well Road, where an old priest with long hairs in a mole on his wrinkled face scrambled the *pa-kua* fortune sticks around. Our driver interpreted in pidgin English: "*Ming* allee samee. *Ding hao!* Velly lucky. You melly chop-chop." (This meant, you two have a common destiny, very good, very lucky. You should marry right away.)

"Now how can you resist that?" Ed laughed and sang on the way to Jessfield Park, and I chimed in.

The driver kept looking back at us with a wide grin of pure delight. He probably knew both our names and our total histories— Shanghai's foreign community was small, and Chinese servants knew everything that went on or failed to go on.

We ambled under the magnolia trees in the big park, the only place a foreigner could walk except the tiny Bund Garden and the Race Course. Chinese families were promenading dressed in silks and satins, and all nationalities were out in the beautiful weather. I looked at the handsome Englishmen in tailoring from Gray's to rival Savile Row.

"My problem is—or was—that I don't like to be tied down." Ed kept trying to bring the conversation around to his point, which I was avoiding. "Until I met you, I thought of a wife as an impediment, not a helpmate. He travels fastest who travels alone. Now all I think about is marrying you before someone else cuts me out. Now I don't even have any destination in mind unless you're with me. I'll do anything you want all the rest of my life. I'll be happy just to be your stooge— really, I mean it. The only thing I care about is your approval. It's the first time I ever had any of those ideas. I'm a captive. It's terrible. I've never been captivated like this before."

(He had already given me his photograph signed "your stooge," and he always called himself that—up to World War II, when he became liberated.)

"You're the only person I've ever met who's going my way," I admitted, but, I told him, I didn't intend to make a mess of my marriage. It had to be Number 1 *ding hao*. Why not? Why have limitations? I believed in marriage. And in divorce. I believed in choice and free will. And I was willing to pay a price for a wonderful marriage. But

I didn't want it to be ruined by frustrated-author psychology. I had to write a book *first*, even if it was never published.

I realized that Ed had a rare—and to me, essential—characteristic. From the first, he believed in me and my talents and future. He was proud of everything I did. Up to the end, he was mystified that I did not become famous and rich, a Great Author, as each of us intended the other to be, there in the sunset of Jessfield Park.

In December I received a telephone call from Ed: "I'm just mailing off my book. Let's take a walk on the bund. Meet you at the Cathay Hotel."

My book was not going well at all. But I was learning prodigiously.

I was wearing walking shoes and my unborn-pony coat with the big shawl collar to ward off the sweeping river breeze. Ed turned up his coat collar and pulled down the brim of his hat as we backed away from the wind. At the customs jetty, a group of foreign sailors jauntily jumped into rickshas, their caps at precarious angles, monarchs of all they surveyed. We knew how they felt—the first excitement of discovery.

Out in the harbor the lowly sampans vied with the sailing junks, while the foreign flagships stood majestically at anchor, emblems flying straight in the stiff breeze.

Ed took hold of my arms and turned me around to face him, literally sweeping me off my feet: "Let's get out of this filthy, dirty place forever. Let's get married and make a trip to the South Seas on a Japanese ship. I've got the itinerary: every place you want to go, and Osa Johnson's never been to one of them—it says so in Japanese. We'll live in Peking while you write your book and I'll finish my travel manuscript there. Then we'll go trans-Siberian and travel in Europe."

"How will I get to the Taj Mahal?" I objected.

"I've already told you—I'll build one for you. Let's go to Russia to see if the future works. And I've always wanted to stay awhile on the Dalmatian coast. And where is that place Axel Munthe wrote about in *The Story of San Michele?*"

I was the one with tears in my eyes this time, as I pulled off one white kid glove and fished the Tibetan ring out of my handbag. "You can put it on now."

We rubbed red noses, Tibetan-style, and a group of amused Chinese workmen crowded around as they always did whenever any foreigners put on a show. In China kissing in public was taboo.

"I don't want to be married in a filthy, dirty place like Shanghai," I said. "Tokyo is nice and clean. I want gardenias and a Japanese wedding kimono. We'll travel through Japan and take the ship from Nagasaki."

"I'll cable John Allison at the embassy," Ed said. "He used to be my roommate."

We held hands and started to run toward the cable office—for the sheer fun of it.

Then I stopped still and announced: "One more thing. We have to stop at dozens of consulates along the way. And you have to make a good impression on your New York publisher, too. I'm not going to travel with anyone in an Untouchable India-tailored suit. We're on our way to Gray's. You can wear Harris tweed for ten years." I still had not forsaken appearance for reality. Why not have both? Why have limitations? Fashion was fun.

Ed didn't like that idea at all. He was glum and disapproving as I picked out the best materials at the best London tailor in the East, not only for a dark suit and a russet Harris tweed, but for a tuxedo dinner jacket and riding trousers as well. Worst of all for the exchequer was a reddish-brown camel's hair overcoat and a new hat.

This may seem idiotic but it was a good investment, considering that he wore the same things for more than ten years. He liked the tweed so much, I could hardly get him to wear anything else all during that time. (It was a two-pants suit, I hasten to note.)

I was well aware that if Ed spent so much money on his wardrobe, it would have to come out of my own clothes budget as his wife. I had no need of new clothes, yet I faced a hard decision. It was like declaring a moratorium on being young and attractive for me to make a resolution not to spend any more money on myself. I did buy, as a bride, a Paris hat, and I had one all-purpose suit made. Then there was a used Japanese wedding kimono. After that, from 1932 to 1939, I bought scarcely anything personal for myself—only the bare necessities. It took willpower.

Causing much trouble, I insisted on being married at high noon on Christmas Day at the American Embassy in Tokyo, with the future ambassador, John Allison, and his fiancée, Jeannette, as witnesses. We wore Japanese wedding kimonos at the Imperial Hotel afterward.

Mine was of heavy black silk crepe, hand-painted and hand-dyed, with a train and sleeves that touched the floor. The top half was lined in bright red silk—the bride must wear red in China and Japan—and there was a red and gold brocade obi. The design around the bottom of the kimono was of a seascape, with blue and white waves foaming and white seagulls hovering over them. I felt like Aphrodite rising from the sea, but properly clad for winter.

We began our honeymoon in Japanese inns the length of Japan, sitting on tatami mats for sukiyaki. At Atami-by-the-Sea we found the perfect Hollywood setting for the perfect honeymoon: a paper-windowed room with bamboos on one side and on the other, where the inn jutted out over the ocean, a Hokusai wave breaking underneath.

We embarked by ship on our halcyon honeymoon in the halcyon days of the winter solstice. "It is the most auspicious time for new beginnings," I told Ed. I had bought some beautiful earrings made of blue-green kingfisher feathers, and I told Ed about the charming superstition taught me by an Old China Hand sea captain: The halcyon days were the fourteen days at the time of the winter solstice when the sea was unnaturally calm, so that the halcyon, or kingfisher, could brood on its nest floating in the ocean. All nature, sun and sea, obeyed the halcyon bird in its breeding season.

The world stood still on halcyon days. It was a time for the birth of Christ and for Joshua to pretend to command the sun and for King Canute to command the waves. It was a time for the Word to go forth upon the living waters, a time to create new worlds. It was a time for sailors to forswear their profane oaths. It was a time for an odyssey under the Southern Cross following in the wake of Magellan. It would always be the time for the big events in my life, though I never planned it that way. I did not like living death or darkness. I struggled toward the light at the winter solstice.

On that halcyon honeymoon, those two young people were unafraid. They were claiming kinship with all of nature in all hemispheres, with all people in all countries, with all minds in all kinds of books.

For reading on the ship we took G. B. Shaw's *The Intelligent Woman's Guide to Socialism and Capitalism*, and H. G. Wells's *Outline of History* as well as his 1932 book, *The Work, Wealth, and Happiness of Mankind*. Americans had not as yet started to think, but we carried along George Dorsey's *Why We Behave Like Human Beings*, which I showed to the British *pukka sahib* Resident in Borneo with one word inserted: Why *Don't* We . . .

We had both read Spengler's *The Decline of the West*—I had read it in the States. In a cursory way we had studied the Age of Empire—that of Japan in Taiwan, of the British in Borneo, Hong Kong, and the China treaty ports, of the Dutch in the Celebes, Java, and Bali, of the Portuguese in Macao.

And now we were visiting all these places. It was a goodly time for Americans to travel—before we poisoned our welcome and our own psychology in Korea and Indochina.

In the chart room of the *Canada Maru*, I studied the navigation maps. There was the island of English Spit (my mother would love that); here the island of Bum-Bum (beachcombers likely). We had passed through the Sulu Sea. The Japanese captain let me take the wheel of the *Canada Maru* in the Celebes Sea. He said he would let me take the wheel again just as we crossed the equator. He liked us because we chose his ship out of all others—it was the one calling at the most unlikely places. He insisted on giving my husband and me his own cabin and private bath, and on turning over his deck to us. He borrowed our books of poetry in exchange. He treated us as if I were Amaterasu, the Sun Goddess, with Apollo in tow. The only other passengers were two or three Japanese businessmen. The warm blue-green South Seas were as clear and smooth as molten glass. Striped-sailed catamarans looked as still and unreal as painted ships.

As we approached Borneo, I appeared on deck in English-tailored white jodhpurs, a white cork helmet, and my very American red-white-and-blue scarf half-mast in wilting heat. Red-painted roofs flashed against a white coral shoreline. Casuarina, mangrove, Nipa palm trees nodded a welcome. This was Borneo—not only Borneo but Tawau! Ten thousand miles from home!

My husband looked at me without approval. He would never forgive me for bringing aboard a big black wardrobe trunk with attire for every possible occasion—from deck shorts to long evening gowns and gold slippers.

"You may think yourself a born explorer," he observed with professional scorn, "but you are no traveler."

The English voice of an ironwood merchant put him in his place, informing me that I was practically the only white woman who had ever stopped at Tawau, except for Mrs. Martin Johnson. He hoped we were not planning to take any movies: "We had to organize a 'wild' buffalo hunt for her in the rubber groves . . . all the buffalo were tame, naturally."

"Did you hear?" I swelled with pioneer pride. "Second only to Osa Johnson." But I suggested that the place must be teeming with white *men*.

"Not exactly. Only two of us—the British Resident and myself. We haven't spoken for years," the merchant said. "It's very Somerset Maugham. He thinks I'm letting down the white man's burden because I make canoe trips with the natives looking for rare hardwoods to sell at a profit."

Borneo was a landmark in my life—a seamark, anyway. Borneo was all but the last outpost of the British Empire to be given up.

Stepping onto the bund at Hong Kong, I felt I was moving backward into the heyday of British Empire, back to the Jubilee of Queen Victoria in 1887. The solid middle-class architecture seemed as permanent as the Empire on that day in 1933, in spite of the fact that George Bernard Shaw was in harbor giving out views contrary to the Kipling thesis—except on the "Recessional" beat. The manager of the Hong Kong and Shanghai Banking Corporation walked with his umbrella and City bowler as if he owned one quarter of the land surface of the earth and one quarter of its population.

We made a cross-country pilgrimage to the birthplace of Dr. Sun Yat-sen at Hsiang Shan, forty miles from Canton. Wandering around the sleepy village, I felt close to history—though this was no longer the center of revolution it had been. That center had shifted to the inaccessible far interior, where the peasants were joining Mao Tse-tung and the mysterious Red Army to fight Chiang Kai-shek and the local landlords.

In Kwangtung we called on the magistrate of the Chungshan Model District, who wore his black satin mandarin cap and heavy glasses with dignity. This was old T'ang Shao-i, who had been secretary to Yuan Shih-k'ai and first prime minister of the Chinese Republic in 1912. Born in 1860, he had been in the first covey of students sent to America in 1873 by the Manchu government, where he studied at Columbia and New York universities. He and his young wife entertained us with a real welcome at their modest country home near Macao, modernized but Chinese in feeling. T'ang liked to talk with newspapermen, and he was far from optimistic about the future of

China and critical of its government. An elder statesman, he said what he pleased on any subject.

As we left for Macao, some junks were loading contraband in a small bay near T'ang's house, and my husband remarked that T'ang was undoubtedly engaged in smuggling. I was horrified to hear this, but Ed had been in China long enough to suspect government officials of any kind of skulduggery.

The Portuguese colony of Macao was on the coast thirty-five miles from Hong Kong. It was known as the center of vice and gambling in the Orient, with opium smuggling the chief business. The city had a monopoly on these two activities and its ledgers were in the black. Macao was an ugly, depressing place, without gaiety or charm. Yet as we walked along the ancient Praia Grande beneath the governor's palace, we felt a rare nostalgic feeling for history to be in this first European outpost in the China trade—established in 1557. The Portuguese were the first adventurers in European Empire—and the last to give it up. (At this writing, Macao has not yet been taken back by China, and the future status of Hong Kong is still in doubt.)

Picturesque on a hill over a fine bay, the buildings were as hybrid as the people—called Macanese, they were a mixture of Chinese and Portuguese descent from the thousand families who originally settled in Macao. Macao, always a free port, had been the chief center of Sino-European trade in the eighteenth century, but Hong Kong took over this role when ceded to Britain in 1842. Most of the 1,800 junks engaged in fishing seemed to be sailing in and out of the port at the time we viewed this busy place.

I was looking forward to seeing Canton, the city known to Americans since clipper-ship days, the only Chinese city for which we have named a number of American towns. It was the strategic center of South China. From Kowloon in Hong Kong, a river steamer took us up the seventy-five miles of broad inlet to Canton. Junks, sampans, and steamers crowded the waterway. Except for the use of steam on foreign ships, the scene was not much different from that which greeted the first American vessel, which arrived in 1784 to start a trade in tea, silk, and cotton.

No railway existed in 1933 between Canton and Shanghai or Hankow. We took the train back to Kowloon and from there a Butterfield & Swire coastal steamer to Shanghai, stopping briefly, then on to Peking, our destination.

First we sailed through the old pirates' nest, Bias Bay, and stopped at Swatow, known for drawn-thread work, lace, embroidery—and for the sweatshops where women produced them. Swatow was also known for its oranges and its typhoons; it was near Taiwan, where storms strike with full force. Just off the coast were two little islands called Matsu and Quemoy, which would become bones of contention after 1949 when Chiang Kai-shek took refuge on Taiwan.

At the original treaty port, Amoy, we visited the international settlement on Kulansu Island, and the American consul. Amoy once monopolized the junk trade with Java and the Straits, and from here went many emigrants; most of the Chinese in the Philippines and Taiwan came from near Amoy.

Foochow was another of the original five treaty ports. It had exported bamboo shoots, lacquer, and the famous Fukien tea, the best.

The Chinese resented the treaty-port system, though plenty of them flocked there to foreign protection to escape from their own people. They demanded the rendition of the ports and the abolition of extraterritoriality. The "unequal treaties" also provided that Christians, both Chinese and foreign, were guaranteed freedom in the practice of their faith, thus becoming communities *imperia in imperio*.

These old treaty ports were dreary dead-end places for foreigners in their concessions, behind their compound walls. Always there was an air of tension and uncertainty, a kind of living death. The foreign communities were places of exile with no inner vitality, no sense of growth. They were waiting for the end like a cancer patient who cheerfully refuses to admit he has any ailment. Imperialism was retreating in China before the tide of nationalism and revolution.

In 1933, a few gunboats and warships of the foreign powers patrolled along the China coast. Foreign gunboats called regularly at Tsingtao, and the sailors made straight for Jimmy's for ice cream sodas, as we also did on arrival there. In Weihaiwei we saw part of the British fleet in the protected harbor hidden behind Liu Kung Island—the foreigners always picked islands and sandbars when building their treaty-port cities. It had been leased by Britain in 1898 as a naval and coaling station, and it served as an important summer resort, as did Tsingtao.

Chefoo had become a treaty port by the Treaty of Tientsin in 1858, at the time that four others were opened up on the Yangtze River, and gunboats were allowed there to protect them. It sat on the rocky Shantung peninsula on the Gulf of Peichili, and was a market for the raw and tussah "Shantung" silk.

Before our steamer could make its way upriver to Tientsin, we were stranded for several days on the sandy Taku bar in a bitterly cold wind. From my decadent American point of view, our ship was practically unheated, but the British seemed to be enjoying enough air for a change. On every ship or train, the British talked and complained constantly about too much heat and not enough fresh air, in marked contrast to the heroic way they always took real danger and discomfort. Finally I gathered that this subject was partly a means of avoiding personal conversation with other people. The other means was judicious verbal worship of the two little princesses, Elizabeth and Margaret, and unreserved adulation for Edward, prince of Wales. As for the Americans, they talked chiefly with horror of Franklin D. Roosevelt, just taking office in Washington, D.C.

There was nostalgia for the "honest old Chinese merchant" and the "loyal old servants" who were no more, now that the nationalist spirit was rising in China and turning them sour and dangerous. The phrase on everyone's lips was "You should have known China then."

Finally we came in sight of the foreign concessions (America had none) on the riverfront of the Peiho in Tientsin, a busy mart of trade. It had become an open port in 1860 when Britain and France occupied it. Its heyday had been under the viceroy Li Hung-chang of Hopei Province from 1874 to 1894, and foreigners still looked back upon him as representing their day of paradise. As in Hong Kong, the solid architecture of the Victorian and Edwardian eras told of bygone glory, and the "Old Lady of the Bund," the Hong Kong and Shanghai Bank, looked sound, substantial but sleepy.

There was death in the air here, a waiting for something inevitable to happen. Japan had taken Manchuria in 1931, less than two years before, and who knew what they would do next? In general, the British passengers were sympathetic with Japanese aspirations and understood them, while we Americans had opposite views.

Looking back on our trip, we had a definite feeling that the era of the white man was passing everywhere in the East, though this was not by any means a common attitude. It was a new birth of anti-imperialism—for non-Communist Americans to be in opposition to imperialism in Asia. What was rising now was anti-Fascist anti-imperialism, not the former "nationalist" anti-foreignism. The native "nationalists" were anti-foreign in psychology but not really nationalists at all. Quite the contrary, they were "the running dogs of imperialism," as the Chinese students graphically expressed it. They were part and parcel of imperialism, junior partners in crime. They were *worse* than the imperialists, with reactionary ethics and prey to all the vices of the West without any of its virtues.

The classic example was Chiang Kai-shek in China, a helpless quisling type, followed by others in Korea and Indochina, paid hirelings or beggars and bottomless pits for the American taxpayer's dollar, the only return being hatred and resentment.

I did not understand all this until I began to study fascism, but by the time I had left Canton and Hong Kong, I had reached these conclusions without knowing exactly what the Chiang Kai-shek types represented. I reacted viscerally and esthetically.

The high tide of Sun Yat-sen's Kuomintang "nationalist" revolution had been in 1925–1927, when Chiang Kai-shek and the right wing turned counterrevolutionary and split with the left wing. From that time until 1949, when Chiang Kai-shek escaped to Taiwan, China as a nation was paralyzed by this split, except for a brief time from 1937 to Pearl Harbor in 1941. Chiang Kai-shek had no program for the future; he had no future, for the same reason that his counterparts had none in South Korea, Indochina, and elsewhere, even with American aid. He was weak and had no base in the population. The people and the youth were against him; he was their enemy and they felt it. There was never any solution for such nations except some form of socialism. It was too late for capitalism, and none of the materials existed to create it.

PART TWO

PEKING

CHAPTER 8

Arrival in
Peking, 1933

The train trip from Tientsin to Peking is about ninety miles. We passed over a rich alluvial river plain with fertile farms everywhere. The houses clustered together in villages, all made of mud or bricks with tile roofs, each with its courtyard surrounded by a tamped-earth wall. As the train pulled into the station, ancient city walls towered overhead. Made of stone blocks filled with earth in the middle, the Tartar Wall was thirty feet high, thirteen miles long, and wide enough for two war chariots.

From the first, we felt the atmosphere of high romance and dramatic history in Peking. We took rickshas through the narrow, unpaved, dusty *hutungs* and along broad main avenues lined with acacia trees. We were jostled by camels bringing in coal for the fires and by mules and donkeys pulling carts among the bicycles and wheelbarrows in the narrow passageways. Only now and then did we see a foreigner in a hired taxi. The yellow loess from the far deserts blew among the streets. It was bitterly cold and we could hardly breathe in the atmosphere.

We went to the old nineteenth-century-type French Grand Hôtel de Pékin, where we were given the palatial bridal suite among the empty echoing rooms, for lack of other tourists. Our rooms were immense, with most of the heat risen to the very high ceilings. (The hotel had changed little in 1972, when I exchanged reminiscences with the *maître d'* of the large dining room, who had been there since the 1930s.) The hotel was only a few steps from the fabulous Forbidden City on the same wide street. It was the social center for foreigners, with dancing in the ballroom, which imitated the Hall of Mirrors at Versailles.

Downstairs was the famous Peking Bookstore and its owner, Henri Vetch, who did publishing and collected rare books, as well as buying and selling the libraries of local residents. There you met everyone who was really interested in China and could spend whole afternoons talking.

Just at the top of the open stairs facing the entrance was The Camel's Bell, a shop owned by Miss Helen Burton, who came from one of the Dakotas. For a low price, you could buy all kinds of beautiful Oriental *objets d'art*, from jewelry to fur coats. I still had about U.S. $500 of my own money, but I had resolved to sacrifice for the greater good everything personal that cost money. (A person could live two years in Peking on U.S. $500 then.) I was in danger of developing a martyr complex, but Helen saved me by making me the only fashion model in Peking. When tourist groups were in town, she asked me to wear her opera cloaks and ballgowns made of imperial silks; some even had trains. I would dance the Viennese waltz—the orchestra always played waltzes when I appeared—and next morning the visitors would appear at the shop to order similar gowns. I also helped Helen design jewelry and bought a few pieces of my own at cost.

I had brought four lovely evening gowns from the States, and I did not *need* anything to wear, but that did not make it easy to forgo such purchases. (The final sacrifice was that I had to sell almost all my Chinese things in 1972 to help finance my trip to China—not only the Camel's Bell jewelry but the mandarin coats and skirts, even my dishes. All I had left was one jade ring, one leopard coat that Ed gave me for Christmas in 1935—it cost about U.S. $200 at Helen's special cost-price—and my short ermine cape. The history of the ermine was this: When Barbara Hutton and her Mdvani prince occupied the bridal suite, she had had a long white ermine cape made, but the fragile bellies were not used. I had these tiny pieces made into a cape for the cost of the labor alone—about U.S. $20. I took great delight in acquiring such bargains. In 1982, I gave my ermine cape to my niece Sheril and my leopard coat to my A-student, beautiful youngest niece, Debra; also the jade ring.)

We lived in Peking during its last days as a paradise for foreigners, from 1933 to 1937, when Japan occupied it. It was a little like old Rome, dominated by dowager hostesses and an intellectual aristocracy. The city of emperors had become the city of students and scholars after the 1911 Revolution toppled the Manchu dynasty. The Legation Quarter had been a fortified enclave since the Boxers had tried to kill all the foreigners in China in 1900, but other foreigners rented Manchu palaces for tiny sums and lived like royalty.

Helen Burton was one of the grand hostesses of Peking. She entertained the celebrities as they arrived at the Peking Hotel. Helen rented a temple in the Western Hills for weekends, taking a staff of servants; such trips helped to make life in Peking rewarding. It was on these weekends that we became friends with Evans Carlson and his wife, Etelle, who was Helen's best friend. Evans later became the gung ho original for the American Marine Corps in World War II—and put that term into the language. But in Peking we had only a few ideas in common with Evans, who was adjutant of the Legation Guard, but we enjoyed swimming in the legation pool and staying there overnight sometimes.

On parade at the Legation Quarter on the Fourth of July, Evans was one of the handsomest officers you ever saw. He also had the unusual gift of instant rapport with people, even with the Chinese Communists when he met them later (in 1937–1938), which was the ultimate test. He was Spartan, stoic, and Puritan, but also overflowing with American goodwill and charm, not to speak of goodness. His father was a Congregational minister in Connecticut, and Evans believed in all these principles. Yet he was starving for more. He was a hungry pilgrim in search of the truth, and he did not quite find it, even at his death. He admired Ed, especially his success as an author, and it was reading *Red Star Over China* in 1937 that was to become the turning point of his life.

Evans was the first victim of the mine (or *mind*) field that was the Snow marriage. He was fascinated by our rapid exchange of ideas and debate, and was caught up in that electrical tension. He was a man of action and did not need any energizing of that kind—but intellectually he was desperate for new ideas to help him cope with the confusion of the world in that time.

"What I always needed was a marriage like Ed's," he said some years later. He felt he had wasted years of his life, because he needed someone to make him think and study, to prod him along. "Don't ever give up criticizing Ed and pushing him," he told me. "That's the making of him."

Evans's problem was that he had a perfect wife. Etelle was pretty, attractive, and totally devoted to him even after he died. She had been a Girl Scout organizer and was efficient, too, the model officer's wife. She was also generous, willing to allow him to carry out his own ideas, and very proud of all his accomplishments. But, he said, she did not debate ideas with him, or contribute anything new. She had a case of true love, but that was not what Evans needed, so he thought. He needed a talking encyclopedia to make up for his lack of formal education, and discussion of all the new ideas then just coming on the horizon.

He was born to command; as a boy he had even refused to take orders from his own mother. Etelle was afraid of Evans in a way and she greatly respected him. He did not like any kind of weakness, so she had to be a "good sport" in everything. She even tried to keep up with his long Yankee legs on mountain hikes. I was with her in the Western Hills when, though pregnant, she insisted on being a good sport during a hike and was suffering pain, not daring even to mention it to Evans. The result was a miscarriage.

One day in the Western Hills, Evans and I were sauntering together among the cypresses and ginkgo trees. Both Ed and I loved Evans and Etelle, but I had been smothered all weekend by talk against Roosevelt and the New Deal. Evans was righteously attacking the labor unions: "If a man doesn't like his job, why doesn't he get out and go somewhere else," he declared, "instead of making all this trouble. He ought to be a good sport."

I seldom lost my temper but I pounced on him: "Don't think you can shoot down Americans like you did the Nicaraguans. Any worker who won't join a union or go on strike is just like a Chinese coolie. That's the best thing about America—that working-class people are refusing to be treated like coolies and want their rights. I don't see how you can be a good sport when you refuse fair play to people just because they are honest and hard-working and want civilized working conditions. Why not? And don't call yourself a Christian, either, with such terrible ideas."

Nobody had ever talked to him like that before, Evans told me years later. "You really woke me up for the first time. I never forgot it. Imagine that little baby face with all those ideas behind it! I decided I'd better go home and find out what was happening when young girls like you just out from home were saying such things."

Evans went home a few months later to command Roosevelt's bodyguard, and became a total admirer of the President.

CHAPTER 9

A Peking
Courtyard

Peking was a suitable backdrop for our Peking Opera experience of the 1930s. The city dated from the Chou dynasty in the twelfth century B.C., when it was the capital of Yen. It was destroyed by Ch'in Shih Huang-ti, the emperor who built the Great Wall of China about 221 B.C., and at the end of the Han dynasty came under the Tartars for two centuries. Then the T'ang dynasty held the city until it was taken by the Khitan Tartars, who rebuilt it in A.D. 986 with walls thirty feet high and thirteen miles long, and renamed it Yenching.

In 1122, the Golden Horde Tartars from Manchuria took the city and enlarged it. Then came the Mongols under Kublai Khan, who named it Cambaluc, built much of the present architecture, and made it his capital in 1267—Marco Polo told of it in this time.

When Chu Yuan-chang in 1368 revolted against the Mongols and set up the native Ming dynasty, the first for 450 years, Nanking was the capital, while "Peiping" was only the "northern metropolis." The Ming emperor Yung Lo transferred his court to Peking ("northern capital") in 1421, and it remained the capital except from 1928 to 1949, when it was again called Peiping and Nanking was the capital. Then in 1949, the Communists restored the name Peking and once more made it the national capital.

Peking was always the frontier post of Empire, only thirty-five miles from the Great Wall. On the north is the gate to the Manchurian steppes, Shanhaikuan, and on the northwest, the Nankow pass leads to the mountains. The city is at the northern apex of the North China Plain, which spreads for ninety miles of level and tilled land to the Gulf of Peichili. The Great Wall follows the crest of the hills like an escarpment at an elevation of four thousand feet. Purple and dusky behind Peking rise the Western Hills.

In 1933, Peking was a city of walls within walls. The streets were narrow, dusty *hutungs*, or lanes, faced with the high, blind brick or mud walls of compounds, where heavily barred doors allowed the only entrance. Walls kept out noise, dust, and robbers, and provided privacy for the courtyard within and the one-story rooms lined up around its four sides. Yet there were a few wide business thoroughfares for traffic, such as Morrison Street (named for the first missionary) and Hatamen Street, where acacia trees bloomed. Houses were made of wattle-and-daub or brick, usually, because of the scarcity of wood.

We were soon taking walks along the tops of the city walls. (Only a few years later, in 1949, Mao Tse-tung would be sitting in the Forbidden City and his government would tear down the city wall to provide bricks for the underground system of bomb shelters against nuclear war.) At the battlemented gates we would exchange greetings with General Sung Cheh-yuan's soldiers, guarding the city with bigswords and rifles. These gates were closed by a curfew before midnight.

Peking was famous as the best-policed city in the Orient. The traffic police were tall, handsome, rosy-cheeked Shantung men with a careless, friendly air—at least to the sacrosanct foreigner. I seldom saw any of the cruelty so common in Shanghai, where the Sikhs constantly banged their clubs on the skulls of the rickshamen and coolies in the streets. The city had water, sewage, electric light, and tramway systems, and the main roads were macadamized.

We rented a house at No. 21 Mei Cha Hutung which had never been lived in by anyone but Chinese. We had modern plumbing and electricity, but no telephone. On August 10, 1933, I wrote to Ed's sister:

> . . . We tried to find a furnished house when we came in March, but couldn't get one, so took this and had to furnish it completely. . . . I soon discovered that Peking is flooded with curios but no usable household articles. . . .
>
> We have servants' quarters of three rooms and bath, and five rooms with bath and kitchen for ourselves. The house is arranged around a courtyard, like a Spanish villa, with high walls on each side and a little garden between the tiles of the courtyard. . . . Ed occupies one wing of the house in the "library," which is Javanese after a fashion, with batik strewn about. . . .
>
> We enjoy it very much here as the climate is wonderful (since March) and our little garden is flourishing beautifully . . . orange trees, lemon trees, pomegranates, wistaria, lilacs, palms, pines, roses. A gardener

comes around every week with the full-grown plants, which he sells at the most astonishing prices, sometimes $1 (25 cents gold) for a hundred, and if we feel temperamental we pull up the old ones and have some new blossoms.

Last month was our "dinner party" month, at the end of which we were all (including the cook and boys) quite "fed up" generally. Some people here have dinner parties for twenty or thirty people. However, with all the nuisance, there are some interesting people here and we have good fun most of the time (except at our own parties). Peking is a last stronghold of the good old tradition of entertaining on the least provocation.

Next weekend we are going on an expedition to the Western Hills, where we shall ride donkeys over the mountains and spend the evenings in several famous old Buddhist temples along the way (which is the hostelry system in China).

We have a Chinese lesson every day and I know about 200 characters now. It is not nearly so hard as it's said to be, and the ideographs are interesting. For instance, a roof with a pig under it means "home," a woman with a son in her arms means "good," the sun and moon together mean "bright" (also intelligent) or "ming"—the Ming dynasty, for example. A man standing by a word means honest, or trustworthy; many mouths mean "gossip." I, with a lamb over it, means righteousness. A door with an ear means to listen, etc. Our teacher is the most modest, quiet little soul imaginable in his gray gown with a spotlessly clean white petticoat peeping through. He teaches us both for $20 mex. a month (about $5 gold) and comes every day (except when it rains; on those days he can't go out, as his street is unusable because of the mud). . . .

Ed had a birthday the other day—28th. . . . He is very anxious to come home, at least for a short trip to see his family, and has been seriously thinking of coming this fall. He might also be able to make some lucrative connections in New York if his book is a success. Or on the other hand, the Chinese and Japanese may decide to facilitate the matter if they take serious objection to the book. . . .

We are both very well (and still friends after six months) and quite an amiable little family withal.

I still remember our first cocktail party. Peking hostesses had one strict rule: Never mix the wrong people. But I wanted to get rid of all our social obligations in one fell swoop. Never was such a salmagundi assembled before in staid, diplomatic Peking. I invited not only Japanese but even a few Chinese, which was rarely done. Most of them were men, of course, due to the shortage of women.

As you came in through the moon gate, the air was fragrant with jasmine, blossoming tuberoses, oleander, and every scented plant I could rent or buy. The small courtyard filled with people, then the living room, dining room, and Ed's study. In the house they took chairs and had lively conversations. I couldn't understand why nobody left—nor why I had to introduce old residents who had been living in Peking ten or twenty years. The cocktails and canapés had long since disappeared when the last two remaining guests looked up into the romantic Peking starlight so reluctantly that I asked them to stay for dinner. These were C. Walter Young and his wife, Gladys. He was the author of books on Manchuria and international law.

"This is the best party I've ever been to in my life," C. Walter declared. "I've met people here I've wanted to know for a long time, and we really talked, too."

Gladys Young had already inspected my house with real interest and asked me to teach a class in interior decorating for the Peking Women's Club—which I wisely refused to attempt. What she liked was my bright, warm-looking living room, more of a conservatory than anything else. Even in winter I kept it full of plants: camellias, gardenias (my favorite), and blossoming orange and lemon trees, among others. I put the plants near the windows so the sun would shine through them to brighten the rooms.

What made the living room not only unique but dramatic was the sizable miniature garden I designed. Under a long glass mirror on one wall, volcanic-ash rocks formed a mountain with a river running around it. The river had a cork to let out the water so that the goldfish and baby turtles could have a change of environment. Miniature trees grew in the rocks. The maples even changed color in the fall.

The curtains and chair covers matched: straw-color with a coarse handwoven texture. I had big concentric circles of many colors appliquéd on the corners in modernistic style, with those on the curtains in heavy paint.

The big departure from the usual dismal ancient-Victorian Peking decor was the furniture I designed and had made by a carpenter who could not speak a word of English. It was ultramodern willow, painted jade or yellow. My half-moon desk had a bookcase running around it. The top was of window glass and held paintings by Grant Wood and Thomas Benton, clipped from magazines. This desk frightened the Middle Kingdom carpenter, but it cost only $15 mex. I had

elegant chairs made with cushions that cost only $5 mex., or about
U.S. $1.

In Peking you could design anything you wanted for the same
price as buying it in a shop. I had a gorgeous time. I even designed my
own silverware, with bamboo sprays. I loved the handicraft character
of China.

Best of all I liked the beautiful, shining-clean golden-straw woven
mats, made to order for the rooms, where the floors were usually of
cold, cold cement or stone. In summer everyone had a big *p'eng* (awning), made of this same straw, over part of the courtyard.

As for the rest of the rooms, Ed had taken a hand in furnishing
them. Never have I forgotten the cold, windy day when I was sick with
a sore throat in an icy, bare house. Coolies began arriving, first with a
sidesaddle, then with some Swedish white leather skates for me. Enormous sideboards and chests appeared, black and brassbound, a hybrid
Chinese style. I thought my fever was affecting my vision, especially
when the most hideous overstuffed chair showed up. Ed brought up
the rear. He was bursting with pride.

"I bought all this for almost nothing at an auction," he said,
breathless with delight, as he occupied the decrepit big chair. "One of
the French Legation men was leaving."

It was fortunate that my throat was too sore to say anything. "Put
the black pieces in the dining room," I wrote, and he happily super-
vised their placement.

Our French Legation dining room was formal, overwhelmed by
this dreary furniture. The only thing in it I could bear was a long
refectory table I found secondhand. For it I bought a beautiful hand-
made lace cloth, which cost about U.S. $10. (I saw one like it in New
York later for $650.) I bought willow-pattern dishes and added willow-
pattern candlesticks of my own design.

The total cost of furnishing the whole house was about U.S.
$100, or some $400 to $500 mex. During our time in Peking our
everyday living cost was about U.S. $50 a month—and we lived in
princely style. The $80 a month for food was about U.S. $20, and
included entertaining on a formal scale. As exchange rates changed, it
cost us less. Rent was U.S. $15, two servants U.S. $8 a month, and
the Chinese tutor U.S. $5.

CHAPTER 10

The Peking
Mystique

The Old China Hand mystique was basically English. You had to have dogs, ponies, English tea (never Chinese), and you had to be properly (not fashionably) dressed at all times, even at home. Always you had to keep "face," even with the servants.

For U.S. $200 a month, you could live royally. "Proper Peking fashion" meant renting a Manchu palace, furnishing it with antiques, training a large staff of servants, and entertaining visiting celebrities. You also rented a temple in the Western Hills on weekends and had a stable of ponies at Paomaochang for polo, riding, or racing. You played tennis at the Peking Club and showed your dogs in the Dog Show.

I was in favor of English etiquette and tailoring, but not of British imperialism. Why should Americans be Number 2 instead of Number 1? I was Young America of the 1930s, still fighting the Revolution of 1776.

In Peking you met visiting travelers from all over the world. It was fun to meet them at other people's parties, but when they came with letters of introduction to us, it meant escorting them to the tourist places, and this became a real nuisance.

Legation custom was followed. The British dressed for dinner punctiliously, but American men like Ed tried to squirm out of it if possible. Women always wore long gowns to dinner when they went out, except on Sunday, and even at home part of the time. You wore a long dress at cocktail parties and to high tea at a legation. The hostess always dressed in a hostess gown, even at tea.

Long dresses served a useful purpose. Even if the top was bare, the dress kept your legs warm. Central heating did exist but the British objected to it, hotly. Houses were usually heated by coal stoves and fireplaces.

For casual wear, women occasionally wore shorts but never slacks. I had a pair of beach pajamas with yards of material in the legs—the only such outlandish costume in Peking.

Entertaining was incessant, but except for tourists, you saw the same people. We had tea every afternoon with scones, cake, cookies, or sandwiches. This was the hour people might drop in. My attempts to become the Madame Récamier of Peking resulted in a salon rather more like an Alice in Wonderland tea party, with Chinese speaking in all degrees of broken English and very few foreigners venturing behind the looking glass. Dinner was never served before eight or eight-thirty.

About seven hundred Americans lived in Peking: teachers, missionaries, doctors, nurses, sinologists, businessmen, artists, and hostesses, together with the legation staff and the Marines (the only American Horse Marines in existence). However, no more than some fifty of these Americans belonged to Peking "society," which revolved about the legation and the hostesses, chiefly "Aunt Lucy" Calhoun, widow of a former minister to China and sister of Harriet Monroe, founder of *Poetry* magazine.

However, you were "in the club" if you lived in Peking, because you had to be a certain kind of person to begin with. You could not earn any money in Peking to speak of—you had to be living on a private income, except for a very few and their salaries were small. The "right" kind of people preferred to live in Peking rather than to earn high money elsewhere. Actually, they had a high standard of living, thanks to the cheap prices. The foreign legations were accredited to the Nanking government; just the same, they continued to be in Peking, which was a charming place, while the capital, Nanking, was insufferable.

Foreigners usually ate foreign food. The cooks had been trained as apprentices by other cooks, so recipes were much the same wherever you went—a mixture of French and English. Water was boiled and kept in bottles in the icebox. Ice was filthy, taken from ponds and rivers full of sewage; it was dangerous even to put the butter on it.

We ate all kinds of vegetables and meat, but no raw salads—to avoid dysentery. Some foreigners washed salads in permanganate of potash and ate them, but I did not consider this practice safe. I had the cook wash fruit in it, but we ate only fruits that could be peeled, or we cooked them. Even with peeling, the knife could carry bacteria to the inside pulp. The Chinese used human excrement for fertilizer, which kept diseases going. Ed had had dysentery in Shanghai, but neither he nor I got it during the years in Peking. (Not until 1937 did I acquire it, when I went to Yenan.) A certain immunity to dysentery and other diseases was built up among those born in China and longtime residents, but you could not count on it. The untold saga of heroism was of foreigners living in Asia in almost constant pain from dysentery abscesses—often ending up with an operation that removed much of their intestines.

My health gradually deteriorated from lack of vitamins. I did not even eat many eggs or drink canned milk as my husband did. And I didn't hear about vitamins in capsules until 1938.

Anything foreign was a luxury. American cigarettes cost $20 or $25 mex. a month—and our rent was only $50 or $60 mex. So our only foreign indulgences were those my husband insisted on: Camel cigarettes, Maxwell House coffee, and Gillette razor blades.

I did not smoke, drink coffee or liquor, except rarely, and bought nothing imported for myself. I would never dare touch a Camel (in 1935, I began smoking cigarettes, but only Hatamens, the kind the rickshamen used, for ten cents mex. a package). I was not allowed to use any Gillette razor blade in its pristine condition—my husband said that if I ever needed one, to cut his throat or my own veins, I must use one of the old dull ones. He had a Japanese invention to sharpen the blades and could use them for quite a while.

As to the coffee, I discovered the cook was using over and over again the same Maxwell House can filled with a cheap variety ground at the store. It was much better coffee, fresh, and my husband never knew the difference, but I had the grocer cut the price down where it belonged. "Squeeze" was the custom everywhere in any small way. You had to pay it and be cheerful about it.

Ed chiefly drank *pai k'erh*, a powerful Chinese wine—which we also used to start the fire in the fireplaces. Vodka was cheap and effective, mixed as a punch with grapefruit juice. Most of the people we knew drank only whisky and soda, and my husband bought these when we entertained. A few bottles cost as much as the rent.

In Peking at least two wines were served at dinner, a Sauterne and a red wine. We had to observe the custom. However, a friend arranged for me to buy wines made by a French monastery just outside the city gates. Janet Sewall and I used to take rickshas and come home laden with enough to last a long time—Chablis, port, Sauterne, claret, plain table wines, blackberry liqueur, Cointreau, crème de menthe. When I got home I transferred them, like my cook with the Maxwell House can, to the expensive imported bottles. Some were old vintage; all were expertly made. The priests drank wine always; this was their own stock, which they supplied to other monasteries in China. The cost was about fifteen cents a bottle in American money; even champagne was only about twice that. They tasted better to me at that price. Visiting Americans thought our cellar fabulous until I told them the origin.

One aspect of English custom that I enthusiastically subscribed to was the British love of dogs and horses. Our dog was white and beautiful, and his name, Gobi, derived from his ancestral desert. He had been a puppy from Inner Mongolia, brought back to Peking by the Swedish explorer Sven Hedin. Someone told us the greyhound was the original dog, evolved in Central Asia. So Gobi was of the most ancient breed.

Gobi took over the entire house the first day. At night he occupied Ed's horrible French Legation overstuffed chair, but in the daytime he insisted on sleeping on our wide bed, which had a real eiderdown quilt covered with real silk. We piled it high with two sets of golf clubs and two tennis rackets in an effort to deter him, but he scratched them away, cat-fashion. Like a Chinese designer, Gobi could never understand why a vacant space should not be occupied. I had a tan camel's hair overcoat tailored for him, and in winter he pranced in it like a winner at a horse show.

Outdoors I always kept him on a leash. One day in a *hutung* in 1936, an ugly, fierce German shepherd took him by the throat without warning and tore his windpipe loose. I grabbed the shepherd's iron muzzle from his attendant and hit the big dog as hard as I could on the nose. He crouched back to attack me, but his keeper got him by the collar, and, by instinct, I ran up and put the muzzle over his mouth quick as a flash. A group of Chinese had gathered; not one of them helped. This was the old custom: They might be held responsible for anything that happened—and also they were terrified of foreign dogs. I soon found the shepherd had been trained by a rich Chinese family to kill burglars, and they were proud of his exploit; they wanted his nature to be well-known publicly. Was his muzzle off in the hope of seeing a dogfight with Gobi?

I have never been more frightened. Gobi's whole chest was torn open, and his body swelled up under the skin. However, the veterinary fixed him up.

Lawrence Salisbury and Edmund Clubb had posts in Peking

when we were there. My special friend was Robert Ward, consul in Tientsin, who came to call on us once in a while. He was influenced by the electromagnetic field of the Snow marriage and was starving for people to talk to about what was going on in the world.

The cubs at the "Language School" in those days ended up a decade or so later as *causes célèbres* because they had sent Washington the facts instead of the usual sleeping-sickness bulletins. John Stuart Service was language attaché in Peking from 1935 to 1938, and Joseph Stilwell of Monterey, California, was military attaché from 1935 to 1939. During World War II, Stilwell was the American put in charge of military affairs for Chiang Kai-shek, who intended to sit out the war and "watch the tigers fight from afar." Washington withdrew Stilwell on Chiang Kai-shek's demand to get rid of this experienced Old China Hand. That moment marked the death of the as yet unborn "American century." It proved that Americans could never handle their puppets, from Seoul to Saigon, but it did not prevent the waste of billions of dollars in useless bribes, and massive devastation, creating hatred of and contempt for Americans all over the world.

Almost every one of the Old China Hands had to be eliminated by the China Lobby-McCarthy inquisitors before American policy could be changed to its wasteful, incompetent suicide course in Asia after 1945.

Peking was prime territory for a changing circle of scholars and students. Of them all, John K. Fairbank became known as "the King," not only of China studies but as the Number 1 scholar on *The United States and China*, as his masterpiece was entitled.* John had a truly honest mind, capable of assessing facts from all sides—and so he was attacked by all sides. In 1933, he and Wilma were bride and groom, as we were.

Herrlee Creel was researching the oracle bones for his excellent book *The Birth of China*, but he did not understand his findings, as he had never studied anthropology. He was reverent toward the past and Confucianism. I remember having him to lunch with Ku Chieh-kang one day, and the battle royal that resulted—Ku had no respect at all for ancient scholarship. Ku Chieh-kang, a famous critical scholar, was one of the most attractive friends we made in China, with an honest, progressive mind—which was even rarer in China than elsewhere.

Karl Wittfogel, a former youth leader in Germany, and his wife,

* Harvard University Press, Cambridge, Mass., 1948; revised 1972.

Olga Lang, were refugees from Hitler, trained in European Marxist scholarship. He was called a Trotskyist. If he had studied anthropology at all, he did not understand it. Olga did a pioneer work on *The Chinese Family and Society* for the Yale University Press. Wittfogel's mind and objectivity had been damaged by his victimization at the hands of the Nazis, who forced him to clean out latrines barefoot to the ankles to humiliate him and destroy his personality.

None of the scholars agreed with one another, and I agreed with none of them. I realized that not one of them had got hold of the key to understanding Chinese society, ancient or modern, though their accumulation of material was important, even so.

CHAPTER 11

Teilhard de Chardin

Early in 1933, I arrived home in my boots from a cross-country paper hunt to find my husband entertaining two strangers at tea. One was an American archaeologist, Miss Ida Treat, who lived in France with her husband, Vaillant du Couturier, head of the French Communist party then. The other was their close friend, a French Jesuit priest, Teilhard de Chardin, who had been exiled to China for his heretical ideas and allowed to publish only his work as a paleontologist. (In December 1928, he and some Chinese had discovered Sinanthropus, Peking Man—he was a woman, Teilhard told me—at Choukout'ien caves thirty miles from Peking.) There was instant communication with both, and they stayed for dinner—and on until it was too late for Teilhard to get to his monastery outside the gates.

Teilhard was one of the most attractive figures of a man I had ever seen, tall, spare, superbly athletic, in excellent health and spirits—and not unaware of cutting such a figure. His handsome patrician face was weathered from paleontological field trips by oxcart, mule, and shank's pony, with fine lines at the corners of his blue-gray eyes, which reflected humor and alertness. He had a manner of sitting tensely on the edge of a chair and lifting his face toward the speaker, eyes crinkling with anticipation and attention.

From the moment of meeting, Teilhard drew a charmed circle around everyone he especially liked, as I later found out. Both Ed and I felt he was our best friend from that first afternoon. But the impact was double. Two circles moved concentrically toward each other but without reaching a common center. Teilhard's vibrations came from one individual, highly developed and magnetized from intensive self-cultivation. The other was the *yin-yang* circle, with its electromagnetic field which I thought of as "marriage power."

That conjunction of the planets at our little Chinese house in

1933 does not exist only in my imagination. Ida Treat felt it, too. We didn't see Ida again until World War II, at a dinner party given by Lewis Gannett, the literary critic, for her and Janet Flanner of Paris. Ida had been caught in Britanny during the war, and all the suffering and disillusionment were etched on her face with ugly Daumier strokes; she seemed blank with black depression. She hated the Soviet Union and everything else, save for a few memories.

"That afternoon in Peking was one of the highlights of my whole life," she said. "It was exalting. How young and gloriously happy we all were that day—we felt we owned the whole world between the four of us—we had all the answers then. I felt rejuvenated for months after that just remembering it. How we all loved Teilhard then!"

Now, she felt, she had nothing left—nothing at all. We had all met just at the time Hitler came into power in Germany and Roosevelt in the States. Teilhard was thrilled that the Catholic Church was being disestablished by his friends in Spain; it proved to him that the Church would end up on the right side—so he dreamed at the time. "The world seemed like sunrise on Easter morning then," said Ida, "not only to Teilhard but to us all, didn't it? We thought of Hitler as only a paperhanger."

"Teilhard is right," I said to her. "Marxism is not enough. Socialism is not enough. I'm an Oliver Twistist—I want more. Why be limited? We want all that and more."

"We all want more," Lewis said, "but what is it we want?" He pointed out that Ida and Janet had been at the top of their professions in France, and right in the middle of the intellectual leadership of all Europe. Now they were doomsayers. He thought there must be something about China to produce Pollyannas like me—"You still seem to be on top, yet China is devastated. You seem to think it's still the best of all possible worlds."

It wasn't China, I told him. I had taken the Pollyanna-ism to China in 1931. It was in my marrowbones. But after the China experience, you never forgot that things could be a lot worse. I had never been one to whine and complain, but if I ever felt like it, I remembered a Korean I met in Yenan. No one else could have survived as he did—yet, though he was almost dying, he was still full of the human spirit shed of its illusions, the same thing Teilhard was always striving for, I said: "pure spirit victorious over all else."

(Lewis wrote a review of my book about the Korean, *Song of*

*Ariran,** for the *New York Herald Tribune*. He did not believe it—he thought it was fictionalized. Ida would not have believed it either. But Teilhard would have realized it proved his own thesis. This Korean had lost everything, yet he had gained his own "soul"—though he did not use that word. He felt he was "God" because he was able to command himself, a victory over the limitation of human nature.)

Teilhard had been influenced by Henri Bergson of Paris, especially by his *L'Énergie spirituelle* (1919) and *L'Évolution créatrice* (1907), but he was determined to find a place for Christianity at the top of Creative Evolution, not outside of it.

Rooted in Victorian optimism, Teilhard believed man was infinitely perfectible and woman more so—he always said women were a higher form of evolution than men. Jesus was the example of the son of man becoming the Son of God, and in his own life Teilhard tried to repeat this. He was engaged in the greatest challenge and adventure of man: to develop by use of the mind, by "thinking energy," into God, and thereby order the universe. To him, becoming God was the nature of man, his special phenomenon, a part of the natural Darwinian evolution.

I have had Teilhard's disciples touch me in a sort of apostolic succession, only because I was one of the few who had touched him. Ed and I used to walk with Teilhard on top of the Tartar Wall of Peking. With our greyhound, Gobi, we climbed up the Ch'ien Men gate, walked to the Fox Tower and on to the Observatory. We would look out through the crenellated battlements from time to time over the gray-tiled roofs of the city. We three felt very much alone and intimate as we walked along.

The wall was deserted, silent, with swallows and bats in the towers and our dog happily chasing imaginary werefoxes now and then. Teilhard took a photograph of me, which I still have, looking out seriously through the astrolabe at the rooftops of the world. Why did Teilhard introduce us to the Tartar Wall and the ancient Observatory built by his Jesuit order over three centuries earlier? Why these two

---

* *Song of Ariran*, first published by John Day Company, New York, 1941. Pearl Buck called it "a grand book." It was reprinted in 1973 by Ramparts Press, Palo Alto, California, and Monthly Review Press, New York. In Japan it was a best seller, especially among the 600,000 Koreans in Japan, with nine printings of the second publication. In 1982 it was reprinted in Japan in a series of Great World Classics.

Americans, instead of two young French or English people—or Chinese? He was symbolically handing over the palladia of French power to Young America in the East, not by wish and will but by premonition.

We used to stand with our elbows on the parapet of the Peking Observatory and think long thoughts. Teilhard identified with the line of Jesuits who first opened up the East—Saint Francis Xavier, the apostle of modern time, who died in the Orient in 1552, and Matteo Ricci, who taught astronomy and science at the Chinese court in the seventeenth century, as Teilhard did research in paleontology and prehistory in the twentieth century.

Teilhard was a real Jesuit, too, and lived strictly by rules of the order; he claimed the right to think for himself but not to express or publish. I could not understand why he did not get out of the order, but now I see that this was the root of his influence. He wanted to take over from the inside, not be a protestant dissenter, of which there were many—but only one like himself.

He well understood the principle of power under percussion—the ancient source of surplus psychic and physical energy among priests of all sects. He preferred women to men, and many of them worshiped him, but he was not the type to violate the vow of chastity, which bottled up this power for other purposes. His attitude toward women was very French, very charming, and cultivated to be charming. He was close to his sisters, and generally favored American women over Europeans because they were emancipated, more interesting, more educated, more on his level, he told me.

To me, he was typically French, especially in appearance and mannerisms. He loved France and always felt exiled from Paris. He especially liked good food and wine, good conversation, fascinating (not pretty) women, and all the amenities of high society. He was not a saint, a recluse, or an ascetic, but a political Jesuit who believed man is also a spiritual animal, the only one.

Born in the Auvergne on May 1, 1881, Teilhard was in his prime when we first met him at age fifty-two. He was a descendant of Voltaire and Pascal, determined to find the logic of the universe and yet to retain the Catholic mystique. Teilhard told me that he did not choose to be a priest; his family ordered it.

He spent twenty-five years in China and the East, after arriving in 1923 to work in Père Émile Licent's research center. Not only was he barred from publishing anything but scientific reports from that time until after his death, but also from teaching.

Teilhard had to develop spiritual power for his own self-survival. He was alone in the world, yet he believed not only that God and Jesus were leading him by both hands, but that he was himself another incarnation of Jesus and therefore of God.

The original contribution of Teilhard is said to be this: that the "spirit" grows naturally out of maximum development of the brain and body; that these three are not separate entities but organic parts of one whole; that the "soul" is not independent of the body but develops out of maximum cultivation of the mind. Of course, I agreed with this totally, and it solved what had always seemed to me an illogical contradiction. It was contrary to the ancient Catholic concept that "saints" can develop spiritually out of sickness, ignorance, and mindlessness. It was also contrary to the Yoga concept of paralyzing the body and mind in order to separate these from the "spirit."

Obviously, however, one cannot develop all three things at the same moment, only in sequence. Meditation is good for the "soul," and tennis for the body. A sickly, weak spirituality can develop from a starved body and mind, but not the kind of spiritual energy that turns the world upside down, as in the case of Mao Tse-tung and Teilhard.

Teilhard rejected the *Decline of the West* thesis of the German Oswald Spengler, which we had all three studied (I had read it in the States and decided to go East to see if the East had anything we in the West lacked). He was absolute in his faith in Western civilization and thought its *élan vital* was Christianity, not science. He totally rejected all kinds of Eastern philosophy and religion, and advised me not to waste my time studying them—this made me think him narrow, bigoted, and limited, so I did not take this advice.

Not until the atomic bomb was dropped in 1945 did I realize the importance of Teilhard's aim, which was to open up the Catholic mind to science and to inform science with Christian ethics, at the same time pushing the evolution of the human species on to higher levels.

Ed and I were typical products of American democracy and we liked it. We could not admit that anyone was incapable of self-government, no matter how many mistakes were made.

Teilhard was an elitist. He did not think China or India or any other colonial nation was capable of self-government, though he was not an imperialist in the Leninist sense, or even in the missionary sense. To him, imperialism was only one process in the long march of Western civilization toward its Omega, just as were other isms like fascism, communism, and Marxism. He was anti-Fascist, but he thought democracy was "moribund." He considered the Comintern a clumsy imitation of the international Jesuit network, and local Communist parties similar to local Jesuit priesthoods, with the adoption of "any means to an end" as a political ethic. He was not anti-Marxist or anti-Communist or anti-Soviet; he thought them childish and inferior to Christian socialism, and like science not informed by the Christian spirit and ethic. He felt himself a victim oppressed by a "Fascist" type of repression even worse than Hitler's, the same obscurantism which brought McCarthyism to America less than a generation later. He was anti-Fascist because it was "anti-Christian" and a tyranny over the right to think, much less to publish. Teilhard was not a part of the old Jesuitism—he was in opposition to it and formulated a "new Christianity" of the "elect," not limited to "Christians" in the old sense.

Before 1936, Teilhard was the only person, except for a few Chinese, we could talk with about the big controversial subjects that were mustering forces for World War II—fascism, communism, socialism, Marxism—as well as the things for which we had no common language then. In diplomatic custom, controversy was taboo—but also nobody in Peking had anything to offer on these new, unknown problems. Conversation was as dull as somebody else's dishwater.

You could not talk at Peking dinner parties about the causes of World War II, which arrived six years later by surprise, but these complicated ideas were common fare with Teilhard. He was not in Peking during the December 9th "revolution" of 1935, when Ed and I became involved with the student movement. Teilhard was in France for three months, then in India and Java, and did not return to Peking until February or March of 1936, at which time he came for lunch at our house. He was astonished by the student movement and delighted, too, though few of the French-trained students participated.

I gave him a small black wooden temple figurine that I had found in Java—an ape-man with a tail. He said he loved it and had never before seen such an ape-man figurine, a "Java Man." After lunch we again walked along the wall, which was only a few steps from our Fox Tower house. We had much to talk about in 1936. Hitler had ordered conscription in 1935, and Italy began the occupation of Ethiopia in October. Hitler occupied the Rhineland in March 1936.

In this black time, the brightest spot on the horizon for Teilhard was the Republican government in Spain, stronghold of the old Inquisition since 1492 and the voyage of Columbus. Spain had been one reason why Teilhard kept insisting: "When the time comes, you will find the Catholic Church on the right side." He meant on the side of socialism, not fascism. Then on July 17, 1936, Franco's revolt began against the democratic government of Spain and won the victory early in 1939, supported by aid from Italy and Germany while the "democracies" watched helplessly.

In June 1940, Occupied France signed the Vichyite armistice with Germany. The soul of France never recovered from that deep wound, yet it was this disintegration that opened the way for Teilhardism and a new psyche, as the white birch springs up in the ashes of a forest fire.

Of all the people I have known, two turned out to be the most important. Both have been virtually deified. Mao Tse-tung became the embodiment of Asia in revolution. Teilhard de Chardin became the spirit of European civilization, of the Christian Omega, perhaps the highest phenomenon of man it has produced so far.

For Teilhard, I became a kind of guinea pig, to try out his complicated philosophy on a youthful, Protestant-secular type of mind. For Mao Tse-tung, I was also Young America in search of the truth— and confronted by the contradictions in China, which he undertook to explain to me.

I can see the Omega point where the philosophies of Teilhard and Mao Tse-tung meet, where the oppositions merge into identity.

CHAPTER 12

Doña Quixote

For a year I struggled against what the Chinese called feudalism, and I was defeated utterly. This was the stupidest thing I ever did. It was my first encounter with real Chinese society.

The first time we stepped out of the Peking Hotel on our arrival in 1933, up came two rickshamen from the waiting line. I decided it would be fun to raise their status in life in the poor-boy-makes-good American tradition. So I gave Wang a job as private rickshaman for less than U.S. $5 a month, and I tried to train Shen I-pei as Number 1 houseboy. I got a cook through the Number 1 boy of a friend—and at first he behaved quite well, until he had enough money to assert "face." I paid each one extra, since I did not hire a coolie.

I had been warned by Old Peking Hands: You cannot do that. You can't beat the system. It's a hierarchy from Number 1, Number 2, on down the line. You can't hire anybody unless he has a guarantee from somebody else's Number 1 boy. Any Chinese would rather starve than lose face by working under a former rickshaman. All the servants for foreigners are organized in a network and nobody new can break in except as part of this network, with *cumsha* all along the line. It's a whole chain of guarantors.

The Peking servant system was considered the best in the world by the dowagers who had been world travelers. You were supposed to have a Number 1 houseboy; a cook, guaranteed by him, who had a *t'u-ti* apprentice, unpaid, doing all the kitchen manual labor; a coolie, guaranteed by the Number 1 boy, who did all the manual work, such as dusting the furniture and cleaning the floors; and a wash amah, at least part-time. This was the minimum. "Aunt Lucy" Calhoun had a large entourage.

Shen I-pei spoke a little English and had been a typesetter fallen into poverty and unemployment. He was rather frail and I thought he needed an indoor job to survive.

Wang was happy enough carrying chits (we had no phone) and exercising our greyhound when he went on errands. He was strong, lazy, and lovable, ruddy from *pai k'erh* wine. It turned out that he owned not only a farm and four other rickshas which he rented out, but also two or three wives. He tried to avoid taking orders from Shen. So did the cook.

It was expected that the cook should take "squeeze," but beyond a certain point it was considered out of hand, and the "missy" lost face for allowing it, as did the Number 1 boy.

I became aware of a passive-resistance effort to break me down and get rid of Shen. I told Shen to discharge the cook and get one of his own, but this solved nothing.

"I have no 'face,'" Shen explained. "To try to make face for myself, I have to have a coolie. The Number One boy cannot do physical work. He has to give orders to a coolie. It is better for me if you cut my wages and pay a coolie. I myself do not want a coolie, of course not. *Mei-yu-fadtze, aiyeh!*" This phrase meant "no way, ah."

"Where there's a will, there's a *fadtze*," I said stubbornly.

The fact that in our small house no work existed for more than one servant was beside the point. I could have done all the housework myself in a couple of hours a day. Most of the time the servants sat around talking to their visiting friends. Janet Fitch Sewall had only a Number 1 boy and cook, which was not uncommon in Shanghai, but there was no such arrangement as I was trying to have. You could not create upward mobility except as part of the guarantee system.

It is no use to get a coolie for your Number 1 boy, I was told, because he would be a *house* coolie and he will also refuse to take orders from a former rickshaman. They don't appreciate being paid extra either. They think you are a fool. You pay only the *exact* wage, no more or less. All you need to do is get rid of Shen and everything will be perfect—all clockwork. Your servants are losing face all over the city by working under a former rickshaman.

Throughout China, foreigners loved their servants and enjoyed a happy family situation, but there was probably no one else who did not strictly observe "the system," a caste hierarchy based on contempt for human labor—but not quite like the Untouchables of India. Few foreigners were murdered in China after the 1900 Boxer time, but when they were, the common cause was loss of face by the cook, who polished off his unsuspecting employer with a meat cleaver.

I don't think even Mao Tse-tung could have got my servants to respect manual labor. (In the 1960s, he did force the top-caste "educated people" out on the farms to learn at least what it was like to do the manual labor that supported them on the top.)

I risked ruining the whole charming Peking experience by this stupid Doña Quixote battle with the windmills. All I needed to do was get rid of Shen. The proper way was to ask "Aunt Lucy's" Number 1 boy or the one at the American Legation to "guarantee" my establishment, and I could have had only two servants and a blissfully happy household all down the line. Of course, I knew this from the first. Yet I struggled for a year. I originally intended to train Shen for another job as Number 1 boy, rather than keeping him myself.

The worst thing of all was that I was dying to get rid of Shen— except on principle. I was worn out trying to teach him his job. No guest ever came in but that Shen would invent some peculiar way of doing things to embarrass us all. The suspense never ended. Ed had no sympathy for my stubborn experiment either.

I felt very sorry for Shen, but I neither liked nor disliked him personally. He had a wife and child who were always sick, and many debts. He was contracting new debts to pay off his old ones, on the strength of having a grand new job with "rich foreigners." He also borrowed small sums from me in "emergencies," which were constant.

Came the day when Shen announced that he had a new baby son and it was necessary to spend a whole month's salary from us to give a feast in honor of the arrival; he had to borrow it in advance.

"Missy, I do not *want* to do this," Shen explained with tears running down his "face." "My wife's family insist on this feast, and I would have no face with them if I did not pay for one. As long as I have a good job, I have to spend this much money."

"What happens if you no longer have a good job?" I inquired, feeling the last straw breaking the camel's-back bridge between me and Shen's future.

Shen looked alarmed: "Of course, I would have no money and no face either."

"Well, tell your wife's family that you have lost your good job because of this idiotic extravagance when you are still in debt. I am simply exhausted trying to change five thousand years of Chinese ways and means. You must begin looking for another job today."

I kept Shen on until we moved to a small village. Of course, neither he nor I could find a job for him. On March 26, 1934, we had a letter from him: "It is your great generosity and kindness that impressed me deeply and fastenedly of having to think and to remember, from time to time, your honorable complexions. As things now stand, I think it may be or may not be possible for me having to be in your employment again. . . ."

Shen came in ricksha (not pulling one) five miles to visit us, begging for a job. But I knew enough about Chinese by this time in all ways to be able to reply with a blank face: "*Mei-yu-fadtze.*" I had got a whole new staff, guaranteed by the Number 1 boy of Ran Sailer, a Yenching professor. Never again did I try to tangle with the system. Never again did I underestimate the power of "labor" in China in its own context. I gave up rickshamen as much as possible, and we bought two Japanese bicycles.

All over China, the same tight network of guarantee-and-responsibility existed, not only by way of the kinship and clan system, but in the big cities by means of gangster *pongs*, which controlled job opportunities for strangers, with *cumsha* all along the line. It was this that had kept Chinese civilization alive over two thousand years. The individual actually did not exist—he was only a link in the chain and could not survive outside of it or in conflict with it. Even beggars and bandits had to send their share of money home, as did overseas Chinese. Women and children were actually in a state of family slavery, and sons were used as old-age insurance. Filial piety was the strict Confucian rule, which was changed to political piety under the Communist party.

It was almost impossible to change China, but holding power was easy once it had been seized. The Communists took over the guarantee system from top to bottom, meantime trying to eliminate the old Confucian nepotism and putting youth in command, or at least in a three-in-one combination of the old, the middle-aged, and the young. The survival of remnants of the ancient kinship system plus the new, well-organized socialist system of guarantees has created the most powerfully cohesive social unit ever devised on this planet. In rural communes, from 30 percent to 70 percent of the membership have the same surname, and the other surnames are of the maternal clans.

What this has meant is that class lines were not only blurred but neutralized by this cushioning from top to bottom as the spine is cushioned by discs of cartilage. Whole families and clans became Communist and others anti-Communist. Mao Tse-tung took his family into the Communist movement, for example, and could never have survived without his status in his family as a shareholder of the property.

Every Chinese had his niche and his status in the old system, with claims on others. Both poverty and wealth were shared from top to bottom as part of the guarantee system. A well-to-do uncle financed his sons and nephews, but they had to pay it back to support his old age and the welfare of his family. A *t'u-hao*, or evil landlord, was one who refused to share with his poor relatives—of course, had he done so, he would have been on their level in no time. A landlord had no "face" in the village if he did not observe the Confucian responsibilities for his clan.

All this was not easy for me to understand, as I had not studied anthropology—which should be compulsory reading at least in Peking, Moscow, and Washington, D.C. I had to learn the hard way, putting the jigsaw puzzle together myself. The most rewarding study was the writings of Lu Hsun, who is still more respected in China than any other literary person, though a non-Communist. His "Story of Ah Q" shows the old concept of face, and all his work satirizes Confucianism.

I picked up many significant ideas from editing translations. For example, you would read of the tragic, starving character about to commit suicide. Then would come the clincher: "I decided to send my maid to my mother's uncle in Tientsin [or Shanghai or Hong Kong] to ask for help, and this solved my problem." Communists did this as well as others. Always the individual had someone to do the manual work on a slave level, even if he or she had no money of his own, and the uncle always helped. Not until I studied anthropology did I know that this was a survival of the matriarchal "avunculate" common to other ancient patriarchal systems—the mother's brother had this responsibility as part of the marriage system.

Mao Tse-tung was helped to get an education by his mother's family, who lived in Hsiang-hsiang *hsien* (county) in Hunan, where everybody was related to Marquis Tseng Kuo-fan, considered the most superior lineage in China.

Many of the old customs of China seemed atrocious to Westerners. For example, infanticide of girl babies was sometimes practiced, so that the other children in the family would have enough. And if a person was drowning, no one would lift a hand to help because he would then be held responsible for his future; also, no one should interfere with obvious *ming*, or fate. In the case of my Number 1 boy

Shen, he and his wife's family were expecting me to go on helping all of them forever—just because I had taken him out of his *ming* situation as a rickshaman.

It is only when one has experienced this rigid, backward system, full of superstitions and cruelty, that one can appreciate the marvelously progressive nature of what the Communists are trying to do in changing China at the grass roots. One can judge China only by its own past, not by any other criterion. Such a simple Boy Scout slogan as "serving the people" breaks down in practice the whole Confucian system of nepotism and requiring "guarantees" as part of helping anyone, especially a stranger.

I felt suffocated by the lack of any kind of elementary freedom in China, but the Chinese liked it because it meant security for them from cradle to grave, at least if the economic level of the family and clan was sufficient.

My wrongheaded experiment with Shen arose from my ignorance of what China was like. Books about China in English were not much help—Ed and I had little but contempt for most of them. We felt ashamed to leave China knowing so little about its real problems. That was one reason we would both risk our lives to interview the Communists in 1936 and 1937. We realized this knowledge was important not only to us but to the West, to the world, and no other way existed to find out what they actually were like.

CHAPTER 13

Art, Literature, and Revolution

Not long after we arrived in Peking, we began to receive regular visits from three artists sent by Lu Hsun, who was then the colossal figure in the arts, encouraging Westernization in all ways. The three always wore foreign-style black serge suits and black bow ties, and looked delicate and sensitive. They could read English but had never before tried to carry on conversations in it. We had instant communication, but Ed could hardly endure the language barrier. He would escape after a few minutes and later ask me to report on what had been said.

They were fellow-travelers—non-Communist, but their jobs and lives were in danger just the same. It was a new idea to me that any mere artist could be a danger to the state. They were small, afraid of our big greyhound, but valiant for the truth. None had ever seen an original Western painting, only photographs, but their admiration was limitless.

In the winter of 1925, they had, with a fourth friend, Hsiang, started in Peking an art society called The Daubers, which in 1933 had eleven members and put out the only art publication in the city. In 1925, Wang Chun-chu and Liang I-chu had been twenty-one, Hsiang and Suhuo, nineteen. In 1929, they had taken forty canvases to Tokyo for exhibition by the Graphic Arts Society. This trip influenced them toward "proletarian art," as they called it, though none of them had ever been working-class. The Daubers were related to the expressionist *sturm* movement in Germany, to Kandinsky and the Russians. They also liked Picasso, Matisse, and Cézanne; and Wang, who loved Millet, aspired to be the Millet of China.

They told me that about fifty left-wing artists existed in all China, with the greatest number in Shanghai, a few at the Hangchow Fine Arts School, and scarcely any in Canton, where suppression was heavy.

When they visited us, they came and left separately to avoid the police. One of their colleagues was in hiding. Another had recently been executed in Shantung, where he had gone to teach. Hsiang was serving a ten-year sentence for painting the Kuomintang flag in the mud; he had been arrested in Shantung in 1932 with eight teachers and twelve students. Only Liang was married.

Their aim was to express the life of the people, these left-wing artists told me. They called themselves expressionists, or students of naturalism, which was new and revolutionary in China. All the Western techniques and materials were new in China, except ink wash and watercolor, which were very limited.

In 1929, Liang had published a book of "modern" sketches, stylized and distorted. This had been looked upon as dangerously radical. Though you could hardly tell "which was the nude and which was the staircase," the female nudes were regarded as proof of the artist's being a Communist.

Around a tray of cookies and Chinese tea, with our concerned greyhound never absent, we talked of Youth, Art, and Revolution. The group's aim was to borrow the Western *science* of art—oils, canvas, woodcuts, lead pencils, charcoal, and, most of all, chiaroscuro and the third dimension. Chinese painting was limited to paper, silk, and the brush. It had no perspective except the aerial perspective. It was *flat*, so flat that some critics suggested the Chinese eye could not visualize the third dimension. It was an escape from reality, a philosophy of escape, not representational but intellectualized.

These artists told me it was no use to go on imitating Chinese art as it had been for a thousand years or more, because it had reached its maximum possibilities. When I criticized them for imitating the West, they were furious: "This is progressive. Why cut us off from all this marvelous art?" They were risking their lives for it.

None of us had any money, but we collected at least fifty valuable woodcuts to send to the magazine *China Today* in New York for exhibition. We asked for their return, but someone kept them and we heard nothing more. (I never again sent anything to that magazine.)

Aided by Teilhard de Chardin, I sent the first exhibition of Chinese left-wing art to Europe. The exhibition was perhaps the first of any "modern" painting, and one of the first shows of any living Chinese artists even in the old traditional style. It was held in Paris, March 14–29, 1934, at the Galerie Billiet. The show later toured Europe, where it was lost—fourteen oil paintings, nineteen drawings, and fifty-one woodcuts, all under pseudonyms (Wang's were Meng Tou and Li Zo).

In New York, Pearl S. Buck and her publisher, Richard Walsh, put out my articles introducing not only the new art but also the new literature of China. Wang and I sent them a big scroll painting he had done of the red-robed monk, pounding on a gate, from the classic Chinese novel *Shui Hu Chuan*, which Pearl Buck had translated into English.

One day Pearl Buck and Richard Walsh came to spend the day with us. We all became friends right off. At forty-three, Mrs. Buck was then in the prime of her life and career—on her courtship journey. In June 1935, the two were married, a perfect arrangement. Dick took care of her affairs from the moment she delivered a handwritten manuscript to the typist. In 1938, she received the Nobel Prize, partly for the biographies of her missionary parents (two real classics indeed). Her books made millions over the years, and she worked almost every day until her death in 1973, at the age of eighty. It was through her novelist's mind that the West, especially America, got its picture of the Chinese. Just before her last illness, she hoped to return to China, but a visa was refused because in her later books she had "vilified the Chinese people," the rejection said.

Pearl Buck had presence and charm, with a lovely voice and blue-green, sea-changing eyes. She was large and matronly, the picture of a Pennsylvania Dutch *hausfrau*. The key to her life was frustrated maternity; she told me that after she had had a retarded child, she dared not try again, and that she hated her divorced husband, J. L. Buck, because he had not told her his family had a history of such births. Out of the lonely compression of the mission compound, she turned to writing. She never lost her identification with the problems of women, and they repaid her by buying her books in large quantities.

Walsh had become editor of *Asia* in 1933; he and Pearl Buck owned the magazine as well as the John Day publishing house, both of which sponsored me in the beginning. We talked to them both about the idea of translating Chinese writing in order to understand the real sociology of the Chinese. They agreed, and Walsh published most of this work. He, more than anyone else, was responsible for introducing Asian writers to the West, since he continued the policy.

In *Asia* magazine I published an article on "China's New Art" and, with Wang Chun-chu, one of the *hsieh-yi* style (December 1935), which museum people talked about years later. I had studied this style with Wang, though I was never able to master it myself. This is the one classical achievement of the Chinese that no Westerner could even imitate; it is the rhythmic brushstroke, unique to China, which flows laterally and creates an organic surface of rare esthetic quality, but does not bend forward and backward to give depth. Mastery of this stroke, similar to calligraphy, was rare. It was limited to line—actually to outline. Modeling in depth was impossible and contrary to intention. You outlined a leaf by putting more paint on one side of the brush. It all had to be done with *one brushstroke* and at one time—to me a silly dilettantism. The Japanese never mastered it, so they outlined everything with a black contour line, which gives their work the "Japanese" look.

Wang was the group leader and the one who enjoyed our discussions most. He painted better in the traditional style than in the Western. Not one work in other than the traditional style could ever be sold in China then, yet these artists sacrificed everything to learn Western techniques.

By early 1935, the others in the group had disappeared and Wang had to escape from Peking. He told us he had no money and no one to help him, and that every kind of Communist apparatus or peripheral group had been destroyed. Some had starved and others died of disease, but the chief government weapon was this: An arrested person could not be freed unless he gave the names of several individuals as "Communists"; usually, he also had to join the new Fascist organization, which was recruited chiefly from ex-Communists who had betrayed others, even innocent persons. This was the ugliest thing in my whole experience, and it was a Fascist technique all over China. As a result, anyone released from prison was suspected of having betrayed others in order to get out. Such a person was considered dangerous because he or she might also have been forced to act as a police informer after release. It was a most tragic situation. The individual might have sacrificed everything for his or her beliefs, and then, having succeeded in getting out of prison after torture and escaping execution—which was legal punishment for any member of any Communist organization—found that no friends dared associate with him or her. Already cut off from the family in some cases, the former prisoner faced death from starvation, as no job could be "guaranteed."

In Peking, Chiang Kai-shek's nephew Chiang Hsiao-hsien carried out this program, and also tortured and executed many young people at the Third Gendarmes headquarters, as well as sending important people to Nanking for torture. (In 1973, I went to the execution ground in Nanking at Yu Hua Tai, where I was told that from 1927 to 1949 the Chiang Kai-shek government had buried about a hundred thousand young people in nameless gravel pits. These were the *best* in China. I wondered how many were there whom I had known or seen at one time or another.)

My original interest in revolution in China was esthetic rather than political. I was astonished to find that the left-wing artists, writers, and students were the intellectual leaders, and were also much more attractive than the others, personally, often even physically. Chiang Kai-shek was suppressing and also killing the *aristocracy* of China—its most advanced youth, those who were developing the human spirit.

We helped Wang escape to Shanghai to get a ship to France, and later had a cryptic note from Moscow, where he was happy. I next heard of him from Yenan in 1939, when he sent me a photograph and some ink-wash drawings using the name Hu Man. In Peking in 1972, I was told he was alive but too sick to see me.

In China it was taboo and always had been to use the female body in art in any way, except for the effect of fully clothed drapery, and rarely in any form but that of the Buddhist goddess Kuan Yin or of the Taoist queen of the fairies. (This held true in 1972. Nudes were still taboo, except to show the muscles of half-clothed workingmen. But for the first time, all kinds of fully clothed women were accepted as subjects for the arts.)

The outstanding characteristic of Chinese traditional art was that it was anti-woman. What was I doing in an alien land where artists had no interest in the female anatomy, where women had bound feet, where young artists and writers were executed for their ideas alone? I thought of the bursting health and vitality of the American artists I knew, in love with life and everything that moved. For the old Chinese, only still-life interested the painters, nothing living. Portraits could not be painted until after death. What, and why, was the terrible gap between these two different worlds?

"You have got hold of a piece of the truth," I had sagely informed the Chinese artists. The West, I told them, was liberated in the time of the Sistine Chapel ceiling of Michelangelo and Leonardo's "Mona Lisa," marking a return to the Greek worship of the human body and mind.

But these artists had something else in mind, and Western art was filtering to them through the prism of Marxism. Why? I could see that revolution was produced by a change in the tools and mode of production, even in the arts. Yet why were the Chinese skipping the whole marvelous epoch of hundreds of years of the Renaissance and capitalism? Was it from choice or necessity?

Before I took up the problem of esthetics in China, I had already decided that the peasants and laboring people of China were much more attractive than the sick, decadent upper classes, not only physically but psychologically. Most foreigners felt that way strongly. The upper classes despised not only manual labor but even walking on their own two feet, much less participating in sports and exercise. It would never have occurred to these fragile, sickly young artists to go out on a farm to develop their muscles and their deficient "sense power." In the 1960s, Mao Tse-tung would order all students to spend at least two or three years doing manual labor. But in the 1930s, the left-wing artists were reaching out across the chasm that had separated the intellectual from the working class in China—intellectually, if not in practice, Marxism glorified labor, not only because it was productive but also because it was beautiful esthetically. Puritanism had had the same idea in the seventeenth century.

When I got to Yenan in 1937, I was hard put to explain why everybody seemed so charming, so attractive, when so many other Chinese I had met were afflicted with such repulsive characteristics as meanness of spirit, cruelty, and so on. I did not even know the word *charisma* then, but that was what each one had—without it he would never have survived, never have established leadership over thousands of admiring followers.

The Gordian knot that tied together the whole of Chinese culture confronted me when I tried to untangle the esthetic principle. Even today this is not understood by many museum curators and specialists in Oriental art; the underlying reasons are unknown to them because they have never studied anthropology and are repelled by its unlovely features. They despise "socialist realism" in China without realizing it is an advance of ten thousand *li* beyond the dead imitations preceding the Marxist period. I loved the art in China in 1972, because I remembered all the terrible problems. When any Westerner has faced the threat of execution for his art, then he is entitled to criticize the current Chinese work. Of course, modern art in China still has a long march ahead.

* * *

A year or two later, we decided to introduce modern Chinese writing to the West, employing several translators. A few Chinese short stories had been translated, and Ed, then teaching at Yenching University, was working with a translator on Lu Hsun's stories. We decided to start with a comprehensive collection of short stories, chiefly for their value in illustrating the real sociology of the Chinese.* We dbalso decided that the way to understand China was to read what the Chinese were writing for each other.

I chose to build up Hsiao Ch'ien and Yang Ping, and insisted on putting two of their short stories, which I edited with them, in *Living China*, though both writers were unknown. The one by Hsiao Ch'ien was the most popular in the book and was adapted for reading on a radio broadcast, which established him in England and the States to some extent. The story by Yang Ping (who used the pseudonyms Shih Ming and Yang Kang) was reprinted in 1973 in a collection titled with the name of her story;† she did not live to see the book, as she committed suicide some time after 1949 when she returned to China from the States.

Hsiao Ch'ien, a Yenching University student, was friendly, lovable, handsome, and gifted. But he was timid, and no wonder. He had been arrested in 1925 at age thirteen, suspected of "socialism," and put in prison without trial, among thousands of others who were arrested and executed. It was declared that those who had a Bible were followers of Feng Yu-hsiang and therefore Bolsheviks. One of seventeen on the same *k'ang* was a nine-year-old student, he told me. Hsiao was born in a poor Mongol Christian family in Peking in 1911 and became orphaned, so he got a job as an apprentice for three years in a rug factory owned by Christians. He had been a devout Christian until he read some literature on socialism at the age of thirteen.

Hsiao believed in ghosts and all kinds of superstitions, yet on the surface he seemed very modern. On graduation from Yenching, he got a job as literary editor of the *Ta Kung Pao* in Tientsin, and soon thereafter, his friend Yang Ping joined him on the staff, with his "guarantee." He was able to spend some time in London later and also in the States, returning to Peking after 1949. (He visited me in Con-

---

* *Living China*, edited by Edgar Snow (New York: John Day Company, 1936; London: Harrap).
† *Fragment From a Lost Diary*, edited by Naomi Katz and Nancy Milton (New York: Random House, 1973), with stories about women in Asia, Africa, and Latin America.

necticut about 1979 and wrote some articles about me which were published in China.)

Yang Ping was much more forceful and masculine than Hsiao Ch'ien, who admired her for it. She was one of the few Chinese I have ever known who was not either naturally charming or artificially so. She was not abrasive, but not far from it. Yet her strong face was handsome, surrounded by careless, Dutch-cut hair. She wore a white blouse and short black skirt, Western style, and lived on the Yenching campus, even though she had not matriculated. Her life had been in danger, and she was befriended by her teachers, one of whom was the famous Ku Chieh-kang. About 1930 or 1931, she had been vice-president of the Yenching student body and in command of the students. She was then put in prison for leading a street demonstration demanding the release of political prisoners.

Yang Ping had a strong, clear, objective mind and she had studied Marxism, which was what caused her to join the Communist Youth League at the time she was a student officer. When Hsiao Ch'ien brought her to our house, she was rather reserved and cynical. I was told she was suspected of being a Trotskyist, and to stay away from her, since she was not trustworthy. I did not believe this, but in any case she was all I could find. She came from a high official family in Hupeh, one of eighteen children. One of her brothers was an important left-wing person. I supposed her family had enough money and influence to get her out of prison, the only way in those days except by "betraying" others. Yang Ping claimed her innocence of betrayal, and I chose to believe her.

Yang Ping became the premier newspaperwoman of China and the first Chinese woman foreign correspondent when she came in the 1940s to the States, where she also attended Radcliffe College. Her face was like a death mask when she visited me one weekend, and I was not surprised to learn in 1973 that she had ended as a suicide.

I also edited Hsiao Hung, who died a few years afterward from poverty and malnutrition. Her husband was T'ien Chun, whose *Village in August* was translated by Robert Ward and taken by the Book-of-the-Month Club. I also edited other stories and poems that were published, chiefly in *Asia* magazine.

Nothing was ever more difficult for me than trying to do the pioneer essay in *Living China* on "The Modern Chinese Literary Movement," though Yang Ping helped on the research. No articles of that kind existed in Chinese, much less English. My essay was published in

Life and Letters Today in London, 1936; and in 1938, *New Writing* in London, edited by John Lehmann, used two short stories I edited.

Ed and I introduced Lin Yutang to my friend Carol McComas, who sent his manuscript to Pearl Buck. Richard Walsh tailor-made Lin's books, which earned a fortune, though Lin had no appreciation of this. He turned to the right and supported Chiang Kai-shek in the end. He might never have been known in the West had he not been on the left in 1933, as we would not have tried to further his career.

I was surprised to find that the left wing dominated the literary movement in China, as in art, though it was imitative of the Russians chiefly. Tolstoy was the most influential writer in China, Korea, and other Asian nations. The only somewhat original, creative impulse in China (even in scholarship, except for science to a small extent) was rooted in the left-wing movement. I did not miss this significance. For many reasons, China had no other road to follow—only the one that led to some kind of socialism. The study of Marxism was the chief inspiration in all creative fields, rather than personal knowledge of the Chinese condition.

After the Communists took power, there was an outcry in the West that creative talent was being suppressed. That was not the case—unfortunately, little existed to suppress: It had to be nurtured, and artists and writers started to receive stipends from the government. Art is still looked upon as a weapon in the "class struggle," but this concept admits a dialectical conflict, which is the root of art. Also, the reach is for roots in the soil, not for sterile imitation. In China today art is didactic, utilitarian, and part of a new transformation, but it is democratic, a mass development. It is also *respected*. As before, words and paintings have magic and power in China. The country is still in the age of parable, but in the future may astonish the world with a "hundred flowers" period, once the roots are established in healthy and fertile earth. China is still paying for over 2,000 years of Confucian stagnation and total repression of any kind of originality. Already in 30 years it has more art and literature than the infant American experiment produced in its first 150.

CHAPTER 14

Year's End

The first year is always the hardest. It had been much against Ed's will that he had fallen deeply in love with the belle of the Shanghai American Consulate General. It was the first time he had ever been faced with giving up his precious freedom. But what is freedom beyond a slave's dull dream, unless it is by choice? Ed actually had much more freedom now than ever before. New options opened up. He had someone behind him to take full responsibility for everything but his own work, and at any cost I insisted that everything else should be subordinate to that. Our division of labor was that he should earn the income—though we both agreed to spend the least possible amount of time and strength on this—while I was responsible for everything else, including encouraging him in his travels and work.

We sorely needed some income after our honeymoon trip, and Ed wrote a long rambling article summing up the observations of our tour of European colonialism in the East. He entitled it "The Decline of Western Prestige." It was an anti-imperialist article that said the West ought to give up its colonies before Japan took them by war. He didn't like the piece—he was geared to the brevity of newspapers and news magazines. But he dreaded cutting down its 7,000-word length to 2,500 words for the *Herald Tribune*, which was a sure market paying $150 immediately—and we desperately needed money at that point.

"I like it," I decided in one of my dead-right moments. "It's a *Saturday Evening Post* type of thing and they're isolationist, too. It's the same breed of cat as the *Herald Tribune*, only the *Post* needs long articles with background for the average American."

Ed had hardly seen a copy of the *Post* since 1928, but he was slightly superstitious about trusting my judgment as his mascot more or less fresh from home. He had, however, built up a peculiar psychology of success: Never risk failure. Patiently he wrote and rewrote all his articles, cut and edited them to make sure they would not be rejected and that they would not bore his reader.

He thought it impossible to get into the *Post* and he wrote as much to the editor in his covering letter, to protect his ego in case of "certain" rejection. I took it to the post office myself in Wang's ricksha before Ed could change his mind. It went by ship mail, insured.

Weeks went by. One day a small windowed envelope from the *Post* came in the mail. Ed almost threw it in the wastebasket, thinking it an advertisement. One of those newfangled machines had written a check. The suspense rose in Ed's office as we studied it. Was it for $7.50 or $75.00 or what? It couldn't be for $750.00—that would have to be a typographical error.

Carrying this tiny piece of paper like the Holy Grail, we climbed into rickshas and set out for the bank, presenting it tentatively as if we were receivers of stolen goods or counterfeiters. The cashier looked at the check respectfully, told us the excellent exchange rate, and credited the sum to our account. In Chinese money the $750 came to about $4,000. We could live more than a year on that—in princely fashion, too.

Ed took hold of my hand; his eyes misted over, and he wouldn't let go even as we rode in separate rickshas side by side down Changan Chieh. The rickshamen kept looking back in delight, trying to keep the wheels from tangling.

We felt like slaves who had just bought their own freedom, and we hoarded this money. This was freedom from fear and worry, freedom to write our books. It was also freedom from fear of rejection for Ed, since he established a regular relationship with *The Saturday Evening Post*, the highest-paying magazine in the world. Thus the *Post* to some extent financed our activities in China, and Ed became the link between China and America. At least he reached the biggest popular audience of any magazine then, with the possible exception of reprints in *Reader's Digest*. This acceptance gave Ed the confidence to carry on with the Watch on the Pacific.

Yet he was careful not to wear out his welcome at the *Post* and sent them only perfectly tailored articles he was certain they would take. They would have accepted many more, had he been willing to risk rejection. As I remember it, the *Post* never rejected one article Ed sent them, nor did they change, edit, or censor anything, except to write their own titles now and then.

The next ship mail after the check brought a long letter from

George Edward Lorimer, editor of the *Post*, inviting Ed to write more articles. Ed continued to do so until the McCarthy time, 1950, when he resigned as associate editor in protest against their new attitude toward China and the East, though Ben Hibbs insisted Ed could write for the *Post* as long as he was editor. (Hibbs told me that whenever Ed's name appeared on the cover, sales at the newsstands rocketed.) For more than fifteen years, Ed wrote for the *Post*; he was the magazine's war correspondent in World War II, allowed to go wherever he pleased all over the globe. He figured they paid him about a quarter of a million dollars over that time.

The astonishing thing about Edgar Snow's life was that at least until 1949, with or without money, he possibly did nothing he did not want to do. He had real freedom, including freedom from worry or responsibility for his wife and home, more or less taking for granted I would provide that—which I did as part of the job.

Until the McCarthy time, Ed never knew rejection personally or in his work, except for those brief months in Shanghai in 1931–1932 when he was ostracized by people whose opinion he cared nothing for. He was so used to having his own way, he was not even aware of it. That was the condition for his success and I realized it—at least after one year of trying unsuccessful alternatives. Ed never came into confrontation with real problems until 1949, and then the succession of blows struck him with lasting effect—the divorce, the fact that he was permanently barred from the Soviet Union, the break with the *Post*, the China Lobby-McCarthy attacks, and rejection by the publishing world (though Random House continued to publish his work to the end).

Ed's first book, *Far Eastern Front*, had made only a few hundred dollars, but he had not as yet given up his work on *South of the Clouds*. After we had settled down in Peking, Ed's job with Consolidated Press was cut out of their budget. Jim Mills of Associated Press offered him a job if he would keep it for two years, but Ed did not want to be "tied down," just as he had refused the best job in the East, reporting from Shanghai for the *Herald Tribune*. He wanted to write and travel as he pleased and never on a schedule. My idea was the same—to sacrifice everything to write our books. We realized there was no future in newspaper work.

I was collecting materials for my own book, but a great blow fell. I learned that another American woman had the same idea exactly. A "pageant" of Chinese History was being published, a popular introduction to the subject.

It is hard to believe anyone could be as stupid as I was. Not for fifteen years did I learn the absolute secret of writing—or of doing any other kind of difficult creative work. Ed practiced it every day, and still I did not see the point. It was simple: You must do your work *first thing* in the morning, and other things afterward. You must go directly from the psychology of sleep to your writing, not allowing anything to distract your mind from this straight and narrow path, not even breakfast talk, the newspaper, or a telephone call. It is a complicated psychological problem—not a question of lack of time. Few women ever learn this vital secret—it is contrary to our natural tendencies.

All during our marriage, I protected Ed completely from any distractions or interruptions until lunchtime, and he justified this by making use of the mornings. As for me, I was always clearing decks early in the day for subsequent free time, which never came. This was my own fault. I had servants and could have done my own work in the morning, just as Ed did. Instead I did what was "urgent," usually for other people. All my best creative energy, my morning energy, went into do-gooding for others. I was not afraid to squander my energies, and I thought the future would be there. But this is not true at all. The future never comes, or if it does, by that time your psychology has been changed, so you can no longer do your own work as you would have earlier. Until 1949, I spent too much time doing other things; then came the McCarthy period, the divorce, and that work has not yet been done.

This was not Ed's fault. He resented the time I spent on various projects at the sacrifice of my own work, because he knew I had to become established before I could make any money or even get my books published. Ed had total confidence in me but most of all in my literary talent. He actually thought I was a literary genius—so did I, of course, though I did not venture to put that conviction to the test. This was the backlog on which our marriage rested. Behind me I felt my husband's total admiration and love.

During our first year of marriage, I had forced Ed to be at the top of the best-dressed list in Peking, to go horseback riding, to build up his health (he had been an Eagle Scout once but had almost lost his health in the East), to go dancing (though he absolutely refused to improve this), to go on weekend hikes in the hills with assorted groups, and to do various other things. He was rather passive by nature and needed to be pushed and pulled and pounced upon, which was exhausting for me, but I was tooth and nail for building him up in all ways.

At the end of the first year, it occurred to me that Ed was not going to change.

"All I ever wanted was your approval," Ed said. "That was what I worked for. Why do you criticize me?" he asked in small-boy bewilderment. "I never criticize you."

I was struck dumb. It was true.

Fortunately, I was perceptive enough to decide on a strategic retreat from my maximum program to a minimum one. I decided to let Ed be himself. He was naturally charming and easy to live with, so long as he didn't have to do anything he did not wish to do. He was also as naturally balky as a Missouri mule. He was not lazy; he enjoyed his work, which was writing, journalism, and travel. He did not waste any money, except on American cigarettes, coffee, and razor blades—in these areas he refused to degrade his Western standards. He was very well-bred and civilized. He hated propaganda, and part of his natural attractiveness was that he never intruded his ideas on anyone, not even in his writing, though we debated between ourselves every day.

I decided I would hold the fort on a few points: 1. We had to keep up Ed's health and work at any cost. 2. I would be even more careful not to spend any money on myself, except for the necessities. 3. I made up my mind not to whine and complain or feel any deprivation, but to enjoy what we had—if I did not have what I liked, I liked what I had. I was not the martyr type, however. I was not even thrifty by nature, though Ed was. I was giving up the little things for the big things, by an act of conscious will.

Oh, how I loved to design things and have them made—for almost nothing. And how cheap the treasures of Cathay were in the 1930s in Peking. It took all my Puritan ancestry to summon up the necessary self-denial and self-discipline. Fortunately, in Peking it was chic not to be chic. I had plenty of beautiful clothes for all occasions brought from the States. But five or six years are a long, long time in a girl's twenties to declare a moratorium on new clothes or any kind of shopping.

One afternoon about 1936, I rode my bicycle to Vetch's Bookstore in the Peking Hotel. My heart skipped a beat when I saw a young woman tourist dressed in the height of fashion—and she walked as such an attractive figure should walk, with a toss of her head in its black high-crowned hat. With one foot on my bike pedal, I looked over every detail. What was *I* doing in the cold, dusty streets of Peking, wearing a gray tweed suit made from one of Ed's India-tailored atrocities? I didn't *want* to be a dowdy YWCA missionary do-gooder with no sense of humor, mired down in a Slough of Despond of Chinese students and missionaries.

Ed and I were under more than one kind of percussion—which is the secret of power. Alone in an alien and cruel land, we were pressed in upon each other in a small vacuum. We were under the pressure of poverty and cut off from the outside. Ed was the happy type and did not feel deprived. But I was well aware of what I had given up for this unique existence. Deprivation, however, is the secret of enjoyment. I was capable of the enjoyment of simple things, the more so by being deprived of others.

Because of this percussion and deprivation, I began to seethe with an explosive mixture of "spiritual" energy, intensified under pressure. It was the by-product of physical and intellectual "energism," as I called it, the surplus over and above those qualities. This was exactly what Teilhard was trying to analyze when he was sure that spiritual power was evolved out by physical and intellectual power, and was not separate from them but an organic part.

There is more than one kind of spiritual energy, and probably it is sex-differentiated. Teilhard's idea was that the individual alone must develop his body, brain, and spiritual power, independently of the opposite sex and even, to some extent, of society; he was himself the perfect example of his theory's success. This was not unlike the ancient idea of all celibate, ascetic priests and mystics, whether sitting on nails in India or in hair shirts in European monasteries and striving by prayer or meditation toward God. All the great spiritual leaders were liberated from women or vice versa.

My argument was this: The division into two sexes was a major advance in evolution and mutation; the more differentiation the more change, variety, and stimulation. Mating was one of the methods of natural selection, and it had evolved over centuries into modern nuclear marriage, a male-female unit with the same electromagnetic power as other cells and nuclei. This *yin-yang* atom (I didn't get the idea from China but I liked the term) could be a generator of energy and power for outside purposes. It could also be a destroyer of surplus energy if not handled with engineering skill to build up steam under percussion and renew that power after its expenditure. Nature provided the miraculous attraction of male and female, and human beings could trap this in the boiler of marriage to multiply all their powers manyfold. The marriage had to be faithful and monogamous, especially for the wife, so as not to break the high-tension power line that bound the two together. Ed was a reasonably suitable partner in such a marriage because he was geared to success and his male ego was sound. He did not understand the theory, but he enjoyed the success of its practice.

"Behind every great man is a great woman, unknown and unsung," runs the old adage. My "marriage power" theory was not exactly new. If the true story of the source of the power of great men could be known, my theory might have many examples. The wife was the powerhouse that generated and regenerated the physical and spiritual energy that not only sustained the husband but made all his higher achievements possible. Such a wife instinctively carried out a one-woman conspiracy, part of which was to keep her powers secret as a natural form of witchcraft, to build up the male ego.

It was easier for a man alone, like Teilhard, to climb to the pinnacle Omega point than for any woman. Teilhard paid no attention to the female saints of the Catholic Church because they lacked the all-around development needed for the climb; they remained on the lower level of the stations of the cross, concerned with healing and minor things. No woman was ever a Jesuit. But Teilhard believed woman was already more highly evolved than man and had a higher potential. He was not against marriage for others, only for priests like himself. Though he did not agree with my "marriage power" thesis, in his own life he was never without a female devotee who helped provide stimulation and new energy, even though no doubt he held to his vow of chastity for political reasons.

The Snow marriage was a gung ho success while it lasted, and provided motive power for quite a few people and historical events.

CHAPTER 15

Village Life
in China

Both Ed and I had a shiny carapace of protection that kept us from being "absorbed," as the term went, in the Peking lotus-eater life, even though we enjoyed it on the surface. But it was hard to escape the social whirl, to save money and get our books written, and especially hard because we were popular in Peking. We decided to move to a village near Yenching University, where Ed taught a course in the Department of Journalism.

It had to be either Providence or *ming* that came up with the ideal place for us to stay from March of 1934 until the fall of 1935—Hait'ien, pure organic village living in a little house set like a gem solitaire on a low hill almost overlooking the Summer Palace. There were even a high lava-rock formation built for looking at the view over the compound wall, and two or three acres for Gobi to gallop around in, among the asparagus and strawberry beds. We had been yearning to breathe free. Here were pure air and our own organic vegetables as well.

The rent was less than U.S. $10 a month, low because owner Jimmy Chuan wanted foreigners to live there. He was head of the Kincheng Bank, which dealt with the Japanese, and he had built the house as a retirement and summer home for his large, happy family. But robbers had broken in and he feared kidnaping—of his children, if not of himself.

The watchman, who doubled as gardener, was afraid to stay alone in the little gatehouse with his family. On one side of this compound at Ch'un Ch'i Ch'u was an uninhabited slope, and the wall was not high enough to keep out prowlers with ladders. Once during our stay, a robber did break a window of the gatehouse and terrified the gatekeeper, who loved having Gobi for protection and treated him well. Near the house was an ancient graveyard; Jimmy had banked on its keeping out robbers, as nearly all Chinese were afraid to pass this graveyard after twilight, including supposedly Westernized students and teachers. But the Manchus and Mongols did not mind. These must have been their own ancestral ghosts, since Hait'ien was a bannerman's enclave for the defeated retainers of the Manchu dynasty overthrown in 1911, and the best court Mandarin was still spoken there.

We made the move on a cold, windy March day. All our furniture was brought from Peking by carrying-pole on the shoulders of the big, muscular Hopei coolies, singing as they jogged the five or six miles. The only alternative would have been Peking carts, which would have broken everything, jouncing over the rough stone-paved roads. Not a crack was made in the thin window glass that topped the jade-green willow tables and my moon-shaped desk.

Oh, how glad I was to get rid of most of the horrible big French Legation pieces Ed had bought at auction and the worn rug and the sidesaddle; I kept the white skates for the beautiful lake at Yenching.

Ed and I, with our friend Yao Hsin-nung, rode on the Yenching bus with Gobi, and inspected our small swimming pool, tamped-earth tennis court, and modern plumbing while waiting for the coolies. A glowing coal-ball fire was started in the Western-style fireplace, and our coal-ball stoves were put up instantly as they arrived. A beautiful welcoming dinner was ready for the table soon after it got there along with the dishes—not one thing broken, not even Ed's bottle of *pai-kerh* kaoliang wine, which he and Yao used for celebrating and also to keep the fire burning bright, practicing long-range spitting on it for fun.

Yao was an editor of *T'ien Hsia*, the leading literary magazine of China; he spoke perfect English, and was the handsome, sophisticated Beau Brummel of Shanghai, always wearing a light dove-gray Western suit with lavender vest and spats and patent leather shoes. He had been staying at our house in Peking while he and Ed translated Lu Hsun's writing.

That first evening we turned off the electric lights and sat around the fire with candles as Yao told ghost stories, each one certified to be true. He believed in them absolutely and had already learned about the graveyard and all the local lore from our new servants. (Our Number 1 boy and cook were properly guaranteed at Yenching University nearby, and each had his *t'u-ti* to do all the work except answer the electric bell.) Yao told us he did not know any Chinese who did not believe in ghosts. The belief was basic to ancestor worship, and may still be alive today. Yet Yao also admired Lu Hsun, who satirized all these old superstitions.

Ed had learned about renting haunted houses cheaply while traveling with Dr. Joseph F. Rock on a *National Geographic* trip. Such houses were clean, free of disease, and safe from robbers, who were all superstitious. No Chinese would go into haunted houses after dark, but Dr. Rock traveled with several Nashi tribesmen, who did not believe in Chinese ghosts, only in their own ancestral spirits. Dr. Rock made fun of all such ideas until . . .

Soon after we moved to Hait'ien, Dr. Rock came on a visit with three of his Nashis. No longer did he ridicule haunted houses. He had once rented a fine haunted house in Yunnan formerly owned by a big landlord. Dr. Rock put his camp cot at the foot of a four-poster bed. Settled down to sleep, he felt the icy grip of death creeping over him, a kind of dead-air suffocation. One by one his Nashis tried the cot and felt the same thing, yet when they moved the cot away from the four-poster, everything seemed normal.

Next morning Dr. Rock decided to get to the bottom of the mystery. He was told that the landlord had been a sadist who bought healthy young slave girls from the farmers and tortured them to death, after which he drank the warm blood and ate the heart. According to old Chinese medicine, this would rejuvenate his health and cure heart trouble. Dr. Rock was stunned when his informant added, knowing nothing of the cot situation: "He used to tie the slave girls to the bedpost to torture them."

From that time on, Dr. Rock checked haunted houses and found he could locate the spot of a crime by the same cold, deathlike feeling he experienced when standing on it. He told us he thought that the tissues of wood and plaster might have trapped the sound waves of heinous crimes, though an earth floor did not retain a memory of murder.

Jimmy Chuan's dream house was the only open one I ever remember seeing in North China, though it also had its distant wall. There were many sunny windows in its open half-square, with a paved courtyard between the two side wings.

One wing of the house was Ed's sacrosanct office, all Java batik and a den of comfort and privacy, which he dearly loved. The other wing was my study, the only time in my life I ever had a room of my own to work in—usually I had to use a bedroom. Gobi commuted between Mount Parnassus and Fleet Street, though most of his time was spent on top of the rock garden hoping for some excitement. For the first time we had a telephone—on the wall near the kitchen and servants' quarters.

Oh, how I loved yellow and sunlight! Every floor was covered with shining-clean golden-straw matting, woven in the room itself to fit exactly. Walls were calcimined in yellow to show off the jade-green willow and bamboo furniture, which fitted to perfection our country retreat. I had curtains made of yellow Korean cloth with hollyhocks appliquéd on them, through which the sunlight filtered onto the golden-straw floors, each reflecting a paradise of warm color. My indoor rock garden was flanked by orange and lemon trees. All my houses in China were like conservatories, full of plants, flowers, and conversation.

I designed for our table some yellow and orange appliquéd linen place mats shaped like lotus flowers. I still wish I had insisted on buying the most beautiful place mats I ever saw: an English garden embroidered on linen in "ten thousand" colors, designed by a Yenching teacher. The price was too cheap to mention now, but it seemed extravagant beyond wishing then. I was under a reign of terror when it came to spending money—just as Ed was under a reign of terror as an example of the model American marriage partner. Perhaps it was feminine deprivation that made me like handicrafts so much. If I had had money to spend, I might not later have had the idea of handicraft and industrial cooperatives to save the skills of women in China.

I dearly loved gardens, both large and miniature. Wherever I went, I always made gardens, and still do. I invented my own type of moss garden, with tree roots for stumps and hollow rocks as grottoes. A tiny maidenhair fern was actually the cousin of the ginkgo tree, one of the oldest living trees and sacred in Chinese temples.

All during our marriage, Ed and I met for tea and macaroons in the late afternoon. That was the time we were chiefly "at home" to callers, though I usually had my Madame-Récamier–style Wednesdays, too. Ed read everything he wrote aloud to me, and we discussed it endlessly, with Gobi sitting on one lap, then on the other, to show his objectivity.

Because of Gobi we were popular in the village, as the Manchus and Mongols liked this type of dog, a native of the same open steppes. Everybody smiled at us and waved. Our servants loved Gobi and were delighted when we took care of another Borzoi belonging to the Larsen brothers of Mongolia, a distemper convalescent with bad nerves and heart who bit my hand the first time I touched him. Gobi civilized Wulfson after a time, but I would not let him out of the compound because of his heart.

Against strict orders, the gateman and the whole neighborhood made bets on the two dogs and let them out to race. They ran all the way to Peking and got lost. The pair were known all over the countryside after the search, with everybody en route involved.

Our language teacher, Huang, was as long, lean, and cadaverous as the two greyhounds. He loved the dogs—he was a Mongol, too—and they sat on either side of him during lessons. We also loved Huang, who was outgoing and friendly. He was a power in the whole area among the farmers, but we could never figure out which secret society he belonged to. He knew archery, and I suspected him of having been one of the Boxers who tried to kill all foreigners in 1900, when his family had been in command of the guard at the nearby Yuan Ming Yuan palace, which had been destroyed by European troops. Yenching University campus was partly on the old palace grounds, with its beautiful lake where Gobi used to swim and astonish the students, few of whom had ever seen a greyhound before.

We taught Gobi to run in a beeline straight in front of a bicycle, with a long leather leash on the handlebars, pulling the rider along at a fast clip. In local legend this ranked with the invention of putting a sail on a wheelbarrow.

When Gobi almost died with distemper, the whole village was concerned. But Gobi was something of an exception. Until 1972, I never thought of China except through a screen of cruelty to animals. The Chinese had a kind of ancient totemic taboo against dogs as pets—though not as food.

We used to ride our bicycles or walk along the narrow paths in the fields, talking to the farm families. Or we bicycled to the Yuan Ming Yuan ruins or the Summer Palace.

Our Chinese class with Huang was fun. We talked about local farm problems. Farmers would not resist the Japanese, he thought; instead they were migrating to Manchuria to take jobs under them. Peasants and students distrusted and despised each other, and the non-Hopei students were thought of as foreigners, just as we two were. Even today this gap is not closed, and students have to be sent to the communes to learn what the farms are like.

My Hait'ien impressions of the peasants subsequently turned out to be correct: They were distrustful rather than innately "conservative," as was so firmly believed by almost everyone then; they would jump on the bandwagon of the winning side if assured of a livelihood. Provided it improved the poverty situation, anything big would snowball of its own momentum. But it was almost impossible to *start* anything new. Huang had heard of the Communists, but they were too dangerous for any villager to get mixed up with, even if their ideas were right. The notion that any Yenching or Tsinghua student (some of whom were involved in anti-Kuomintang activities) could be trusted by a local farmer was beyond Huang's imagination—and he was right, at least for then. The student revolutionaries would urge the *lao pai hsing* to fight, but none of them would do anything so manual as that.

Ed learned to write Chinese but I refused to do so. Though I was fascinated by the ancient pictographs or ideographs, I objected to the whole principle of the old characters, and thought the Chinese should be taught in latinized script instead—a new idea just heard of, though the Soviets in Siberia had already started *latinhua*. Learning a pictograph was the same as learning by pictures: You could never escape from the same old meaning.

I decided to drop the study of Chinese except for what I needed for everyday use. We could get excellent full-time translators for about U.S. $10 a month or less, including typing and secretarial work, and I felt that if I spent my time learning the language, I would never learn about China.

CHAPTER 16

Fascism and Marxism

We had moved to Hait'ien in time for me to matriculate for the 1934–1935 school year at Yenching University. I took most of the classes available in English, plus one in Chinese—that course was on "The Logic of Hegel," under Chang Tung-sung, known as the top Chinese Hegelian, who became a friend and subsequently supported our various projects.

There were five other foreign students at Yenching. One was Derk Bodde, who later became the sinologist pride of the University of Pennsylvania. Another was Margaret Bryant from Michigan, taking a degree in China studies. Under Harry Price we studied what few books were available on Chinese economics, including a little information on cooperatives. I was influenced by the unique classic *Land and Labour in China* by R. H. Tawney, and also studied Tawney's *Religion and the Rise of Capitalism*. Tawney was my cup of tea, and opened up new horizons in understanding the civilization of the West. I also took a popular course, in English, under Lucius Porter on the general History of Philosophy in the West. Another class, taught by P. C. Hsu, dealt chiefly with Confucianism and the family system. (Hsu was a Christian who hated Confucianism almost as much as Margaret and I did.)

Alone, I had a special class in Chinese Esthetics under L. T. Huang, Dean of Fine Arts, which explained the recondite philosophy behind Chinese arts.

We also bicycled to nearby Tsinghua University to take Fung Yu-lan's class in the History of Chinese Philosophy, and Bodde later translated his book on that subject. Even in the icy wind, with sleet and yellow dust blinding our eyes, we pedaled the five miles to the city of Peking to take a special course in Buddhism and Taoism from Hsu Ti-shan, the best Chinese scholar on those subjects.

This year of very heavy research and study was highly productive for my mind, and I knew where I was on the China terrain. In old age Edgar Snow said he was "something of a Fabian." We were reading the Left Book Club editions of John Strachey and G.D.H. Cole. We used the Yenching University library. We had no money to buy books or magazines and subscribed only to the organ of the British Labour party, the *London Daily Herald*, for which Ed was correspondent for the whole Far East from 1932 to 1941. We borrowed from Helen Burton *The Saturday Review of Literature* and *The New Yorker*. We felt cut off from the rest of the world and were only vaguely aware of the swing to the left and toward Marxism that was occurring. Our ideas developed by themselves with a life of their own, based on grass-roots necessities, not theory.

One day at Yenching we heard an enthusiastic talk, given to an attentive student body by a woman Quaker who had just returned from Mussolini's Italy. Not only did the trains run on time, but the youth movement was inspiring and beautiful in such a slovenly place. Ed and I were shocked, so shocked that we went to the library and got out two new books on fascism, written by Italian Fascists. They actually made us both sick at our stomachs. We took a dislike to everything in the books, especially to the total lack of logic, the irrationality—not to speak of the castor-oil treatments for leftists.

Harry Price, my economics teacher, from his Yale studies was inclined toward the idea that irrationality was a big influence in human thinking. I used to argue with Harry as he and his wife, Betty, and Ed and I took long walks around the campus and nearby fields. I thought you could explain everything by uncovering cause and effect, by reason and scientific research. I felt that both Ed and I were in league with history, which meant that we were in touch with reality and not deceived by appearance. We were *dead right* and continued to be up to the end—this conviction was so firm under my feet that I still feel that way, even though many earthquakes have shaken the terra firma in my life.

Yet during our China years, the only other English-speaking person who was consistently right was Madame Sun Yat-sen. All three of us had learned from experience, not theory. Our ideas were part of a daily learning process. Also we had a wide perspective. We knew all kinds of people. Ed and I had open minds, able to suspend judgment and to be selective in the end. We were *free* to think for ourselves; others earned a living by adjusting to their employers.

Madame Sun represented the active opposition to Chiang Kai-shek's counterrevolution. I had talked with her in Shanghai, where she had given a farewell dinner for us when we left for Tokyo to be married. There we had met Yang Ch'uan, a non-Communist, one of the most impressive Chinese I ever encountered. He was secretary of the Academia Sinica, very Westernized, and a member of Madame Sun's league for civil rights, formed in 1932, which was trying to get fair trials for some of what Madame Sun referred to as the "fifty thousand political prisoners" in China. To terrorize this league—which it did—Yang was assassinated by Fascist Blue Shirts on the steps of the Academia. This happened early in 1933, about three months after we had met him. Another league member, Lin Yutang, was threatened, and the league dissolved.

This was a Fascist blow directed at the top of the intellectual establishment of China, and none of these Academia Sinica scholars ever again dared stand up for even elementary, Western-type rights. Dr. Hu Shih had been a member of the league, and he was so frightened that he would even refuse late in 1935 to support the December 9th student movement in Peking; he told a faculty meeting that the movement "was started by Mrs. Edgar Snow, with money either from Moscow or President Roosevelt. Therefore, we have no reason to support such a foreign idea." This incident was probably the lowest point in the history of Western-trained persons in China—Dr. Hu Shih was even attacking *his own* constituents, the Westernized students of Yenching University.

We "lost China" when these Americanized scholars refused to support the December 9th movement, and, earlier, when the Christians as a body did not take a national stand against the killing and suppression of the Westernized democratic intellectuals by the new fascism beginning in 1932. In that year six young writers had been buried alive by the Kuomintang in Shanghai at Lunghwa after digging their own graves. Most shocking to me was that it was the intellectual aristocracy that the Fascist regime of Chiang Kai-shek was arresting and killing. Most of those under the "white terror," as it was called, were non-Communists.

It was almost impossible to find any facts about the "underground" in China or about the Fascist movement, which was supposed to be a kind of secret society. In 1937, I was told a little history by Liu Ting in Yenan. He said the Fascist movement started in 1932 as a result of the Shanghai war when Chiang Kai-shek had no other way to turn. It was started by some Whampoa Kuomintang cadets who had studied in Moscow. They had been sent to Russia by the Kuomintang, but the right wing did not trust them, so they escaped to Japan about 1929. After Japan took Manchuria in 1931, the cadets wrote to Chiang Kai-shek personally and offered to build up his power to save himself. They were invited to Nanking. A few had been arrested in Moscow as spies connected with Trotskyists, and they referred to the Soviet Union as "Red Imperialism." These were the Fu Hsin She.

A second Fascist group of former Moscow students who returned about 1930 were "*all* former Communists," Liu said, and "translated many Fascist books—those of Mussolini and Hitler, too." They used the word *Fascist*, said Hitler was the hero who had revived Germany and that Chiang Kai-shek could be the Hitler of China.

The third Fascist group was the C.C. clique of the brothers Chen Li-fu and Chen Kuo-fu, a kind of secret political police force which was not only anti-Communist but also against other Kuomintang cliques.

Early in 1932, Chiang Kai-shek established a school for political training in Nanking. There were a thousand students and all the teachers were Fascists. Chiang also established in 1932 a Fascist investigation bureau headed by Tai Li, the man closest to Chiang Kai-shek and the most dreaded name in China. (He continued to work with Americans up to 1949, when he had to escape.) Chiang Kai-shek also got men from Germany to organize his political work.

"The second and first groups were called Blue Shirts and the others C.C.," Liu Ting explained. He went on: "Subjectively, the Fascists want to drive out all foreign powers—all imperialism—and also the Red Imperialism of the Soviet Union." The slogan for "national socialism" was used, but they "are not anti-capitalist," he said. "The Fascists do not oppose feudalism; they welcome the New Life movement slogans from the old feudal Chinese philosophy."

Of course we did not know all this in 1934 and 1935. We knew only that the Chinese were trying to create an illogical type of what I called sub-fascism. I think now that it is basic to fascism to be illogical, to tell lies, to be contradictory.

In Hait'ien we also began to study Marxism for the first time, though Ed had borrowed some books on the subject for a short time in India. Our minds were not as congenial with these old Marxist tomes as they were with the new left wing in England. I took a dislike to *The Communist Manifesto* immediately because it was obviously anti-woman. I didn't like the whole tone of it—it was not the type of thing an All-American Girl would find inspiring. Karl Marx analyzed capitalism as of the nineteenth century, and he had obviously found and synthesized a bit of the truth. But he had little to offer two young people immersed in China. Lenin was close to the realities in the colonial world with his new thesis on imperialism. It was his work that inspired all the anti-colonial revolutions in Asia and elsewhere, even though such men as Gandhi did not understand or agree with Lenin.

We could not get hold of the most important book for understanding China and the nature of its revolution: Engels's work on the family. Though Engels knew nothing of China to speak of, he had found the key: ancestor worship. Mao Tse-tung, from personal experience, realized as early as 1927 that the key problem was the clan (the *tsu*), which was the vehicle of ancestor worship and Confucianism. Yet even today it is obvious that the Soviet Union and Marxists all over the world have failed to understand the nature of the problems in China.

To many Chinese, Marxism was the first theory to illuminate the murky depths of China's complicated problems. They took to it like ducks to water. And it is true that the Marxists in China seemed to be the only ones who actually understood the objective situation, but there were few of them.

The Marxist concept that the economic and social class of the individual determines his ideas and behavior is basically true, I have found, even though many individuals transcend this limitation by an act of conscious will and intellectual study. In China the lines were not only blurred but actually mixed—organic status in society was still the cohesive element, through the province, clan, and family relations of a prefeudal nature. The horizontal class structure had not as yet divided the kinship system into classes, though big general classes could be said to exist, such as "rich" and "poor." Terms like *capitalist* and *proletariat* belong to Western capitalism, where these classes had been differentiated from the feudal and tribal kinship systems by way of the bourgeois revolution.

Mao Tse-tung knew what his terms meant in the context of China, even though to Westerners these only compounded confusion. Many Chinese still think *proletarian* means an intellectual attitude that can be achieved by study and changing the mind. But orthodox Western Marxism is based on the concept that proletarian ideology has to come from a real economic working class—industrial workers in a capitalist or socialist society. Some Chinese think the Communist party can substitute for the proletariat because it has the ideology of Marxist socialism, whether or not the members originate in the technical working class. This is actually the key problem in China today—and the reason for the "proletarian" revolution there in 1966.

The Marxist idea that change occurs by a change in the mode of production is important. Thus you can hand over millions of tons of modern weapons, and teach English to the upper classes in Seoul, Saigon, and Phnom Penh, but it is impossible to create "democracy," as Americans imagine; this change has to come from the farm and factory in a changed mode of production with new tools. All over the preindustrial world this situation exists: The upper classes do not engage in socially useful production, and never have. Hence their minds cannot be liberated from their previous social attitudes, no matter how many foreign languages they may learn, except in a few individual cases when by becoming professional revolutionaries they become salary earners, so to speak, in a new structure and may be transformed by this.

Thus in China, Mao Tse-tung sent students to the farms and factories to ensure a "proletarian" ideology, knowing that if they went first into a big professional bureaucracy—as university and middle-school graduates hoped to do—they might not be trusted to carry out socialism, but would transform it to their own "elite" interest.

In 1934–1935, I was shocked into action when Chiang Kai-shek's government started to revive Confucianism and its four principles in the New Life Movement, imitating Mussolini's *Vita Nuova*. It was hard to understand, but I finally came up with the idea that it was "sub-fascism," later called quislingism in Europe. In the end Chiang was not a quisling, though he refused to resist the Japanese, saving his resources for survival in the interior. However, looked at from the angle of "imperialism" and the multinational companies, all such puppets are quislings. They are the servants of international foreign capital, utilized to try to destroy the imperative revolutions of their own people.

CHAPTER 17

Peitaiho: Missionaries by the Yellow Sea

By the end of 1935, we were in a situation where the most complicated problems of China and of the world converged, in total uncertainty. The 350 million Chinese were sitting helpless as turnips while Chiang Kai-shek flirted with fascism in hopes of saving no more than his own little regime. Most of the West was asleep, while the Italians, Germans, and Japanese were out to change the status quo. The League of Nations was already dead. Ed and I did not want the United States to be involved in Asia or to intervene in China, and this was still the policy of the State Department. Yet only Americans could act—everyone else was tied down by Empire or other problems.

Ed and I had no confidence in anyone, no guide to theory or action. On the contrary, we felt a whole new era had to be inaugurated, at least in Asia.

At Yenching University everything was as usual, with the common denominator a belief that the Chinese would absorb the Japanese in a few hundred years, so why worry? The foreigners actually expected that they would be able to stay and work under the Japanese, as did their students. Yang Ping, the ex-Communist writer, told me Yenching was hopeless in all ways and that "the Christians," whom she disliked and considered totally reactionary, had control of the student body. Ed's students that year in the Department of Journalism had no ideas at all beyond earning a living.

When Harry and Betty Price invited me to spend part of the summer at Peitaiho, where they had rented a big cottage (I would also stay with them there in 1936), I was happy to accept. For a year I had been in the midst of the most successful Protestant missionaries and converts in all China. But the *élan vital* for China was lacking. The whole development seemed artificial, all at the top. Now, for two summers at Peitaiho, I came into contact with "the Missionary mind" from all over China (except those from the South, who summered in Kuling near the Yangtze River). These gatherings were like camp meetings and made life tolerable for the rest of the year.

A terrible murder had occurred in Hupeh Province. A young American missionary couple, the Stams, had been beheaded by Chinese. The "Communists" (specifically the army led by Chu Teh) were blamed for the murder, especially by the Kuomintang, which saw the value of the propaganda for the right wing. This welded the missionaries into a fraternity of fear of "Communists." Even if no Communists at all had been involved, the missionaries were anxious to believe they had.

Circulating in Peitaiho in 1935 was a pamphlet called *The Red Scourge*, written by a missionary. I could see it was only a fanatical document, yet I could also see it was dangerous for missionaries to take such a strong anti-Communist stand. Even some right-wing Chinese did not like this attitude; they called it imperialism, just as the Communists did.

The uproar over the Stam murder was utilized to collect funds for the China missions and also for the Chiang Kai-shek regime. The murder had so much influence that it was possible to believe the Kuomintang itself had paid to have it committed in order to mobilize foreign opinion against the Communists and for the Kuomintang.

In 1935–1936, I could hardly understand why the missionaries were making so much of one isolated incident, however distressing, and risking the future in China for it. Yet they understood the Chinese village better than I: This was an earthshaking incident, and they realized how insecure their foundation was in China. The Stam murder would assume even more significance if the local villagers had done it on their own—this the missionaries realized with horror, so they *wanted* to blame it on the Communists.

One had to remember that it was as recently as 1900 that the Empress Dowager had ordered all foreigners and Christians killed in China, and hundreds had paid the price. The men who engaged in this killing were for the most part still alive in 1935. About 2,000 Chinese Protestants and 30,000 Chinese Catholics were murdered, along with 221 Western Christians. Not a few missionaries I met had been in China in Boxer times, some of them born there.

I made a point of trying to find the truth about the Stam murder. In Yenan two years later, nobody had ever heard of it, and I was told that Chu Teh's army had never been in that area. He was hundreds of miles away, and yet he was blamed for it. They were sure no Communist had done such a thing; not only would it have been idiotic for them, but also they did not as a rule allow beheading, and certainly not of any foreigner. Later, in Manila, I met the Chinese consul who had gone to Hupeh to investigate the Stam case, Kuangson Young, but he had not the slightest proof of who had done it.

I concluded that no real Communists had been involved, but perhaps some partisans among the local people—"wearing armbands," it was said—had murdered the couple just as a kind of accident of history, perhaps with no logical reason at all except anti-foreignism. But the point is this: Permanent hatred and resentment were created among the Communists, who thought the attribution of the murder to them a Big Lie to discredit them and make them out to be savages. They still resent the "lies" told by missionaries over the years, and believe them to be intentional.

Only fourteen years later, all missionaries and nearly all foreigners were pushed out of China. What I was sensing in Peitaiho in 1935 and 1936 were the tremors of premonition.

In the mid-thirties none of us knew anything factual about what kind of Communists were in the far interior and whether or not they enjoyed beheading harmless young American couples. Someone had to find out the facts.

In the 1930s, I had the Puritan horror of lies. I was too unsophisticated to realize that the Big Lie and the Little Lie and innuendo are standard weapons in the arsenal of war, especially civil war, and most of them are repeated by innocent believers. I still believe that truth is always on the right side and that it is the best policy, too. Otherwise, trust is destroyed and with it morale, political and personal.

The first Protestant missionary had been Robert Morrison in 1807, and the last was Miss Talitha Gerlach, still in Shanghai, though not technically a missionary but a former YWCA secretary. In 1935, China had 5,875 missionaries of 107 Protestant sects and 512,873 communicants. Of these, 37 percent were single women—mission work was part of women's liberation for Protestants. In 1936, the Catholics claimed 2,934,175 members with 12,499 nuns, priests, teachers, and layworkers.

I well realized that Christianity was a revolutionary and progressive religion compared with all the others in Asia—this was Teilhard's firm idea. I had never thought otherwise, except that I needed my year of study at Yenching to find the proofs of it. It was clear to everyone that a vacuum existed in China, and that both Catholics and Protestants had the raw materials to fill this vacuum; yet neither took on this role. Why? And why did Chinese seem to be hostile to the Christian ethic, even when they had no alternative to it?

I had never studied religions much but I was open-minded on all subjects. I was only vaguely aware of the history of religion as a power for change, though I knew about the Protestant Reformation, the Puritans and Cromwell, and so on. In those terrible years in China, I had to come to grips with my own Western civilization—what it was worth not only for me but for China. I was for it all the way, yet I knew it had not penetrated the bamboo curtain to speak of, not in the best sense.

It was obvious that what China had needed for a century were Christian socialist missionaries. In China, real native Protestantism would have been far more radical than the present Puritan socialism which has evolved—so radical as to be impossible. Overpopulation makes the individualism inherent in Protestantism impossible in China and in other such nations; this marvelous development of the individual in the West is a luxury China cannot afford to cultivate. A mass society was easy to slip into in China. Individualism never existed there; it was forbidden under the Confucian principles of a rigid kinship structure following ancestral rules.

The most individualistic Chinese we knew was Hubert S. Liang, a product of YMCA education. Yet he realized at the same time we did that what was needed in China was a whole new ideology related to socialism.

In other words, the missionaries did not bring the highest type of religion or Western civilization to China, both because they were not socialists and because they were hardly aware of the revolutionary implications of Christianity. By 1911, they were compromising and adjusting to all the old evils and sickness of Chinese society instead of fighting them as the nineteenth-century missionaries had, tooth and nail and in the face of real danger. Up until about 1911, the Protestants had actually been converting the poor and working-class Chinese and fighting against the upper classes, real revolutionary action.

As for the Catholics, early apostolic Christianity was fanatically revolutionary against the old society of tribalism and clannism, and it civilized the barbaric tribes of Europe year after year, bringing with it the nuclear family and a new anti-tribal ethic against revenge. Roman Catholicism was the ideology of feudalism, destroying the previous tribal-clan system, all kinds of ancestor worship, totemism, and so on—including slavery as a mode of production—and replacing the slave with the serf.

Of course, that was exactly what China had been needing since the days of Ch'in Shih Huang-ti, who was in power exactly at the time Jesus Christ was preaching in the Mideast. Why did Catholic missionaries fail when their religion was so very valid against the old Confucian ancestor-worshiping clan-tribalism? Partly because they compromised with it, and partly because pure Catholicism, as it had been in its classic, evangelical time, never came to Asia. What arrived was the Counter-Reformation in the form of the Jesuits and other orders, who were concerned more with destroying "revolution" by the Protestants than with creating a new society in Asia. Christian charity and compassion were not undesirable as personal qualities in China, but they did not fit into the historic necessities.

It was singularly appropriate that Teilhard, a Jesuit Old China Hand, should signal the Counter-Reformation's end which Pope John carried forward in the early 1960s. A few years later, Pope Paul stated that Catholics should realize Christianity was developing in China under the name of socialism. He saw that a new religion was being born in China, with Mao Tse-tung as its prophet, growing out of the same conditions that gave birth to Christ in the Mideast, and to Mohammed as well.

I had to think hard about what the essence was of Christianity and Western civilization. It was alarming to find that the missionaries had stopped opposing Confucianism and were not encouraging resistance to the pagan Japanese. They even referred to Chiang Kai-shek as a Christian, an idea certain to destroy any prestige they had left among young Chinese.

Religion is not enough and Marxism is not enough—Teilhard was right. The hominization of man requires that above and beyond both of these there must be created a surplus, which has always been known as spiritual power, which grows out of suffering and deprivation as well as out of conscious will. The price is very heavy and can easily be death.

I had no wish to be a Christian martyr or any other kind, but I resented the fact that the so-called Christians failed to set the example they should have in China, and not only were taking no leadership at all when it was most needed, but were actually being non-Christian in the historical sense. *Someone* had to act.

I was the victim of history, which was squeezing out of me, like wine from new grapes, the surplus I had by nature and development. This wine was being handed out to the Chinese to intoxicate them with will and determination to act. I was still developing intellectually, but history was channeling my studies into narrow paths, contrary to my whole nature. I, who set out to be the Renaissance woman, was being cut down to size as a worker in the vineyards—a researcher on the nature of revolution in China.

In Peking I began to realize vaguely that "spiritual" excellence was bypassing nearly all the "Christians," except for Madame Sun Yat-sen and Teilhard de Chardin. That department was being taken over by young Communists or believers in socialism. Missionaries had what I considered a cheap, easy type of spiritual development, which took little courage because they firmly believed God was taking care of them and that to do the will of God was enough. Even Teilhard believed this. But real courage is an act of conscious will, with no idea of any "God" protecting one.

The essence of all religion is to be willing to risk your life for a belief—not for survival. This implies sacrifice of your personal advantages for others, for society, or for the future. This is the test of "spiritual" quality. The Communists in China had to have this quality to a very high degree, and today are teaching and trying to develop it on a mass scale. They follow Mao Tse-tung's teaching that you cannot become a Communist except by being reborn. In 1982, Hu Yao-bang, head of the Communist party, established the principle of developing a "socialist spiritual civilization," using that phrase.

Individual spiritual development is not enough. It has to be productive and in league with history, not in opposition to the future. Of all people, I was a prime individualist, believing in the maximum development of the individual, especially the woman, who had not as yet often demonstrated this capacity. Yet by the end of 1935, I was socialized against my will. I was being destroyed as an individual, sacrificed for that great mass of people known as China. I actually lost my sense of self-preservation.

From the first minute in China, I had been incessantly busy. All my sense of immortality and accomplishment had been concentrated on my determination to write one classic book, and I was too involved in China to work on it.

This has been a peculiarly female dilemma, which is why we have produced so few classics in any field. All along the way, we are pulled to pieces by the urgent needs of others. In my own case I knew none of the things I got started would have been done, through sheer accident of history, except for me—I was the only person in that place and at that time. Hence, the imperative of history was bigger than my own will, my own ego, and my own well-being. I became an involuntary "Christian" in China, for lack of others to take on this sacrificial role.

Yet at this minute I still believe in the immortality of art for its own sake. I believe in monuments, the legacy of achievement; I believe in the Human Adventure, in trying, in building Parthenons. What I believe in and love most is the American experiment—the American persona. I always have. We have not been excellent insofar as producing deities is concerned. But since 1607, we have produced millions of individuals working hard for the highest standard of living ever known, and developing at the same time a high "spiritual" worth in the sense of maximum generosity, kindness, friendliness, good humor, and true democratic instincts for judging by merit. I would not give up the real American people for all the Parthenons, all the Beethoven symphonies, all the English literature, all the French cuisine, all the Taj Mahals, and all the Russian and Chinese revolutions, all combined.

This American persona created one great monument to the Human Endeavor: the Constitution and Bill of Rights, written in the midst of a revolution by its participants. Our ancestors fought at least three brave and terrible wars to establish the American experiment and its principles—the Puritan civil war between Englishmen in the seventeenth century which destroyed "feudalism," the Revolution of 1776, and the Civil War of the 1860s. China had to fight all three of these wars at once, and to fight against modern imperialism as well. They had for their use no ancestral weapon in the shape of democratic change and rights. Only war could make the big telescoping changes.

CHAPTER 18

Our Haunted House
Near the Fox Tower

While I was at the seashore in 1935, Ed had gone to Manchuria to see what the Japanese conquerors were doing. His book, *Far Eastern Front*, was an attack on them. We were not exactly nervous, but we did know that Japan was poised to take over North China at any moment. There was only one deterrent: The Japanese did not want to alarm Americans, who were then completely isolationist. They planned to rule through Chinese puppets.

At the top of Japan's blacklist were the names of J. B. Powell and Edgar Snow. It seemed like a good idea to move inside the Peking wall, especially as Ed had had enough of the village idyll and was champing at the bit to get back to newspaper work.

In the fall of 1935, we found another ideal home—a house haunted by werefoxes, lost and desperate students, and refugees from Manchuria. Because No. 13 K'uei Chia Ch'ang was haunted, the rent for half the place was about U.S. $10 a month, and we shared the staff of servants with the principal tenant, Dr. E. T. Nystrom, a monarchist Swedish geologist who was at the Peking Club every night and spent half the year in Sweden with his beautiful wife, who refused to live in China. Nystrom had founded his own Nystrom Institute for Scientific Research in Taiyuanfu, Shansi; and in Europe he consorted with denizens of the *Almanach de Gotha*, whose autographed photographs covered the walls of his living room.

We lived in this Kiplingesque setting during the last legation days. The big semiforeign house was intended to be an English stately home, though it had only one story, with a long glassed-in conservatory, full of plants and flowers, in front between the two wings. Our separate bathroom was palatial, with marble equipment and modern plumbing. The big rooms had fireplaces and steam heat as well. A high-walled compound enclosed about an acre, with stables at one end, a tennis court, and a glassed-in pavilion for formal garden parties of the leghorn-hat-and-black-velvet-sash variety. Near the gatehouse was a garden potting house; I fixed it up for Ed's den, and he growled happily there in solitude.

On Saturday nights, Nystrom would go to the Grand Hôtel de Pékin with one or another legation party. "Wear your apple-green dress with the court train," he would beg me, and would ask the orchestra for a Viennese waltz as soon as I arrived in the long red-velvet opera cape that was one of Helen Burton's gifts to the local fashion model.

No. 13 was in the corner of the ancient wall where the Fox Tower stood, empty and desolate except for bats, swallows, and werefoxes. Farther on was the Jesuit Observatory where we walked with Teilhard. Nystrom had his own five-hole golf course there, with short-distance holes crisscrossing. At one side of the immense compound wall was the Boxer Cemetery, where the foreign victims of 1900 lay buried; the Chinese believed every grave was haunted by its ghost.

About a mile from Hatamen Street along the city wall was a vacant mall or glacis-type space where all the walled compounds were blind—no doors opened onto the mall—and the high tops were covered with sharp pieces of glass. This was a sinister, spooky place, and the Chinese did not like to go along there, but we rode our bicycles, with Gobi on the long leash. It was dusty but clean and private.

Did I ever see the werefox that haunted No. 13? Yes, I did, once when neither Ed nor Nystrom was at home. A werefox was similar to a werewolf, only the Chinese kind was usually a woman who had been mistreated in life and had come back to take revenge. To look upon her was to die. The Fox Tower itself was full of werefoxes after dark, and the earth at its foot was saturated with the blood of the guilty and innocent; this spot, where the walls of Genghis Khan were still scarred by arrows, had been the execution ground. (Executions now took place outside the city wall, and tuberculosis sufferers attended so that they might drink the blood while hot as a cure. Communists and bandits were considered good medicine, because they were so brave.)

Werefoxes would come only to the second story or higher, which is one reason the Chinese did not dwell in two-story houses. Our one-story house had an almost-flat tile roof, with no more space than a foot or so between it and the ceiling. It was kept carefully sealed all around with cement so that no outside animal could get in.

Alone in our big living room one evening, I was reading a borrowed copy of *The Saturday Review of Literature* when I distinctly
heard what sounded like slow, measured footsteps on the ceiling—
from above, but not on the tile roof. Gobi's hackles rose and he
whimpered. I was almost too petrified to ring the electric bell for the
Number 1 boy.

"*Something* is walking overhead on the ceiling," I whispered,
pointing upward.

"It's the werefox," Han said. "It's been heard here before."

Both Han and Ch'en, the coolie, brought their bigswords and
straw pallets to spend the night on the living room floor, after they had
patrolled the grounds and left several other men on guard with bigswords. I went to the bedroom to try to sleep.

Not long afterward, both boys heard the same sound. We went
into conference. I wanted to get a ladder to look through the small
trapdoor in the hall, where the electric wires came through. But they
refused to look or to allow me to look.

"No, *T'ai-t'ai*—look-see, die; no look-see, no die," they explained.

When morning came, I insisted on getting a ladder and flashlight
and put my head through the trapdoor for a look-see. The whole
neighborhood knew about the werefox by that time, and about twenty
people had gathered in the room in ten minutes. The men were carrying bigswords.

Heavy yellow loess dust carpeted the rafters, with no obvious sign
of disturbance. I started to climb down as my audience heaved an
audible sigh of relief.

But wait! What was that wide board doing there, lying across the
rafters? Up again I climbed to restudy the terrain, with total silence
restored below.

The board was warped. One side curled so that the rounded bottom could rock in a cradle motion. Yes, a mouse had run along the
curled edge at just the right angle and set the board to rocking so that
one end hit a rafter with a distinct hollow sound like footsteps. I didn't
have to be Archimedes to understand the principle of a mouse at the
fulcrum of leverage. You could move the world that way.

I put the trapdoor back and looked down at my suspense-filled
audience. I didn't want to ruin a good tradition, or to have the rent
raised, or to encourage robbers afraid of werefoxes. (I didn't even tell
Ed, knowing he would not keep it a secret.)

"*Huli meiyo*," I reported—no werefox. "Is this werefox weather?"

"Yes, it is," I was told. "We have had heavy rain and now we have a hot, dry spell. That is when the werefoxes are heard."

Peking had sharp changes in humidity and temperature. Floor cracks widened an inch and closed up again. Loose boards could curl and creak as they dried out and cracked. Nails could pull out of warping boards with anguished yelps. Doors opened by themselves as the wood panels shrank in the heat.

On such a wet-dry night, the whole Fox Tower would be yelping with shrinking boards.

Now who had laid that wide board in just the right position to make werefox footsteps? It had to be someone who wanted to keep the rent cheap, or to make robbers think the house was haunted.

In 1972, I walked again in the narrow, dusty *hutungs* around No. 13 and took photographs in the twilight of the Fox Tower and Observatory. The wall near the Fox Tower was being torn down, but no one had as yet dared confront the werefoxes.

The house was a feudal monarchist castle, a remnant of the Manchu dynasty, which was forced out of the Forbidden City in the 1911 Revolution. The Number 1 boy, Han, was related to the imperial family. He looked and acted like a king. The cook and his apprentice were of the same ilk. The coolie, Ch'en, whom we dearly loved and who adored Gobi, was a long, lank Mongol—he had probably been a bannerman warrior as late as twenty-four years earlier, and he looked the part when he carried his bigsword to patrol inside the spacious compound. The gatekeeper, Kuan, was the only youngish servant and lived in the gatehouse with his family. Fifteen persons lived in the servants' quarters.

Considering all our nefarious activities in Peking, we were very lucky to have these particular servants. The Manchu-Mongol element were very discreet for their own reasons and owed no allegiance to the Peking police or the Fascists. The Japanese were wooing them and had made Pu Yi emperor again in Manchuria, but the servants of foreigners knew enough to mind their own business or they might lose their jobs. Any one of our servants could have made a lot of money turning some of our revolutionary student friends over to the police, but they never did.

Another safety element was that Nystrom's politics were probably to the right of Attila the Hun, but we never discussed such things. He was a friend of Sven Hedin, one of the famous pro-Fascists of Europe, whom we also knew distantly.

The etiquette at No. 13 was actually that of Manchu royalty. When Dr. Nystrom returned at eleven o'clock at night, or at any other time, two lines of servants had to greet his royal progress at the gate, kowtowing with foreheads to the ground—all but the Number 1 boy, who bowed. I had learned my lesson about interfering with the Peking servant system, but this I could not endure. When the gateman and his wife started kowtowing to *me* at the gate, I ordered them never to do such a thing. *"Pu shih meikuo kueichu,"* I declared. "That is not an American custom." (None of them understood any English.)

In spite of all I could do, however, most of the servants lined up to greet us, all proud smiles, when we were formally dressed to go to or come from some social event. How they wished I looked and acted like a queen all the time—they identified with us! In the big kitchen, intended for preparing legation-style dinner parties, the cook and the boys entertained their friends constantly. One of their frequent topics of conversation was whether or not their "missy" had been the belle of the ball—which I often was, actually, dancing the Viennese waltz with Dr. Nystrom and assorted Fascists; the non-Fascists were never good dancers.

It was not easy for me to give up any chance to dance the Viennese waltz in the Grand Hôtel de Pékin, where the two best dancers were also the two most attractive men in Peking: one the Number 1 Italian Fascist, a friend of Count Ciano, and the other a young Nazi Junker recently arrived from Germany. An apolitical bridge came down when the Viennese waltz began, and we maintained a silent truce till it was over. Each of them was trying to be the Nietzschean superman in every way. But they had more respect for Ed and me than for anyone else in Peking, and both were very pro-Anglo-American, as Ciano himself was (to his ultimate undoing: He was executed by the Fascists for it in the end). There was so much dialectical energism in opposition between me and this young Fascist and Nazi that electrical sparks flew. Pathos was there and high tragedy and frustrated romance, the attraction of opposites, enemies by circumstance, not by choice.

During the summer in Peitaiho, the Number 1 Fascist had been prevalent, but I had been avoiding him since 1933—except for the waltz bridge over the Danube. He managed to be on the same train returning to Peking from Peitaiho, and we fenced verbally all the way. He was the first real Fascist I had ever tried to talk with. Despite his politics, he was witty and charming, and tried his best to be irresistible. He seemed to be the first person I had met in China, except Ed, who had a real sense of humor. I still had a sense of humor, and wit—which I was gradually losing year by year. Oh, how homesick I was for the bright young people at home, who were fun and who loved me, even at a distance!

It was not easy to get rid of my Fascist, who escorted me against my wish to the big brass-studded double gate at No. 13. But when the servants lined up on both sides to welcome me, he was intimidated. As he got back into the taxi, he said, "I dislike Fascist women. I'll never marry one. I like anti-Fascist women. Fascism is for men only."

That dueling train trip from Peitaiho may have been the last time I ever felt young and witty and fascinating and amusing and "teddibly, teddibly Amedican," as this young Oxford-educated Italian put it. A few weeks later I had to grow up fast. I declared war on all kinds of fascism and Nazism, and so did my husband, in spite of any local Gestapo or Chinese Blue Shirts.

This Fox Tower corner of the Peking wall held the special mystique of our China experience. Here we two foreigners alone became a two-man party and a two-man diplomatic corps on the folk level, at war all by ourselves against the Japanese and all the Fascist powers and their local protégés. Here the December 9th movement flowered. Here *Red Star Over China* was written in 1936–1937, just at the time Japan occupied North China. From this house was forged an entirely new Chinese-American entente, which would reach its diplomatic climax many years later when Ed got Mao Tse-tung's permission for President Nixon to visit Peking, a historic reopening of relations between our two countries that occurred a few days after Ed's death in Switzerland in 1972.

CHAPTER 19

The December 9th
Student Movement, 1935

The end of 1935 was the absolute nadir in China, a time of living death. I felt suffocated, as if the air itself were dead, full of the carbon monoxide and methane gas of putrefying vegetation. Ed and I had each other, but we felt alien to the rest of humanity, at least to the part then dying in North China. We felt totally alone.

It was no news that Peking was dead. It had been dead for a thousand years, except for the May 4th movement in 1919. I did not want Peking to be fought over and destroyed, but also I did not want the Japanese to take it in "a screaming silence . . . cold in heart and limb . . . not vast high-walled cities of thick iron gates and battlemented towers . . . there should be at least the night-wind moaning of forgotten ghosts of glory."

That was the tone of a long poem I wrote called "Old Peking," which *Asia* published and which was subsequently anthologized.[*] (Like many young literary hopefuls, I had begun as a versifier.) The December 1935 issue of *Asia* was made up chiefly of my work—with that poem and a long article on painting, done with Wang Chun-chu, called "The Four Gentlemen of China." The poem was translated for both the Yenching and Peita University magazines, and Ping Hsin, the most important woman poet, also translated it. It expressed so exactly what Chinese youth were feeling, was so right for that moment in history, that it was total communication in any language. Ed thought it proof of my great literary genius and used to read it to dinner guests when I was away.

It was at this maximum point of suffocation and paralysis that the Yenching students injected adrenaline into the dying tissue of

[*] Alan F. Pater, *The Anthology of Magazine Verse and Yearbook of American Poetry,* 1935 (New York: Poetry Digest Association, 1936).

China. Every other school in China was under total Fascist suppression, with the possible exception of nearby Tsinghua, also an American-supported university.

In January 1935, I had begun writing anti-Fascist articles, though I hardly knew what fascism was. I set myself up as the chief dispenser in North China (in all China, I guess) of any kind of anti-Fascist materials I could find—all of which I had to type and retype. I was handing them out by the briefcaseful to the university students.

I was collecting material for a history of student movements in China. At that time students were more important than they were anywhere else—because they represented the country's top aristocracy. That students could endanger the state was a new idea to me.

I had been in Shanghai during the 1931–1932 student movement, and I identified with youth and women in China from the first. "They are holding up the train services on the trunk-railways for hours . . . they demand that General Chiang Kai-shek shall personally proceed North to lead China's armies against Japan . . . drastic action is imperative now if the Government—not the student body—is to claim to rule China." This was written by the chief British Tory, H.G.W. Woodhead. He said about fifty thousand students had got to Nanking by commandeering whole trains.

On November 27, 1931, *The China Press* had reported that ten thousand students "win passive clash with Chiang." They had waited twenty-eight hours, demanding that Chiang Kai-shek appear, and finally he did. From that moment on, Chiang waged a vendetta against students—and they hated him. He probably thought all of them were Communists—he included in his definition of that term anyone who hated him and his regime.

In 1931-1932, students believed that Chiang Kai-shek could fight Japan if he wished, but in 1935 no one knew what the situation was. The 1931–1932 leaders had been arrested—and their bodies ended up in the gravel pits of Yu Hua Tai in Nanking.

In my articles I wrote: "Over three hundred students, professors, and intellectuals generally were arrested, and an unknown number executed, during 1934, in North China alone. . . . Chiang set about the formulation of a definite political theory along Fascist lines. . . . His sworn-brother, Chang Hsueh-liang, now No. 2 Fascist of China, returned fresh from talks with Mussolini and full of plans for a Confucian-Fascist Revival. . . . Chiang put in Italian aviators instead of

American at his Nanchang airdrome and invited a staff of some two
hundred Italians and Germans as advisers."

Ed hated propaganda—he never in his life wrote any that I know
of—but he allowed me to do it, even though it was dangerous for us
both in several ways. He taught his journalism students to hate propaganda, too. At the same time, I was teaching them how to *make* propaganda. I was naturally an activist and had always been a student leader,
from grade school to the University of Utah, just as Ed was naturally a
real journalist, always on top of his subject and nearly always minding
his own business, except to support me at strategic moments.

October in Peking is supposed to be lovely with bright sun and
orange persimmons in season. As I sat at my desk in the big bow window, tanned and healthy from the Peitaiho swimming but stifling in
the depressing atmosphere of the city, Gobi began to bark.

"It is a student from the Department of Journalism of Yenching
University," the Number 1 boy announced. "His name is Chang
Chao-lin."

Gobi ushered in a tall, handsome youth, the new president of the
student body and a refugee from Mukden in Manchuria. He had never
called on us before, but he may have been in Ed's journalism class the
previous year.

"I want to talk to Mr. Snow about his impressions of the Northeast," he explained.

I wrote a note for the Number 1 boy to ask Ed to come to the
living room. Ed had stayed in Manchuria and Dairen during part of
the summer, but he had learned little of what Chang wanted to know
about: the volunteers reported to be fighting the Japanese while hiding
in the millet fields.

Chang Chao-lin was certain that Chiang Kai-shek would never
fight for North China, or any other part of China, but would do as he
had done when he betrayed the Tungpei provinces. "We can never
believe anything in the Chinese press," Chang Chao-lin said. "Only
foreigners have any information on what is happening anywhere." He
looked not only despondent but desperate as he expressed his feeling
that, bad as it was to suppress anti-Japanese activity, it was worse to
suppress news of it when it occurred spontaneously.

This was Ed's favorite subject: freedom of the press. We both
loved this student instantly. He was frank, open, sweet, likable, but
angry and bitter, ready for anything, even nervous. *This boy has power,*

I thought; *he is capable of action.* He had qualities of leadership, obviously, not only intellectually but physically, a rare thing.

Chang saw no future for himself, for journalism in China, even for China. He did not know where to turn or what to do. But he decided he liked us as much as we did him, instantly.

"If there's any hope for China, you're it"—I said what I was thinking.

That afternoon we were like three blind children in the dark, reaching for a nonexistent bridge over a black chasm.

We talked a long time and before he left, Chang stood a moment at the window, shy and miserable, trying to hide his tears.

I collected a big folder of my "anti-Fascist" materials for him to take back. Chang later told us he belonged to a secret anti-Japanese group, but it never entered my head that this group might be "Fascist." Not long afterward, Chang Chao-lin confided in me that the group was the Youth Corps started by Young Marshal Chang Hsueh-liang in imitation of Mussolini, but it was being split by the leftists.

Recently returned from his trip to Europe to learn about fascism for himself and for Chiang Kai-shek, the Young Marshal was a friend of Mussolini and also a favorite of his daughter, Edda, and her husband, Count Galleazo Ciano, Italian minister to China. The Number 2 Fascist in China, the Young Marshal was likewise a favorite of Madame Chiang Kai-shek and admired her. He was eventually converted to the cause of anti-fascism, chiefly by his students. The afternoon Chang Chao-lin first came to see us was the beginning of the end of fascism in North China. From that moment, I felt we might win the local Peking war against the Axis—even though the Nazi-Fascists had got Nanking in their pocket.

(Chang Chao-lin joined the Communist party about February 1936, as the other leaders did. In 1983, he was teaching at the University of Jilin (Kirin) in the Foreign Languages department, and was also writing a history of the Sian Incident for the Communist Party History department. He writes to me now and then, though I have not seen him since 1936.)

The Yenching student government now began to make calls at No. 13. I dearly loved all of them! It was as if I had been drowning in the Slough of Despond and was being rescued.

K'ung P'u-sheng, vice-president, later became the fiancée of Chang Chao-lin, though she eventually married Chang Han-fu, who became vice-minister of foreign affairs. She was tall, dignified, poised, and sure of herself even then. (Until 1966, she and her sister K'ung P'eng, wife of Ch'iao Kuan-hua, minister of foreign affairs, were the chief women in that ministry, working closely with the premier, Chou En-lai. In 1972, it was K'ung P'u-sheng and Huang Hua who arranged for my VIP tour of China, and I had a December 9th reunion then with several of the students in Peking. K'ung P'u-sheng is a lovely personality, combining the best of East and West, as her late sister also did. Both had YWCA training but became Communists. K'ung P'u-sheng was national student secretary of the Y for over ten years, and later chief of the International Section of the Ministry of Foreign Affairs. In 1979, she came to New York on a United Nations delegation, and soon after became ambassador to Ireland, the second Chinese woman to be an ambassador.)

The student-body secretary was Li Min, who came to call oftener than the others, small, quiet, loyal, affectionate, and the A student of Yenching, a protégée of Ran Sailer, as were the K'ung sisters. Li Min was not anti-foreign—quite the opposite. She was a native of Kwei-chow in the far interior, daughter of a Han Lin scholar and official, making her way through Western studies by scholarships. She had to move from the old Confucianism into a pro-Communist stance, without the mediation of Christianity. (When I saw her in 1972, her face was a mask and she seemed, and said she felt, "very old," though well enough to teach both Chinese and English at the diplomatic corps. She was wearing my old pin as vice-president of West High School. I had also given her my short mouton lamb coat, light and thick, so she could run fast at demonstrations and be protected from bigsword hits. In the 1940s, she wore this Chinese-American friendship coat in prison to keep warm and wrote to me, "Your image is always shining in my mind.")

Chang Hsu-yi was pretty, with dimpled apple cheeks, healthy and robust-looking, her face usually wreathed in an engaging smile. (This was still true in 1972, at which time she was a leader in the Federation of Women. For many years after 1936, she was national industrial secretary of the YWCA.)

These were the three girls among the seven Yenching prime movers of the December 9th revolution. The other three boys, in addition to Chang Chao-lin, were Huang Hua, a native of Hopei and Peking, and an economics major; Ch'en Han-p'o, a journalism student (at the time both also belonged to the secret Youth Corps); and

Ch'eng Chieh, whose grandfather had been tutor to Emperor Pu Yi. Some young students at Tsinghua also helped start the movement, such as Yao Yi-lin (who became a vice-premier and was one of the chiefs of government in the 1980s.)

(Ch'en Han-p'o and his friend Chang Chao-lin later ran a newspaper in Sian which had a big influence on the officers who would engineer the arrest of Chiang Kai-shek. Chang would be my escort around Sian in 1936, and Ch'en would perform the same service in 1937, when he had to escape to Yenan. Ch'en Han-p'o became the premier journalist of China for a while, and when we had a 1972 reunion, he was "a leading member" of the Peking government publications department, tanned and healthy from a May 7th "vacation," doing manual labor. By 1979, he was head of the national department and president of the Association of Journalists, resident in Peking.)

(It turned out that Huang Hua was probably the proudest product of Yenching and the most successful of the 9th Decembrists, developing also a singularly attractive personality adapted to his posts as vice-premier and minister of foreign affairs, after being the first Peking ambassador to the United Nations. In 1982, he resigned both posts, but remained a state councillor. An article I wrote about him was published by Harrison Salisbury in *The New York Times* the day Huang arrived in New York in 1971. It was a happy moment when I saw him again for the first time since 1937 in Yenan.

"What happened to that beautiful red wool shirt Jim Bertram gave me for my trip and which I gave to you when I left Yenan?" I asked as he drove me back to my hotel. "That was his socialist Oxford Union shirt. That was the talisman link between Oxford, Peking, Yenan, and Madison, Connecticut."

"I wore it and wore it and wore it," Huang Hua said in his deep, slow, throaty voice, flushing easily, as he had always done as a young student. He was unusually emotional for a Chinese and embraced his friends Western-style in 1971, though without kissing.)

In 1935, Huang Hua was a proud, moody, self-possessed boy. One felt he was responsible. (He joined the Communist party "in the spring of 1936," he told me in New York. Before that, he had been imprisoned for a few days as a student leader, in danger of being tortured. He was a liaison figure with Chou En-lai and Yeh Chien-ying during the "United Front" era in Hankow and Chungking, and for the last American-British negotiations in 1949, dealing with his old college president, Dr. Leighton Stuart. He was the China representative

at the Panmunjom discussions on the Korean War. As a senior diplomat, he was a big success in Africa and Egypt, the last to be recalled
during the Cultural Revolution, 1966–1969, at which time the Yenching-Tsinghua dynasty in the Ministry of Foreign Affairs came under
ultra-leftist attack, and he and others went to May 7th schools for re-
education in manual labor.)

Around November 1, 1935, Huang Hua and the group composed
their famous petition of that date, "For the Right of Free Speech,
Press, and Assembly and Against the Illegal Arrest of Students." A
mimeographed copy was brought to our house to be translated there by
some of the group. It was strong and dangerous. I told them it was too
radical. It read in part:

"After the establishment of the government at Nanking, according to newspaper reports, the number of youths slaughtered totalled no
less than three hundred thousand, and the number of those who had
disappeared and been imprisoned cannot be even estimated. Killing
was not enough; they were even buried alive; imprisonment was not
enough; they were even subjected to torture. Hell itself has been
brought to humanity!"

The petition then attacked Nanking for not resisting Japan and for
using anti-communism as a pretext so that "any activity on the part of
us, the people, might be branded as a crime. Anyone stood in danger
of losing his life. . . . The number of publications suppressed and of
writers arrested cannot be even estimated." It also told of the arrest of
Dr. Fung Yu-lan at Tsinghua and of others.

It was signed first by "The Students' Self-Government Associa-
tions of Yenching University," followed by ten others, including
Tsinghua University, with six of them middle schools. Some two
thousand copies were mailed out to schools all over China.

I tried to get the foreign press to publish the manifesto. I took a
copy to Frank Oliver of Reuters.

"Why, we couldn't possibly publish such a thing," Frank said.
"It's nothing but propaganda."

In Asia this was the opening salvo of the World War II alliance
against the Fascist Axis—the children of Nanking officials were openly
attacking their parents and Chiang Kai-shek. These students were risking their lives right in the lion's mouth under martial-law conditions,
yet this was not news to Reuters!

I got back on my bicycle, with Gobi on the leash, and proceeded to the Hotel Du Nord, where F. MacCracken Fisher was United Press correspondent. Mac sent the news to Earl Leaf of the U.P. in Tientsin, and the two of them supplied the student news from then on. That, symbolically, was the moment Americans took the torch from the British. Fighting the Fascist Axis was our war, too, and the U.P. vaguely cottoned to this. The sleepy British Empire crumbled into dust on that day, symbolically, and all unaware, as usual. The absolute minimum required for their own survival would have been for the British to publish news from the most conservative university in China on "freedom of the press."

Frank Oliver of Reuters had been hostile, intimidating. But his Chinese assistant was even more so—he knew exactly how important the piece of paper was. I had no doubt it would be in the hands of the police within an hour or two, probably of the Fascist element first. Gobi scented the atmosphere and sat at my side protectively with an anti-Fascist glare.

I pedaled slowly home in the lavender twilight along the spooky mall beside the ancient Tartar Wall, the November wind moaning along the crenellated top. I was worried. The worst thing that could happen was for the students to risk their lives for nothing—without any publicity about it. We were alerting the enemy and doing nothing worthwhile. Obviously, either the movement would be nipped in the bud—or we had to make some news that could not be ignored.

Back at No. 13, I said to Ed: "I think I'll start smoking cigarettes—and I'll have some of your wine." (I hardly ever had anything to drink—it made me sleepy.) We were sitting around the coal-ball fire in the fireplace.

Ed was horrified. "Why waste money on cigarettes? My Camels cost almost as much as the rent."

"Because of Frank Oliver," I explained, "and Doihara." (General Kenji Doihara, known as the "Lawrence of Manchuria," had arranged the Ho-Umetsu Agreement in the summer of 1935. This agreement was a quisling understanding under which parts [or all] of North China would be taken over by the Japanese by means of puppet regimes. Much depended on secrecy and deception, which is where the importance of Reuters and the foreign press came in. A brief lull or hiatus existed between the old and new power establishments in North China. In October 1935, an anti-Communist autonomous government was proclaimed in East Hopei, and Japan pressed demands to the maximum for this government to cover all North China—100 million people. Doihara placed his bets on General Sung Cheh-yuan as a puppet, offering him $100 million in cash and threatening him. But General Sung was undecided. Doihara's ultimatum to Sung was to expire on or about December 10. The student movement would put an end to this situation temporarily, until 1937.)

I began smoking small pink packages of mild Hatamens, the brand the coolies used. I would never dare touch one of Ed's Camels.

Nothing happened. There was no way for the news to reach the public or schools all over China except through United Press and my article in the *China Weekly Review*, whose editor, J.B. Powell, now began to turn anti-Fascist, though he had been since 1927 the chief foreign apologist for Chiang Kai-shek.

Obviously, action was necessary, to make news that would reach the public. A demonstration had to be held, at any cost.

Before I left the United States for China, I sat for a formal portrait.

Above: In the "golden, glamorous Orient," with the statue of the Laughing Buddha in Hangchow, 1931.

Below: "For Peg from her stooge Ed" reads the inscription on the first picture of himself Edgar Snow gave me. "Peg" was one of my nicknames.

Photograph by Edgar Snow, from the Helen Snow collection

"Ding hao!"

Helen Snow collection

The ministrations of massage amah Mei were relaxing after a hard day's work.

On the eve of our
wedding, December 1932

Photograph by Sanzetti, Shanghai,
from the Helen Snow collection

Honeymoon shuffleboard
on the *Canada Maru*,
January 1933, wearing the
red-white-and-blue scarf
which was to see a lot of
action

Helen Snow collection

Above left: Teilhard de Chardin snapped this picture with my camera, by the old Jesuit astrolabe atop Peking's Tartar Wall.

Above right: Former rickshaman Shen I-pei, Number 1 boy at our first home in Peking.

Below: At home in Hait'ien, relaxing in beach pajamas and kimono with our greyhound, Gobi

Above: Edgar Snow with Evans Carlson, whose World War II Marine Raiders served to put the term *gung ho* into the English language

Left: With visiting author Pearl Buck.

Right: Our servant Ch'en with Gobi at No. 13 K'uei Chia Ch'ang in Peking

Photograph © Helen Foster Snow

Among the prime movers of the December 9th student movement were: (*above left*) Chang Chao-lin, in student gown and Western hat; (*above right*) David Yui, in uniform in Yenan; (*below*) plotting strategy, Constance Chang at left, Huang Hua and Ch'en Han-p'o in goggle helmets, unidentified woman at right

With Jim Bertram on the beach at Peitaiho

Generalissimo Chiang Kai-shek at right,
Young Marshal Chang Hsueh-liang on the left

May 1, 1937: a mass meeting at the village of Yun-yang, where I stopped on my way from Sian to Yenan. At lower left you can make out the red-starred caps of two Communist soldiers; in the foreground, the bound-footed women of the village; at right center are the uniformed children of the village school, backed by the banner-carrying men. By 1949 the Communists had won all China with meetings of this type: slogans, banners, and songs.

Above: Kempton Fitch, having delivered me to Sanyuan, appears to be eyeing the Red guard's cap covetously. *Left:* Mao Tse-tung, Chu Teh, and Agnes Smedley, in Yenan

Above left: With General Chu Teh in Yenan, 1937

Above right: With Chu Teh in Peking, 1972; K'ung P'u-sheng, one of the December 9th students, is in the background.

Below left: With K'ang K'e-ching, Chu's wife, in Yenan

Below right: Ping-Pong was always popular with the Red armies.

Above: The crossed flags of the United Front. *Below:* The Kuomintang sign on this wall near Yenan welcomes Red soldiers to come over to the government side. Beneath it, I chat with a group of Tungpei soldiers who have done just the opposite, leaving Chiang Kai-shek's army for the Red armies.

This is a famous photograph in China, in the museums now along with Ed's portrait of Mao. From left to right: Lin Po-ku, Mao Tse-tung, Chu Teh, and Chou En-lai, at the time of the United Front negotiations in Yenan, 1937

My bodyguard Ko Sun-hua, on the road from Yenan to Sian

We were both exhausted but happy in Tsingtao in October 1937.

Left: Rewi Alley

Below: Spinning yarn in one of our gung ho industrial cooperatives. The machinery used was also made in a gung ho cooperative.

China's famous Soong sisters (in dark coats) in Chungking during World War II. At left is Mme. Sun Yat-sen (Ching-ling); center, Mme. Chiang Kai-shek (Mei-ling); right, Mme. H. H. Kung (Eling). One thing they all agreed upon was support for our cooperatives.

Above: Farewell to China, December 1940. J.B. Powell, at right, entertained us at the American Club in Shanghai just before I boarded ship for home.

Right: The picture that Hollywood photographer Piver put in his window, because it "looked like Joan Bennett"

Top: Reunion in 1977, at a New York reception for my old student friend, China's Foreign Minister Huang Hua.

Above: I finally deliver Mao's letter to Teng Hsiao-ping in Washington, 1979, more than forty years later.

Left: Pao-an, 1978

CHAPTER 20

Action

The lowest point of barometric pressure in China, as indicated by the maximum "white terror" (the Chinese name for it), came just before the Japanese forced Chiang Kai-shek's Third Gendarmes—commanded by his nephew Chiang Hsiao-hsien, then the most sinister Fascist in China—to leave Peking for Sian. This was a monumental blunder. It meant that Japan would fail to establish a quisling Fascist regime in North China, that they did not even know how to engineer the kind of arrangement that Hitler would soon make such brilliant use of in Europe.

No patriotic or anti-Fascist movement in Peking would have been possible—would even have been dreamed of—had the Third Gendarmes not been removed. We would have thought such a movement certain death. The Third Gendarmes had totally annihilated all anti-Japanese activity along with the left wing. Not one Communist was free that we knew of, and if one existed he had lost all connections with the destroyed party.

It may be a law of political science that when such a point is reached, new leadership rises—and has to rise; at the maximum point of contradiction, the "Fascists" turn into anti-Fascists. That happened in Peking—and in Sian.

In a recent article in *Beijing Review*, Ch'en Han-p'o writes:

> The student-body movement surged ahead despite the bitter winter. Finally, the day we had been anxiously anticipating arrived. On December 8 . . . Huang Hua brought us the word for action: A parade was to be held the next day.
>
> The next three hours were devoted to preparations. We conducted an intense student meeting that night and passed a resolution to take to the street the next morning.
>
> We then informed the Snows of our plans, including the slogans we

intended to use, the route of the procession and the site for gathering. On December 9, students from Yenching and other universities took to the streets to protest the government's capitulation to the Japanese invaders' strategy of taking Chinese territory. Snow and his wife joined the marching students. [Actually, we took photographs from the sidelines.]

The parade met with armed suppression. Shouting slogans and using their bare fists, the students fought soldiers. *

Only about eight hundred students were on the Peking streets in the December 9th demonstration, but it was this forlorn hope right at the political and military front that galvanized all the students of China when they heard of it. This act of total courage at exactly the right moment made possible the big demonstration on December 16, with perhaps ten thousand students, which David Yui helped to plan— professional among total amateurs.

From October 1934 to October 1935, Mao Tse-tung and the Red armies had been on the Long March of six thousand miles to the far Northwest near the Great Wall. We had no way of knowing what their policies were in the midst of their civil war, though in August they had started to stress fighting Japan instead of engaging in civil war. We learned about this long afterward, but Peking had to formulate its own ideas until David Yui arrived, the first real Communist made available.

Soon after the December 9th demonstration, Huang Hua brought to our house a youth whom he introduced as David. He was fairly tall, pale, tired, ill-looking, and ill-kempt in his long Chinese brown wool gown (most male students wore gowns then, a sign of aristocracy). His handsome face was open and changed expression easily, but it was also aristocratic and you felt the self-assurance. In manner he was easy, well-bred, and dignified. He did not seem nervous, yet his hand shook when he held a piece of paper. He had an air of mandarin authority, though he was only about twenty-four.

No one ever looked less like a conspirator, yet he had a quality possessed by nobody else I had met. What was it? *Experience*, I thought: This must be the real McCoy, a real live subterranean member of the Communist party, or at least the Communist Youth. How

* "Amidst the Student Movement," *Beijing Review*, February 15, 1982, at the time of the memorial meeting for the tenth anniversary of Edgar Snow's death in 1972. My recollections are not quite the same.

did one find out—and still be able to say one did not know? Member-ship in the party, or even close association, was a capital offense. One never asked such questions. It was better not to know, of course. But was that prison pallor on his face? How could he be so casual if con-stantly hunted by police and Fascists who were paid high prices for the real McCoy? Our servants, too, would have been well paid to uncover a real or even suspected Communist.

David wasn't afraid of our friendly greyhound, as nearly all Chi-nese were at first.

"Gobi's a card-carrying charter member of the Peking Student Union," I informed David. "He has to have his nose into everything going on."

David sat down in a big overstuffed chair and Gobi climbed in beside him. From then on, even in brief notes, David never failed to ask about his friend Gobi.

A few minutes later, three other students arrived. David looked them over with a distinctly patriarchal Confucian air of appraisal. The five of them actually did sit in a circle, with their black heads bent forward almost touching in a ring as they talked in a low key, intense beyond description. Gobi pushed his long, black nose into the ring beside his old friend Huang Hua.

From my desk at the big bow window, I warned the circle: "If you don't want our servants to turn you in to the police, don't look like such a Hollywood-movie ring of conspirators. You'll have to sit back and discuss the *wu wei* of Lao Tzu when they come."

Our royal Manchu Number 1 boy appeared with a tray of tea and cookies, silent as a cat in his felt-soled slippers. Gobi warned the stu-dents, and their heads bobbed up in guilty alarm. The instant the servant left, the heads formed a ring again, the tea forgotten.

I couldn't help smiling the whole time. *This is revolution*, was my thought, *when any Chinese forgets to drink tea*. I dearly loved all five—if only because they *had* forgotten to drink their tea. But I was on pins and needles for their safety.

I already knew Sung Ling, the energetic, fearless, bright-eyed, squirrellike Tungpei delegate who had led the December 9th demon-stration in the streets, marching into the armed police. He soon be-came the liaison with Young Marshal Chang Hsueh-liang in Sian, who befriended him, even sending troops to get him out of prison. (Sung Ling became chairman—equivalent to mayor—of the impor-tant port of Dairen (Dalian), and got in touch with me in 1982. The

9th Decembrists have been having national reunions the past couple of years in Peking.) Yao Yi-lin was the Tsinghua delegate, a sophomore at the time, aged only about seventeen but brilliant and a natural leader, who joined the Communists. I have forgotten the name of the fifth "conspirator," but he may have been from Peita or Shihta University.

These five were the "brains" of the student movement. They directed it, not only for North China but all over the country, as the rest of China took its lead from the Peking Student Union, dominated by David.

This group of liaison delegates sometimes met at our foreign house; it was too dangerous elsewhere. I could see they were taking instructions from David, who seemed to be an expert, but I had no idea that he was anyone important. I thought he was just lucky to be the only real Communist, or one of the few, out of prison and alive. From the way he talked, I felt sure he was making his own decisions— he seemed to be alone.

Both Ed and I, and the students, had been wishing to make contact with a real Communist, and David had searched out the Yenching leaders, apparently on the evening before December 9. So far as I knew then, no Communist apparatus of any kind existed in Peking before David arrived. A professor we called Peter came to see us once or twice, but we were told he was a "social democrat" and not to trust him. He may have been a real Communist who had lost connections, which may have been resumed later. He was active among teachers. I think "Peter" was Hsu Ping. In those days everything was secret and everybody was under suspicion, a legacy of the Fascist techniques. Hsu Ping probably worked with Liu Shao-ch'i as soon as Liu arrived to mastermind things in February 1936. Liu had been in prison in Kiangsu before that, I was told by Wang Ling, mayor of Sian, in 1982.

I asked David to stay after the other four had left.

"I wonder when you last had something to eat," I inquired. "Can you have some foreign food with us?"

"I have no need to worry about money for eating," he replied, "but my stomach does not behave well when I eat." His problem, he said, was that sometimes he couldn't get any sleep. He had a heart condition. But yes, he could stay to eat with us. "I have nowhere safe to stay anyway."

I soon learned he moved every three or four days from one boardinghouse or hotel room to another to avoid discovery by the police. His address could have been betrayed any day by one of the persons who knew him. He dearly loved his mother, who supplied the only money he had and seemed to live somewhere in the Yangtze Valley; as I remember it vaguely, he was staying with her when he first learned about the Peking student movement and came to Peking instantly. His mother worried about him but did not interfere.

The first personal history I learned was that David had been the chief student leader at Peita University during the 1931–1932 demonstrations, which had caused Chiang Kai-shek to resign for loss of face. (David never did tell me that Tseng Chao-lun, a professor at Peita, one of the most distinguished scientists in China, was his mother's brother. Tseng was sympathetic to the student movement in 1935–1936. David's mother was a great-granddaughter of Marquis Tseng Kuo-fan of Hunan, worshiped by Chiang Kai-shek.)

It was not until February 25, 1936, as my old, yellowed notes state, that David told me about having been arrested in Tsinan in July 1933, hands and feet in chains, in prison for six months. "My uncle saved me when I was sentenced to death in 1933," he said. "He is a close friend of Chiang Kai-shek and one of the Four Great Elders of the Blue Shirts." (David's real name was Yu Ch'i-wei, but he took the name Huang Ching. His Blue Shirt uncle, I later discovered, was Yu Ta-wei, who became Chiang Kai-shek's minister of defense and was in Washington, D.C.—in the embassy, I think.)

David said he was one of forty students among three hundred in the Tsinan prison, and that twelve important Communists had been executed while he was in prison. He added, "Every day Communists are executed in Nanking." He told me Peking had about a thousand political prisoners in 1936, taken by the Third Gendarmes, mostly students, and there were around fifty thousand in all China.

(David also mentioned that some girls were in danger in Tsinan when he was, but I paid little attention to this. Not until 1968 did I discover that his special girl friend, Galatea, whom he influenced to join the secret Communist party in Shantung just before he was arrested in 1933, was Ch'iang Ch'ing, the most powerful woman in modern Chinese history from 1966 to the death of Mao in 1976. About 1938, David escorted her to Yenan, where she met and married Mao Tse-tung, as David may or may not have hoped. Thus David's influence on history exploded in the 1960s with Ch'iang Ch'ing's rocket rise to power. Ch'iang Ch'ing and her "gang of four" were arrested soon after Mao died. She was sentenced to death on some kind of conspiracy charge, but this was changed to life imprisonment in 1983.)

David had decided not to be married, but to sacrifice everything for the revolution, so he explained to me. His health was permanently harmed by the Tsinan experience and later stress and danger.

"But, David, you have to rest and get away from danger, or you will die." I tried to persuade him to take a vacation now and then.

"It's no use," he replied. "I'm worse off. My heart's worse, too. I've tried it, living with my mother. I feel better when I'm active. You see, there's nobody else to carry out my work for me."

My old notes of March 7, 1936, state that David told me he and Huang Hua had barely escaped arrest "last night." He gave me a list of students arrested, betrayed by "spies," and said the Fascists had now organized to destroy the left wing. He said he was on five Blue Shirt blacklists, and that the "Third Gendarmes laugh at them."

David was always cool, calm, gentle, quiet, self-possessed, and judicious. He acted more like a judge than an activist making history, never hurried or ruffled and without fear of danger or death. In his superior manner, he referred to the students as "petty-bourgeois radicals," and "much too leftist." He made good-natured fun of "heroics." He was not anxious for me to influence the students, but he realized *he* could never have got the student movement started.

I do not know if David had ever talked to a foreign woman before, though his English was good, but he hardly knew what to make of me at first. He understood Ed immediately and they were good friends, though Ed did not talk much to David, who called on us often because he had no safe house to spend his time in. I never had more real fun than discussing Marxism with David and analyzing "the objective situation." We had perfect communication. Once in a while I overwhelmed him: "You certainly are a good agitator," he would say.

David was a totally superior and admirable type, an ideal Marxist. Since all options were open to him, his decision to become a Communist had a high ethical quality of choice, not economic necessity or class hatred. His mind was clear, brilliant, totally honest, open to any kind of facts (so long as they did not contradict his own). He was *normal*, with a healthy mind and psychology—that was the attractive thing about him, as it was about nearly all the Communists I talked with in China. He was anti-fanatic, nonreligious in his Marxism, yet he used it as a sharp tool to think with.

I didn't always agree with David, but for the first time I had a clear view of the whole political picture in China, especially of Chiang Kai-shek and the Kuomintang, which he thought too weak to defend China or to carry out any historical tasks.

In February 1936, an important Communist arrived in North China, and with him a change of policy. This was Liu Shao-ch'i, who criticized the student movement as being too leftist, and established a much broader policy for a "national United Front," to include "Fascists" if they wished to join.

(Liu became Mao Tse-tung's successor for a while until the 1966 Cultural Revolution against his policies. In the 1960s, Liu was accused of having gotten Communists out of prison in 1936 by having them "repent" to the authorities instead of being executed for refusing, a difficult ethical point. "They should have died instead of repenting," I was told in 1973. Nothing is easier for a pietistic Communist to say— one who has never risked his life or even seen the inside of a prison. In 1935 and 1936 in Peking, it seemed quixotic to rot in prison when you could get out and go to work again. But this question has two sides: No one would have trusted such a person, not even I. In 1980 Liu was "rehabilitated" along with his followers.)

David informed me that we in Peking had an "anti-Fascist front"; he considered this incorrect—we should have had a "broad anti-Japanese front."

"Would it ever occur to you that *I* would never have devoted my time to that?" I said. "And also I don't think the student leaders would have risked their lives for such a 'broad front,' though it is all right that it has evolved into it now. We were *anti-Fascist* first of all and we broke the 'white terror' in Peking just because of that. My time is too valuable to me to waste it on anyone who is not anti-Fascist."

David looked at me very respectfully. "History moves in stages, of course," he offered.

"I'm a prime mover, an initiator," I said. "You're an organizer and a theorist. All the students who started the movement were anti-Fascist. That was the momentum."

Looking back, I see that Ed and I had a special role in turning students and everyone else anti-Fascist, including previous Fascists. David and Liu Shao-ch'i came along and recruited them as Communist followers. I noticed that Ed and I were psychologically much more anti-Fascist than the Communists seemed to be.

(I never saw David again after he called on me in Yenan during the summer of 1937, at which time he told me with pride that he was the Number 2 of the Communist party in North China. But he sent regards to us through Evans Carlson in 1938, when Evans met him on his trip in Central Hopei, not far from Peking, where David was political director in the resistance forces.

He became minister of machine-building, vice-chairman of the State Scientific Planning Commission, and a member of the Communist Central Committee. A semi-invalid from sacrificing his health and youth in the most dangerous underground political work in Chinese history—in any history, perhaps—David died in 1958, at the age of forty-six. His widow, Fan Chin, became vice-mayor of Peking until she was purged in the Cultural Revolution.)

When travelers to China speak of the "new socialist man" and changing human nature, I think of Chinese I have known like David, who had to find his own way and make his own decisions. I cannot recall that he had any unfortunate characteristic—he was not anti-foreign, he was not pietistic, he was not obscurantist; he was highly civilized and in favor of more civilization for everybody, including the Chinese. He was charming and likable, with no abrasive edges. Through the worst ordeal of China, he survived, and even kept his sense of humor and proportion. I am not sure, though, that he was quite human enough.

By December 16, all the Peking students were alerted. So, too, were the authorities and the Japanese. We had not much idea what would happen, as the demonstration on December 9 had been a surprise.

Early on the sixteenth, Ed and I were warmly dressed and in a taxi, picking up Mac Fisher of the United Press. We cruised around to find the various units on different streets. My report for the *China Weekly Review* said:

"We arrived in a motor car just in time to see a squad of bigswords charging directly, and without any warning, right into the student leaders. . . . As the parade reached the square in front of the Ch'ien Men gate and halted . . . the police—who had no superior officer and seemed completely disorganized, half-dressed, hatless, nervous, and excited—ran out in wild distraction on the veranda . . . and fired three volleys of blank shots directly into the mass of the students, not over their heads. . . . The crowd vanished with scarcely a trace but instantly surged forward again. . . . One station coolie with presence of mind began serving as a middleman in the negotiations with police."

That night we received a telephone call that a terrible melee had taken place in a dead-end lane where three hundred students were trapped and about thirty so beaten with bigswords that they could not walk.

On December 16, every newspaperman in Peking was on the streets. Even J. B. Powell had arrived from Shanghai for the *Chicago Tribune.* At Ch'ien Men, the medieval gate on the city wall, Ed and Frank Smothers climbed on a tower, where Ed took the only movies of the student movement that I know of. (This camera was a big investment for us, bought for the purpose, and Ed later took the first movies ever made of the Red armies.)

I was at the side of J. B. Powell, propagandizing him, when he saw the prettiest girl at Yenching wearing a leather jacket.

"Now that's my ideal girl revolutionary," he said, taking photographs.

I ran out to the line of marchers and brought Constance Chang over to introduce her: "She's the daughter of lettuce growers in California."

J.B. was so delighted to find an American he could identify with that he allowed me as much space as I wanted in his magazine afterward.

Arthur, brother of Constance, was also in the demonstration, with his future wife, Liang Tzu-yi, daughter of one of China's most famous scholars under the Manchu dynasty, Liang Ch'i-ch'ao.

(In 1972, we had lunch on December 9 in the Peking Hotel, at which time Arthur was head of the Friendship Hospital; they had both spent several years in the States. Constance returned to the United States and married a brilliant young newspaperman in New York, T'ang Ming-chao, who became chief of the Decolonization Commission of the United Nations. Their daughter, Nancy, born in Brooklyn, became confidential interpreter for Mao Tse-tung, and was in that post for President Nixon during his 1972 visit. [And so the wheel comes round again.] In 1974, Nancy was elected to the Communist Central Committee, but after Mao Tse-tung died in 1976, she more or less disappeared from public notice.)

The December 16 demonstration was estimated to have had from 6,500 to 10,000 participants. On December 16, Reuters reported:

"Student demonstrations on a larger scale than ever before known in Peking took place today. . . . The police were inclined to be rather unnecessarily brutal, but the presence of a number of foreign pressmen with cameras helped the students a good deal. . . . immediately cameras were levelled police ceased beating students. . . . between ten and fifteen students are reported to have been struck and injured by swords in this melee. . . . No violence was shown to Japanese, many of whom watched the demonstrations."

On December 18, 1935, Reuters reported that the mayors of Peking and Tientsin called on Major-General Doihara to apologize for the student demonstrations. I never met Doihara, though I saw him, but Ed talked with him. He was well aware of our influence over the students. We were in direct confrontation, as Doihara was in Peking during those fateful days and saw the December 16 demonstration.

On December 26, 1935, the *Manchuria Daily News*, Mukden, quoted Doihara as saying: "It has become almost certain that the Kuomintang is behind the Chinese student movement . . . the Chinese Communist party has been availing itself of the student movement. . . . Certain countries are reported to be engaged in underground activities regarding the North China question. I am inclined to believe that they will discontinue such activities. . . ."

The *China Weekly Review*, December 21, said: "Shanghai 'Nippo' blames American influence for student movement in China, that . . . behind the scenes . . . someone is pulling the wires . . . the bulk of students . . . were students of missionary schools . . . the student movement has been carried out under the leadership of professors who are graduates of American universities."

About this time, the Japanese press published an article saying that a young American woman had started the student movement, no doubt financed by President Roosevelt. I was quite frightened by this—there in the midst of dangerous Fascists. But I think that actually it was the publicity in the foreign press that blocked the Doihara plan. Getting that publicity was my special role, and I worked on dispensing it from November to the time school was out in June 1936, meantime teaching the students how to get news to the foreign press; it was an entirely new idea to them, and they were shy about doing it.

Doihara was publicly repudiated by his government for purposes of face. It is a charming irony that Doihara and all his mobilized armies had to retreat when faced with two little anti-Fascist Americans living on U.S. $50 a month—but armed with a piece of the truth. In

1936, Roosevelt came forward handsomely to help with his "Quarantine the Aggressors" speech. But both before and after that, in North China no one was quite certain just how much American support the student movement was or was not receiving through the Snow connection. The answer was zero. But that mystery was our big weapon, worth whole armies.

The student movement continued till the end of the school year in June. Then the excitement was transferred to Sian, where a revolution in men's minds was in progress, as the Tungpei students rushed there to influence the armed forces—real power at last!

One of the most important outgrowths of the student movement in 1935–1936 was the conversion of Young Marshal Chang Hsueh-liang to active anti-fascism, from his previous position of Number 2 Fascist of China. This was brought about chiefly by his own students, who had belonged to his secret Youth Corps, and several of whom initiated the December 9th movement. In 1936, the Young Marshal would arrest Chiang Kai-shek, trying to persuade him to end the civil war.

It would be hard to devise an operatic plot more incredible than this. Japanese General Doihara had masterminded the peaceful occupation of Manchuria in 1931. The Old Marshal, Chang Tso-lin, father of the Young Marshal, had been secretly assassinated by the Japanese, and Japan had restored law and order. Obeying his superior, Chiang Kai-shek, the Young Marshal retreated south of the Great Wall with his army, the "Tungpei" Army—meaning "of Manchuria." Our house became the rendezvous of many Tungpei refugees, and we influenced their conversion to anti-fascism.

In 1935, the medieval walls of Peking resounded to the slogans of the anti-Fascist youth. The medieval walls of Sian had become the center of fascism, and headquarters for the civil war against the Red armies, which had just completed the Long March from the South in October. The Young Marshal was in command of this anti-Red war, while inside the walls of Peking, we—who were independent, non-Communist, and known to be so—were engaged in winning the hearts and minds of the young. When one of the Young Marshal's Youth Corps members, Sung Ling, now anti-Fascist, rushed to Sian soon after the demonstration to report to him, the Young Marshal not only voiced support for the student movement but also favored the United

Front with the left wing and soon made a de facto truce with the Red armies.

All of us were instinctively aware that something new was stirring in the world: The anti-Fascist alliance that would win World War II was born in part at Yenching University.

(In 1981, Hubert S. Liang, on a lecture tour in the United States, told me that his Journalism Department at Yenching had been partly financed by the Young Marshal in the 1930s.)

The December 9th student movement marked a historical epoch, the fourth stage of the six listed by Mao Tse-tung in the history of China from 1919, as published in his thesis "On the New Democracy." The December 9th movement and the Sian Incident of 1936 influenced the Communists and were part of the recipe by which Mao Tse-tung finally won the victory and established a coalition-type government in 1949. On the basis of this "new democracy," in 1944–1945 he was willing to cooperate with Americans; had such cooperation been achieved, the history of the world might be quite different. Instead the "Fascist" power began in the United States, and the China Lobby-McCarthyist influence cut us off from China until President Nixon opened it up again in 1972.

Never again were foreigners at the point of leverage in China that we were in 1935 to 1938; after the American intervention against the Communists from 1947 to 1949, it seemed impossible to them that such progressive and happy Chinese-American cooperation had ever happened.

Yet from 1935, it was these Yenching-Tsinghua students who were the liaison with the West for the left-wing and Communist elements in China, and they were the engineers of the rapprochement of 1972—when it was Edgar Snow who got Mao Tse-tung's permission for President Nixon to come to Peking. Thus the "New China"-America friendship was born in the December 9th movement of 1935 in Peking.

CHAPTER 21

James Bertram, Rhodes Scholar from New Zealand

It was a happy day for me when James Bertram arrived in Peking early in January of 1936; he and Ed and I formed a charmed circle. In the midst of our travels, Jim would publish four books on China, Ed nine, and I five (as well as amassing six volumes of historical notes).

Except for Ed, Teilhard, and the Chinese, I had had no one really to talk with in Peking since 1933, yet I was bubbling over with ideas and desperate for more intellectual companionship. Jim was already anti-Fascist as a result of his travels in Germany, Italy, and the Soviet Union. He later wrote: "At Oxford in the year that Hitler came to power in Germany, Marxism was in intellectual fashion as common in All Souls' as in Morley's Gymnasium." He explained, "In Oxford most of us were [socialists], and we meant it. G.D.H. Cole and Dick Crossman were our tutors, John Strachey was our prophet, Auden and Spender . . . our chosen poets." * Yet his first love seemed to be Rainer Maria Rilke's poetry, plus Shakespeare, whose works he carried on his China travels.

Jim was a Rhodes scholar from New Zealand who had studied English Literature, which he later taught in a New Zealand university. He had joined the Oxford Union, swearing that never would he "fight for King and Country." Yet only three years after we met him, he had to come to grips with World War II and set out to join the army. (I hope I had some influence in preventing this; I tried to keep him in our tiny circle of China Hands where he was most needed. But the war caught up with him in Hong Kong in 1941.)

Jim was very attractive—tall, muscular, athletic, and handsome,

* James Bertram, *Beneath the Shadow* (New York: John Day Company, 1947).

with curly hair and a sensitive Scottish-English face, quiet, well-bred, diffident, sweet, and shy, and though deeply emotional, totally self-controlled. His blue eyes were full of quest; he was reaching out for new experiences. He was my Sir Galahad—and I had to keep him from becoming my Sir Launcelot. I had to be "cruel" to him, as he put it. He was the son of a clergyman in Auckland, and ideal for the sort of relationship we had—the sort we had to have.

The code in the East was very strict, especially for the British. But British or American, we shared a common Puritan inheritance of correct behavior in all situations. As Betty Price put it in Peitaiho, "It's lucky you are a lady and Jim is a gentleman."

My situation in China was much too important to me to let it be ruined by a "mess." I had to be Caesar's wife, double-distilled. I might have several "special relationships," but only on condition that I keep the appearance as well as the reality of fidelity, and establish these ground rules in the minds of my admirers from the start. With caution, I steered clear. Ed took it for granted that I would—but underneath was raw subcutaneous jealousy.

With Ed's help, I also had to build Jim up. He was part of the team—though Ed was always on the verge of pushing him out, for personal reasons. I got Ed to send him to Sian as his correspondent, for one thing, and I referred him to Ed's and my agent, Henriette Herz, and my publisher.

The anti-crisis came the first year, when Jim was anxious to travel with me—always on the platonic level we had established—to Korea and later to Sian. I was afraid to be alone, especially on the dangerous trip to Sian. But I knew Ed would be furious if I traveled with Jim, if only because of the public appearance of it. I never told Ed anything about this crisis—nor did I tell Jim how hard it was not to have him come along. I let him think I preferred to be alone for journalistic scoops.

I think back on how well-behaved we all were in those days—in contrast to the present. Meaning is created by value. We placed tremendous value on ourselves and our purposes and our relationships, and so they had real meaning—not only for us but for the Chinese. I marvel now at what I could do then. Not only was I involved in the difficult art of dealing with the Chinese, but also in the almost impossible art of dealing with several male admirers and keeping them on the line.

The years 1936–1937 were big years for Jim, as well as for Ed and me, full of travel, danger, achievement, and close, gung ho *esprit de corps*. Jim's books made him the most famous Britisher of his years in China, along with our other gung ho member, Rewi Alley, also from New Zealand. Jim was the China wing of the British left-wing movement.

Jim paid a heavy price for his China experience. He was captured fighting in Hong Kong in 1941 and spent four years as a prisoner of the Japanese, laboring as a dock coolie. We knew nothing of what had happened to him until I received a note written just as he embarked on the American ship that took the liberated prisoners aboard in 1945. Not until 1959 did I see him again, when he visited the States with his wife, Jean, on his sabbatical, traveling on a Rockefeller grant.

I often think back on the youth and health and high hopes and real talent destroyed before they could flower or reach their prime, especially among the British, in both the World Wars.

CHAPTER 22

Edgar Snow Goes to See the "Red Star Over China"

The student movement had spread all over China. By the end of December 1935, about sixty-five demonstrations had occurred in thirty-two cities.

On the whole the police treated the demonstrators quite well, with good discipline. I used to look at the big, strong Shantung policemen in Peking and wish this type of Chinese were on the right side.

By February 1936, ten thousand police were mobilized in Peking day and night against the students. They raided several universities and made some arrests, though student guards kept watch at all times. At Tsinghua a regiment of the Twenty-ninth Army, armed with big-swords, surrounded the campus. They were looking especially for Liu Tsui, a pretty, lively girl who had been the heroine of the demonstrations when she rolled under a big city gate and tried to open it from the inside. But she was hiding in a closet at our house, and we spirited her off to Shanghai, from where she went to the States to stir up sympathy for the student cause.

Our house was full of student refugees, as well as Tungpei exiles from Manchuria. One of these was Fullsea Wang, the son of the president of Tungpei University; he used to sit shyly in a corner, saying nothing but intently observing the menage like a sociologist. (A year later, Wang volunteered to be my interpreter on my trip to Yenan, and his father hid in our house when the Japanese attacked. Wang Fu-shih [Fullsea] got in touch with me after the 1972 rapproachement with New China, and we exchange letters—he publishes mine. He became editor of an encyclopedia.)

Our big greyhound was a member of the student union, but our Chow, Ginger, was a Fascist and tried to bite every student he could get hold of through their padded gowns.

By this time a National Salvation Union had been formed of

"Cultural Circles," with 149 members. At Yenching, Hubert S. Liang was a leader among teachers. Peita, cradle of the May 4th movement, was under two kinds of suppression, chiefly internal. Tseng Chao-lun, a leading scientist of China, was one of the four open supporters of the students. He was David's uncle, though I did not know this until later. Professor Shang Chung-yi was in prison for several weeks and lost his job. He often came to our house in a dither of indecision and eventually went south. Some months later Hsu Teh-heng, also of Peita (and later one of the founders of the 1949 government), came to tell us that Professor Shang had been drowned when a bus drove off a ferry.

At Yenching both the president, Dr. J. L. Stuart, and the chancellor, C. W. Luh, gave moral support to the student movement—an act of Chinese-American friendship whose repercussions would extend down to the present.

A death penalty for "agitators" had been promulgated, and the Peking Student Union was outlawed from Nanking, but on March 31, about twelve hundred dare-to-dies of twenty-four schools took a desperate stand, protesting the prison death of one young student and the arrest of others. Our foreign-correspondent group was present as usual—Ed and I, Mac Fisher, and Jim Bertram.

Meantime, forty-three Tungpei University students had been released in Sian on demand of Young Marshal Chang Hsueh-liang, whose army was already affected by the patriotic movement. The Young Marshal gave his "personal guarantee" for them. He was kept busy saving students in those days. Of course, we knew the students could not fight or even be among the troops in any war—they were too feeble. Only real Communists would dare to go with the troops. Yet nothing was more important than the magic of *knowledge* to stir up the people and the armies.

In 1936, no outsider in China had any idea just what kind of people the Red armies had, not even David Yui. But the students and intellectuals had nowhere else to turn, even if the armies' leaders turned out to be nothing but "Red bandits"—which was what Chiang Kai-shek's side called them always, with plentiful lies about atrocities to stir up hatred of them. At that time, it was hard to believe that any Chinese could possibly be a Communist, though history was full of bandits and peasant rebels who never changed anything.

For nine years the Red armies had been blockaded. Now they had ended the Long March after a year on the way and were in the far Northwest near the Great Wall. Here was the first chance to see them.

Ed considered making a trip to the Red armies as early as March 1936, but nothing could be arranged then by David, who wrote to us on March 25 from Tientsin: "The problem of Ed's shall be settled a few days later. One of the both men shall tell you this consideration. On this problem I have explained to them as possible I can. I think they have no reason to refuse your requirement. I hope it shall be realized. Please write to me before your travelling."

To his publisher, Harrison Smith, owner of *The Saturday Review of Literature* and his own publishing house, Ed confided his idea for a trip. Harrison encouraged him, as he always did everything we proposed. One spring afternoon, at our usual teatime rendezvous in the big living room, Ed and I made a big decision.

"It's *dead right*." I felt very certain in one of my categorically imperative moments. "You'll have to go at any cost." I would have gone with him if I could, but that was impossible, though I would have been good camouflage.

Ed said he would go to Shanghai immediately. "Madame Sun Yat-sen can help if anyone can." He couldn't try to go to the Red areas without some kind of clearance. And the trip would have to be kept strictly secret. It could ruin him with the *Post* and the *Herald Tribune*. "Still," he said, "it's the biggest scoop in Asia in my lifetime, even if the Guggenheims don't think so." (Ed had been stunned when his application for a grant to study the Communist movement in China was rejected by the Guggenheims—and when it was given instead to a student to study "facial expressions of the Chinese"!)

On April 29, I wrote to Henriette Herz, our agent: "Ed has to go to the South for a business trip but will be back soon."

Ed was back home from Shanghai by May 19, when a letter came from David, who had escaped to Tientsin wearing one of Ed's old suits for disguise, as it was by then too dangerous for him to stay in Peking. The letter said he was reading English magazines "to be a man of the modern age"; in Peking he had felt he was in "the 18th Century." David was organizing a student movement in Tientsin and obviously would have been conferring secretly with Liu Shao-ch'i, who was then the chief Communist in the North China Bureau, one of seven, including David, Huang Hua, Yao Yi-lin—our student friends—and Po I-po, Ch'en Po-ta, and Hsu Ping, though at the time we did not know who were Communists.

In May two Southwest generals, of Kwangtung and Kwangsi— Pai Chung-hsi and Li Tseng-jen—raised a rebellion against Chiang

Kai-shek because he refused to resist Japan and was starting another internal war. At first the students demanded that the Communists "support the Southwest," but Communist policy was to stay out of it, to prevent civil war at any cost—which was the prevailing policy of the Soviet Union.

The armed forces were fast developing an anti-Chiang Kai-shek posture, but the situation was very confusing. We knew that in the Northwest, the Young Marshal was in a secret truce with the Red armies, which was why it was at all possible for Ed to attempt a trip there.

There was not a minute to spare because of the dangerous, uncertain civil-war situation. Early in June, a Peking professor gave Ed a letter, in invisible ink, to deliver to Mao Tse-tung. Ed packed up his sleeping bag, his Camel cigarettes, his Gillette razor blades, and a can of Maxwell House coffee—his indispensable artifacts of Western civilization. He was feverish with excitement, and with inoculations. Late as always—and, too, he had hardly expected the trip actually to materialize—just before leaving he took his injections against smallpox, typhoid, typhus, and cholera. We also knew that the black plague was endemic in the Northwest, but there was no known inoculation for it, nor was there any really for typhus. I took most of the shots as well— just in case I could get to Sian somehow.

Life was very sweet and our work very successful at that moment. We had no wish to risk all this for a totally unknown adventure—yet it had to be done. No one, including the Chinese, had any idea of just what kind of people the Red armies represented. Someone had to find out, and no one else could or would make such a trip. Then, too, we were intoxicated with power, all kinds of power: power to influence history, marriage power, and, though we would never use such a term, a high sense of spiritual power over and above all mundane things.

Ed was always casual about risking his life. It was taboo to mention danger. I would never mention such a delicate subject as insurance for either of us.

With movie and still cameras around his neck, Ed petted the bouncing puppies, and all the servants lined up at the gate to say goodbye as we departed by ricksha for the railway station. Our dear sweet Mongol coolie, Ch'en, was in a third ricksha with the luggage, and Gobi rode in the seat with me as always. Clutched in my hot little hands was Ed's nasal oil. He usually had sinus problems from the dusty Peking air plus smoking. I knew he would forget the oil if it was not put into his pocket on leaving.

It was dark midnight with no light on the streets but the bobbing ricksha lanterns. We insisted on going along the clean spooky space by the old city wall as usual, though the rickshamen tried to avoid this haunted area—also as usual. Overhead were the immense desert stars and a crescent moon. Gobi was seeing things in the dark shadows and trying to jump out of the ricksha to investigate. We were silent, except for the slow pad-pad of the jogging rickshamen.

Out in that dark unknown space, new worlds were aborning. This was the great adventure of our generation—but neither of us had any idea that anyone else would think so. We did not have the least idea that what Ed wrote about this journey would become a best-selling book. But we were aware that his eight years in China needed either a climax or an anticlimax to be justified.

As usual, we almost missed the train bound for Sian. I put the nasal oil in Ed's pocket as he climbed aboard. He stood on the steps, grinning as if he were Caesar at one of his triumphs, and saluted: "Heil, Hitler!"

"Don't lose your nose oil!" I commanded, and the noisy, coal-burning locomotive wheezed on its way.

On June 16, I wrote our agent that Ed "has gone on a long trip into the interior."

From Sian, Ed wrote of his need for an interpreter. Huang Hua had earlier been released from a short time in prison, and had come directly to our house. Back at his Yenching studies, he received a telephone call from me. I told him Ed was asking for an interpreter immediately for a secret trip to the Communist areas. He volunteered to go, though he had to give up his graduation. I gave him all the money I could scrape together, and Huang Hua took the next train. As interpreter, he became a partner in the *Red Star Over China* project.

I received a few notes from Ed full of annoyance and discouragement, telling of delays and all kinds of problems. He was homesick and had "missed too many boats" already. Then I heard nothing more whatever, not until September, when a secret Red courier brought a letter: "I wish you were here to share my experiences. . . . What lively conversations and discussions you could have here; the air sparkles with intelligence. But then the bugs and the filth you despise."

I had not expected to hear from Ed. I well knew how impossible communication was. In the letter he asked me to send by the courier copies of the *Reader's Digest*, bars of milk chocolate, coffee, and a map-making instrument. He also asked for his secretary, Kuo Ta, to make a copy of an article on chemical farming in *Harper's*.

Kuo Ta became a partner in *Red Star Over China*, just as Huang Hua did. He typed every line of it and loved every word.

CHAPTER 23

Interlude

Ed and Huang Hua were on their way to the Red areas, but the rest of the Yenching leaders had a secret celebration at graduation time, on a stone boat in the Peihai lake. It was a triumph and a farewell. All of us dearly loved each other, with the extraordinary feeling you get only from the knowledge that together you have changed history. Two of the girls were becoming national secretaries of the YWCA in Shanghai. Two boys were going to Sian as journalists on the Young Marshal's newspaper, intending to influence him and his soldiers—which they did. Li Min had been elected again to the Yenching student government. The police could have picked up the whole lot in one swoop.

All the students were real Puritans. Ordinarily, they never went to movies, or to dances either. But I made sure the students went to three movies, usually with me. There was only one movie house in Peking, and it had been playing *The Tale of Two Cities*, *Les Misérables*, and *Mutiny on the Bounty*, the first two adapted from favorite books of mine.

"It was the best of times, it was the worst of times," Dickens had begun his *Tale*. All the students began using the phrase. Nothing so well fitted the China situation.

During the winter, I was told, the students in prison had sung "A Cuban Love Song," "Rio Rita," "Old Black Joe," and "Goodnight, Ladies." Now, in the summer of 1936, a new "Song of the Volunteers (*Ch'i Lai*)" and the "Budyenny March" (learned from a movie) spread like wildfire. The first song became the national song after 1949.

From November to the end of school in June 1936, I had been busy every minute with the student movement, not only typing and retyping, but also having to think hard for the first time in my life on subjects far beyond my experience. I was being ground into mince-

184

meat as an unpaid do-gooder. But I didn't *want* to be that type; I liked myself as I had been. So did Ed, who never got over his horror that I had changed from "perfection" into whatever it was I was becoming.

I was very tired by the time Ed left for the Red areas, and I had given up my physical-culture ideas. By now, I hoped only to recuperate and to regain some of the 20 pounds I had lost of my usual 120. The summer of 1936 was my last opportunity to see Manchuria and Korea, I figured. Ed's name was anathema to the Japanese everywhere, so my trip would not be without some risk, especially as General Doihara and his friends knew all about our student-movement activities as well. Jim Bertram, new to China, was actually afraid for me and wanted to go along for protection—aside from any personal attraction he may have felt for the task. That was impossible, though he did not entirely understand my reasons for saying no. It was also amusing that because I was so secretive about Ed's sudden disappearance, some foreigners, including Jim, probably suspected we were trying a marital separation.

Before I set out for Manchuria, I needed to rebuild my health at Peitaiho, where Harry and Betty Price had again invited me to stay. Peitaiho was my last summer idyll in China. I was surprised to find that Jim had been invited for part of the time, but this did not detract from the scene. We all went to the beach, slept under mosquito nets, climbed the sand dunes, and watched the fishermen, home in the early day, spread their dripping nets to dry by blue Peitaiho bay. We talked about youth, art, and revolution. We talked Marxism and capitalism and socialism, and about China in all its mysterious phases.

One afternoon Jim and I went alone to the village for some shopping and stopped over in a little nightclub-type place where we danced a few times. Of course Jim was a very poor dancer—being anti-Fascist. Still, it reminded me of the States and the wonderful times I had had with all my old admirers so long ago.

Having recovered some of my health—and even a few pounds—I set out on my trip in August, first to Manchuria. In Dairen I stayed with the American consul, John Allison, and his wife, Jeannette, who had been attendants at our Tokyo wedding in 1932. Jeannette and I wore beautiful long blue and white cotton kimonos with red woolen obis, and had fun gossiping. It was delightful to have a woman friend to talk with.

In Mukden I was royally entertained by the consul, Johnny

Davies, son of missionaries, witty, bright, and full of fun. (In the Mc-
Carthy time, he was a victim of the China Lobby, but by 1971 he was
invited to testify in congressional hearings.) Always in the East, the
tiny foreign enclaves were starving to see a new face and listen to a new
voice. The hospitality was like that of American frontier days in its
open delight.

When I left, Johnny Davies gave me letters to the consuls in
Korea. From the Uchi-kongo Hotel in Choanji, Korea, I explored all
the mountain paths and tried to swim in the icy, crystal-clear mountain streams. The Kongosan was one of the most beautiful mountain
places in the East, sacred to Buddhism since about A.D. 513. We
visited some of the thirty-two monasteries and talked Buddhism to the
monks. Our modern hotel with food was only U.S. $1.50 a day. What
a place for hippies!

I sat on the veranda with close-mouthed missionaries who hated
Japan and felt a special responsibility for Korea, the only Protestant
community of importance in Asia. Korea took to democracy as no
other nation in the East. I loved the country and the people, as the
missionaries did. These missionaries were all anti-imperialist and always had been. The Protestant youth of Korea had been the first to take
up Marxism in the East, and later I undertook to write the life story of a
Korean Communist, *Song of Ariran*.

You have to be able to think in dialectics to understand or begin
to comprehend all the complexities of Asia, where one contradiction
has belied another since these nations were first opened up by force to
Western influence. Western civilization did not actually reach the
Asian mind until the medium of Marxism made it possible—especially in the thinking and theory of Mao Tse-tung.

I made friends with an English instructor at the Japan War College, and his wife. And Mr. Gohring, the rotund, jolly owner of our
drugstore in Peking, was at the hotel, too; he yodeled and sang the
"Song of the Valkyries" from the mountaintops. (Mr. Gohring belonged to the only Alpine Club in the Far East and nominated me as
the only woman member after I got back to Peking.)

We embarked upon a two-day climb to the highest peak in the
Kongosan, Mount Piroho, without warning that the worst typhoon in
thirty years—and for twenty more to come—was about to hit the area.
Using chains and alpenstocks, we reached the top just half an hour
before the fury broke. Cozy in a low Korean grass-thatched hut beside
a precipice, I found it a thrilling experience for two days. My favorite

sport had always been mountain climbing. To me, Piroho was small potatoes—I had lived within sight of the Grand Tetons until the age of nine.

Coming down was dangerous, since the chains had been destroyed in the typhoon. I was tied between two strong Korean guides, and we had to pole-vault the swift icy streams. I was very frightened in a tiny cockleshell of a boat on the angry river, with pigs, chickens, and human bodies floating past. Later at Seoul I saw the immense flood from the bridge.

I felt the tragedy of Korea, a stepping-stone between Japan and the Soviet Union and China. Then, in 1950, a battleground for the United States and the United Nations. It was one of the worst days of my life when the United States sent armed forces into Korea—I well knew it was a new beginning of "imperialism" for Americans. When the United States finally got out of Vietnam and Cambodia, it was a great spiritual victory for Western civilization, and twenty-five years acoming.

In 1936, the imperialism of Japan had nothing progressive to offer the East—only more degradation and obscurantism. Japan was building big industry everywhere, using Chinese slave labor, while at home the army was drafting Japanese youth and setting their minds back to samurai times. The defeat of Japan in 1945 was a great liberation for the Japanese, and very progressive.

CHAPTER 24

My First Trip to the Northwest, 1936

Arrived back in Peking, I found no word of my husband, but I expected him to stay as long as possible to get a good story.

The autumn days were glorious in Peking, and I had recovered my usual good health. Jim Bertram showed up again, after traveling alone to learn about China. As before, we kept the high-tension relationship charming, veddy British, strictly not personal. I needed an escort, since it was not possible for a foreign woman to be alone with Chinese except in the capacity of student or paid employee, such as an interpreter or guide; and Jim and I went on picnics with one or two of the excited Chinese who were desperate for someone to talk with about the "situation." We went to the T'ai Miao in the Forbidden City, the entire place empty except for a few caretakers. We also rode bicycles out of town to the countryside, where Gobi chased the ducks in the moat by the city wall and at one farmhouse was confronted by a huge black Chow. A young farmer ran out to hold the dog back, putting his arms around him with real affection—the first time I ever saw this except with my own dogs.

"You have a beautiful big dog," I said, smiling.

"*You* have a beautiful big dog," he said, looking friendly.

I looked at the red peppers and garlic and persimmons drying on the low roof and hanging from the eaves, with ears of corn and kaoliang. "You must be very happy here," I said.

"We are very happy," he agreed, and somehow a moment of real friendship was established.

In those few golden days, Jim and I talked of everything under the sun—or at least I did. Jim was far from talkative; he was quite reserved, but he missed not an overtone. Some of Jim's Oxford friends were fighting in Spain; one of them was killed there in November 1936. Jim was on a high peak of revolutionary romanticism, a kind of Byronic identification, experiencing a poetic, exciting time. He was on the *qui vive*, willing to do anything and everything.

One September day, I heard our dogs holding off a dangerous Red invasion. Rushing out through the conservatory, I found the boys protecting a strong, muscular stranger who refused to retreat into the gatehouse, as most callers did. There was a broad grin on his face as he handed me a letter from my husband, the first news since June. I loved Wang Ling immediately—so did Ed, I soon found out. He wore voluminous knickers, which the Communists then thought the best bourgeois disguise. Here was a secret Red courier direct from the Red armies behind the blockade—the first I ever saw.

"Snow has smoked up all the cigarettes in our districts and is dying for coffee," he announced in Chinese (he knew no English). "He's having the time of his life, though. He's very popular."

The long letter was dated August 3, and enclosed a letter from Huang Hua to Chang Chao-lin (who was in Sian, however). Ed's chief comment was: "They all seem extremely optimistic, and cheerful. They go at the difficult labor of discovering a new scientific world like schoolboys to a football match."

"I'm going back with you," I announced to Wang Ling. "If you try to leave Peking without me, I'll turn you over to the police."

"*Hao, hao ti-hen!*" He actually rubbed his hands at this thought of marital felicity. "Won't Snow be surprised and glad!"

"Surprised, not glad," I said, astonished that he would agree. "You'll be spoiling his vacation from his ball-and-chain."

Wang Ling was full of mischief and humor, always teasing. He pretended to be taking me to surprise Snow—and he never did tell me that Ed had asked him to bring me to the Red areas on his return trip. I didn't find that out till weeks later. (As mayor of Sian in 1978, Wang Ling held a banquet for me together with General Wang Chen, whose autobiography I had written down in *The Chinese Communists*.* He even remembered the name of our dog Ginger.)

I had to be ready to leave in a few days. And I had to tell Jim Bertram so that he could take care of things in my absence, and also Mac Fisher, whom I asked to handle Ed's newspaper work, which I had been doing up to then. Mac was horrified that I would make such

* Reprinted 1972, Greenwood Publishers, Westport, Conn. This book was originally published in 1952 by Stanford University Press, California, under the title *Red Dust*.

a dangerous trip, and Jim was desperate to go with me, even just to be platonically on the same train to Sian, where he might negotiate for his own trip into the Red areas. I was afraid to go alone, and even more anxious than Jim to have him come with me. But I knew Ed would be furious if we traveled together. I did not even invite Jim for a farewell dinner; it would not have looked right to our servants, and in China the servant system was a network of information on every subject.

I could not explain all this to Jim, however—I never did tell him the reason I refused his company—and he never forgave me. He thought I was rejecting him altogether, and I had to let him think it was that simple.

I underwent the terrible experimental typhus inoculations (I had had the other necessary shots at the time Ed had his), and had my long hair cut and permanent-waved. Off the wide bed came the beautiful eiderdown quilt, for a sleeping bag, and the North China Industries also made me a camel's hair coat for travel. (Ed had given me a magnificent leopard coat for Christmas to keep me warm during student demonstrations, but it was not for traveling. It was my best friend for the next forty years.) Then I had fleece-lined boots made for the cold Northwest. Jim brought me his red wool Oxford shirt for good luck.

The plan was to meet Wang Ling at the railway station but never to show any recognition during the two- or three-day trip to Sian, where a Red Army liaison man would call on me at the Sian Guest House. My official explanation would be that I was doing newspaper work and studying archaeology, with Chang Chao-lin, our Yenching student friend, as interpreter and escort.

Jim came to take me to the station in plenty of time. He snapped my photograph in the courtyard. He was totally disciplined—as I was—but he could hardly contain his flushed emotions. Anger was there and competitive envy, along with the buildup of a frustrated nine months of being my only special admirer. Jim was also protective, a real gentleman in all ways—more so than Ed, who took his wife as much for granted as he did all other acts of Providence.

My sleeping bag and equipment were in a straw suitcase in one ricksha. I said good-bye to the dogs and to the servants, lined up as usual on both sides of the gate. Then Jim and I set out along the deserted road by the ancient city wall, just as Ed and I had done four months previously.

"Of course, you're only going to the end of the world—and beyond," Jim remarked glumly.

At the station Wang Ling made sure he and I saw each other, but without acknowledgment. I waved good-bye to Jim as the old-fashioned train pulled out in big clouds of white steam and black coal smoke, rattling along the city wall and whistling loud enough to wake all the dead in China.

Sian was an ancient walled city, with authoritative big gates that seemed intended to keep out young American females with anti-Confucian unbound feet. All foreigners were met at the station by police, passports were checked, and travelers were allowed to stay only at the modern Sian Guest House.

Soon after my arrival at the Guest House, I was visited by a re-turned-student type of Chinese, with freckles, tweed golfing knickers, and cap. He was casual, open, had a sense of humor, and was quite nonchalant.

"Call me Charles," he introduced himself in vernacular English, doffing his jaunty tweed cap. My second Red Army acquaintance—unlike Wang Ling, the tiger cub anxious to claw away any number of mountains in the road—seemed unimpressed with my project.

"We have only one little truck," he informed me, and there was very important other baggage to send. It wasn't easy to make space for me anyway. It was very hard to get their truck through the lines now because of troop movements. He was very daunting.

"Call me cargo instead of baggage," I said, pleading that I weighed only 108 pounds.

But engineering graduate Liu Ting (Charles's real name, I later discovered) said he hadn't the least idea where my husband was or what he was doing. Besides, I didn't look strong enough to be making such a trip. I didn't look like the type. "Why do you want to go?" he asked.

Why did I? Why did it seem so important? I finally convinced him that though nothing like such valuable baggage as my husband, still I was worth a little hiding space.

He told me that the truck would leave at daybreak any day. I would have to take a ricksha alone to get to the secret place where the truck was kept. Liu would phone me ahead of time. "You must be ready to leave on a few hours' notice."

"It must be very dangerous for you here," I said.

He grinned. "No more than it is for the Young Marshal; I'm living with him in his house."

Just at this time, Sian was the center of political and military power and intrigue in China. Some of the officers were guests at the Sian Guest House, and the air vibrated with conspiracy and uncertainty. Fascists were becoming Communists, or at least neutrals, and ex-Communists were being paid by Fascists as spies or double spies. The situation was at the point where opposites reach identity. But Chiang Kai-shek was a psychotic anti-Communist with a closed mind, and the anti-Japanese Southwest revolt against him by the Kwangtung and Kwangsi provincial armies, begun on June 2, 1936, had not changed him in the least. The settlement was made public on September 8, 1936, just at the time of my travel, and Sian was seething with resentment.

At that time, Liu Ting was the only liaison man in Sian for the Red armies. (He was in Peking in the 1970s and often saw Rewi Alley, but I missed him.) Every ten days or so, a single conspiratorial Tungpei military truck with a guard in Tungpei uniform made its way in and out of the network of spies and police infesting Sian. As such, the truck could travel with *carte blanche* through White territory to Yenan, which was then headquarters for the Young Marshal's army. From there, one had to have *carte rouge* to travel by horseback to the Red capital of Pao-an, which was where Ed had spent most of his time.

For about two weeks in Sian, I died a thousand deaths every day, expecting to leave next morning on a perilous trip to an area where, Liu Ting said, I might be marooned indefinitely. I was too nervous and excited to eat or sleep. I wasn't the brave type at all. But I had willpower, and a sense of destiny.

Our old student friend Chang Chao-lin was an editor on the Young Marshal's newspaper. Every day, dressed in a foreign-style suit, he took me around the city—to the Drum Tower, the Bell Tower, the temples, the museums, the curio shops. We talked and talked about the "situation."

Chang was full of suppressed excitement. Here we were again, the two of us, right in the midst of the biggest storm that had brewed up in China since 1927—just as we had been in 1935 on the eve of the December 9th student movement initiated by Chang and his friends.

Chang Chao-lin was in danger himself. The Blue Shirts from Peking had been transferred to Sian under Chiang Hsiao-hsien, the ultra-Fascist nephew of Generalissimo Chiang Kai-shek. Terrorist "Special Action Corps" were kidnaping students and others. But the

Young Marshal had wired Chiang Kai-shek that he would "defend any men who loved their country." And he did.

In September, around the time I was leaving for Sian, the Fascist gendarmes in Sian had kidnaped Sung Ling, our friend and one of the three student leaders "most wanted" by the police. The Young Marshal was furious and sent two companies of soldiers to surround the gendarmes' detention house and get the student released. Sung Ling had been the student liaison with the Young Marshal from the beginning. He lived in his house when in Sian and had a big influence on the Young Marshal's thinking.

On March 9, 1936, Sung Ling had come to see us in Peking and had reported on his talks with the Young Marshal, whom he quoted as saying: "I think you will be satisfied with my eventual policy. I cannot tell you my true feelings now. I deeply sympathize with your movement, though, and will do everything to make your ideas known to our men." He took Sung Ling to a meeting of five hundred officers and introduced Sung Ling's two-hour speech against civil war.

A virtual truce had existed between the Young Marshal and the Reds by the time Edgar Snow reached Sian on his trip in June. But Chiang Kai-shek planned a new "extermination campaign" against the Red armies. Early in October, the Fascists seized three student delegates from North China. The Young Marshal closed all city gates and surrounded the headquarters with troops, who broke down the door and rescued the three.

Thus in Sian a kind of cold civil war was already beginning between Chiang Kai-shek and the opposition to his policies. Since early October the Young Marshal's army had been ready to fight to protect the Red armies from attack. That was where I came in.

Liu Ting had telephoned me several times to inform me of the nonarrival of the little truck. After two weeks he came to see me and said it was being held up on the other side of the Wei River due to military maneuvers. He could not find out when my husband would return but thought it would, of necessity, be almost immediately. He advised me to leave Sian forthwith, partly so as not to draw attention to Ed, who stood to lose his films and notebooks if discovered.

I had no wish whatever to leave Sian. I was a poor newspaperwoman, but I knew a good story when it was handed to me on a silver platter, and a good story was under cover there now. This might be my last chance to record history. Just during those days I was in Sian, two

Red armies from the South, commanded by General Chu Teh, were fighting their way in Kansu to meet up with Mao Tse-tung's columns in October, ending their separate Long Marches.

The Young Marshal sent for me, as the only available foreign correspondent, to explode the situation in Sian by way of the *London Daily Herald*, Ed's paper. I would not have been surprised if the Young Marshal had been given the impression that the Snows were in league with all the democratic chancelleries of Europe and America. It was almost inconceivable to the Chinese that two young people would do entirely on their own the things that Ed and I were constantly doing—with no "guarantee" from anywhere. It was great to be an American in Asia in those days. The waves parted before us as before Moses at the Red Sea—especially a *red* sea. We were welcome everywhere. Any American was likely to be looked upon as the next best thing to Roosevelt himself.

A few Chinese reporters were also invited to the interview, but were not allowed to publish anything.

I had not met the Young Marshal, Chang Hsueh-liang, before, though he evidently knew all about me. He was thirty-seven and had been the ruler over 30 million people in Manchuria when Japan took it away from him in 1931. Since 1930, he had been vice-commander in chief of all Chinese armed forces, Number 2 to Generalissimo Chiang Kai-shek. He had been Chiang's catspaw and "little brother." In 1933, he went to Europe, where Mussolini and his son-in-law, Count Ciano, had converted him to fascism. This Number 2 Fascist of China had been shaken out of all such nonsense by the student movement, and also by his admiration for the Red armies who had defeated his troops. He was proud that his own Tungpei students, some in his own Youth Corps, had helped initiate the December 9th movement. This took away some of the disgrace he felt for having lost Manchuria. By the end of February 1936, he was already anti-Fascist, as reported to us by his favorite student, Sung Ling.

On October 3, I put on my blue suede beret and my red-white-and-blue scarf. Chang Chao-lin and I set out in rickshas for a six o'clock appointment with the commander in chief of the "Northwest Bandit-Suppression Headquarters." We could hardly contain our delight.

We were greeted in excellent English by a young intellectual in glasses, the Young Marshal's secretary, whose name was Ying Teh-tien. His air of triumph was even greater—and less disguised—than

ours. (Two months later, Ying would be one of the "Three Mus-
keteers" who conceived and engineered the kidnaping and imprisonment of Chiang Kai-shek. These three men were originally influenced
by the student movement, but their imaginative kidnaping of the Generalissimo was their own idea.)

Chang Hsueh-liang, the Young Marshal, was in mufti, a simple
gray gown—a nice Confucian touch inasmuch as he was announcing
the mutiny of himself and his army against the high command. The
suspense was electric. I couldn't help smiling at him—with all the
history of the past year in my eyes. He was a little flustered. He had
protected Ed's trip to the Red areas, and he had been willing to protect
mine, to the maximum. He and I had one thing in common: We were
always hiding students in our houses from the police. The Young
Marshal laughed out loud when I mentioned that he had secured the
release of forty-six arrested Tungpei students in Peking on his personal
guarantee.

I had submitted five questions in advance. The Young Marshal's
answers were precisely opposite to Chiang Kai-shek's policies. His explosive formal statement was this:

"If the Communists can sincerely cooperate with us under the
leadership of the Central Government to resist the common foreign
invader, perhaps it is possible that this problem can be settled peace-
fully, as in the recent Southwest case."

At the end, he crossed over to shake hands with me. This was a
kind of covenant.

On the street, Chang Chao-lin and I shook hands solemnly. This
was *it*—the Rubicon.

The Kuo Min News Agency sent out a fabricated account, daring
to quote falsely the Number 2 commander in chief.

The telegraph office in Sian refused to send my cable. I had to
take the first train to Peking. I hated to leave Sian right in the middle of
the biggest story of my lifetime, but Charles—Liu Ting—insisted. No
one knew how soon the Young Marshal himself might be in danger.
Total uncertainty existed. Chang Chao-lin decided to be my bodyguard on the train trip to Peking.

Not far from Chengchow, a young Tungpei officer entered our
compartment. He introduced himself as Colonel Wan Yi, and he was
bursting over with indignation. "We must cooperate with the Red
Army," he declared. He spoke in open defiance of Chiang Kai-shek,
saying, "The soldiers will act themselves, without orders."

Outside the train window, we saw several troop trains of Nanking's best soldiers being rushed to the anti-Red campaign. We knew they were also being sent to surround the mutinous Tungpei Army and to squelch officers like Colonel Wan Yi.

Chang was in tears when the colonel shook hands and left us at Chengchow.

"Here we are, two little mustard seeds," I remarked to Chang. "Lo, what a mighty harvest of dragon's teeth."

A year ago, we had been suffocated in an atmosphere of living death. Now we had the whole 150,000 Tungpei troops with us, on the side of the students and ready to act; in my purse was the Young Marshal's statement committing himself to lead them. We had not only Peking but all North China.

But we didn't have Chiang Kai-shek as yet.

As I watched Chang Chao-lin and the colonel, I thought, *This must be why I stay in China.* One or two little students can start whole armies moving in the field, with less than a year of propaganda. The combination of intellectuals and men of action was like tinder to matchwood. (Later on, I realized this was true in all pre-industrial nations where there exists no middle class with a real voice except among the young students.)

Back in Peking, I cabled my write-up of the interview with the Young Marshal to the *London Daily Herald.* United Press sent it all over America and China. It was also published in the *China Weekly Review* and the *North China Star,* and nearly caused a premature Sian Incident. The Japanese demanded an explanation from Nanking, which repudiated the interview.

But great was the rejoicing among the students of China.

CHAPTER 25

Red Star Over China— Edgar Snow's Return, October 1936

I had returned home from Sian about October 7. Back at my desk in the bow window, I rushed out some articles and letters. I was now North China correspondent for Powell's *China Weekly Review*, a regular writer for *Asia*, a substitute correspondent for the *London Daily Herald* and the *New York Sun*, and the all-China correspondent for *The Nation*. Our agent, Henriette Herz, had offers for me to do a book of verse, articles, all kinds of things. (Always she was a co-partner in the Snow-Bertram-trio joint enterprise. We loved her from a distance. Every letter she sent was full of wonderful heartwarming news—and money, a little anyway.)

I was also in the midst of buying tea, silks, and other items for some of the new friends I had made in Korea and Manchuria. Life was very sweet, overflowing with success.

Around the twenty-fifth of October, I was busy at my desk as usual, with Gobi and Ginger sitting at my feet, bored and yawning. A formal knock at the side door startled us all. This was a surprise bandit proceeding. All visitors were formally announced by the gateman to the Number 1 servant, who in turn announced them to master and missy with royal etiquette.

There on the step stood my husband, grinning triumphantly behind a grizzled beard.

"Mrs. Livingstone, I presume?" he inquired, bowing.

"You look like the canary that swallowed the cat," I replied.

"What have you been up to?" the dogs demanded to know in full chorus, jumping all over him.

In he came, carrying all shapes of bundles, which he put down in the middle of the floor. Out of one he took an old gray cap with a faded red star on it, pulled it over one eye, and capered around the room, Gobi and Ginger leaping and dancing with him. He was exploding with pride of achievement, and happy just to be alive. All his files, films, and notebooks were there on the floor, safe.

I was ringing the electric bell before he made the usual demand: "I want some scrambled eggs, Camel cigarettes, Maxwell House coffee . . ."

"And Gillette razor blades," I finished for him.

"And canned peaches—American canned peaches." This was a big luxury for exiles in the Far East. For once, I did not mind spending money on imported luxuries.

The servants mobilized in all directions—roast beef, apple pie, hot biscuits.

Ed demanded his mail. I put the box of letters, all answered, in front of him beside the big armchair.

Ecstatically, he skimmed through the letters and threw them down on the floor—letters from his publisher, from *The Saturday Evening Post*, from his father and sister and brother, most of all from Henriette Herz.

I handed Ed the first photograph we had seen of Henriette; she was beautiful, with warm, sympathetic eyes. I told Ed she was getting married, to Philip Cohen.

"Time to go home," Ed commented in admiration. "If I'd known she looked like that, I'd have done better work." We both remembered this old remark from the first time we had met.

"What are those people like?" I tried to pry something out of him, but he was having too much fun teasing and keeping up the suspense to answer. Suddenly I recollected the importance of getting Ed's films processed before anyone knew what they were.

In ten minutes I was in a ricksha with the films on my way to Hartung's. I also took, for reproduction, some rare old photographs that had been given to Ed by Mao Tse-tung himself in Pao-an—the only ones in existence taken before the Long March began. Hartung's was German—perhaps, I speculated, Nazi—and in the photographs the red star was visible on every tattered cap of the Reds. We lived in fear that the films might be "lost" at Hartung's, and hoped that the Chinese who processed them would not realize their value.

These pictures had already almost been lost in earnest. On October 21, Ed had been near Sian, in the secret Tungpei Army truck. The bag containing all his film and notebooks had been tossed off by mistake at Hsienyang, twenty miles from Sian. Fortunately, the truck went back for them.

And fortunately again, when I picked up the developed photographs later at Hartung's, they were all beautifully done, no questions asked.

It was important to keep Ed's trip secret until his films and articles could be on their way to the States. Peking had been reading and confiscating mail since the student movement began, but so far they had not dared to touch foreign mail. As soon as his trip became public knowledge, everything would be watched. We really did not know how much trouble to expect. The Japanese were very much present in Peking, of course.

About two days after Ed's secret homecoming, the telephone rang. It was the Associated Press—Jimmy White.

"When did you last hear from Ed?" he asked, his voice full of warning.

"Just a little time ago," I replied guardedly.

Jimmy said that a report had come from Sian that Ed had been executed by the Chinese Reds. The news was already on the A.P. wires in the States.

That was one of the worst dangers: A traveler could be assassinated as a means of discrediting the Reds.

Consternation at No. 13 as I whispered to Ed, who was already alert to the situation.

Ed came to a decision. He took the phone and gave Jimmy his story.

Queries began to come in from Britain and the States. Ed's obituary was in type in Kansas City. A big investigation was about to be launched in Sian for the two of us. We immediately wired Sian military headquarters that both of us were safe in Peking.

Just a few days before Ed returned, a newspaper report had appeared that I had been killed by bandits in Sinkiang. Now a missionary was reporting Ed's death in Kansu. Snows were being massacred all over the Northwest, and all unknown to Chiang Kai-shek's best army and police.

This was no routine matter for the security forces. There had been a time not long before when foreign powers had taken over territory the size of Shantung as a reprisal for the murder of one of their nationals by Chinese; China had been on the verge of being carved up among the powers. The fear inspired in the Boxer days was still operative. Chinese everywhere were under strict orders to account for every foreign traveler at all times, or heads would roll.

All during October, both when I was in Sian and especially on the day Ed was in the city—which coincided with Chiang Kai-shek's October 21 Sian conference with Chang Hsueh-liang—the best Gestapo and Blue Shirt Fascists were supposed to be operating with maximum efficiency. If these security forces knew nothing of two errant foreigners, the loss of face would be tremendous. They were kidnaping Chinese right and left. Foreigners were usually sacrosanct in China, but travelers to Red areas might not have this immunity to arrest.

Our safety lay in the multiplicity of suspicions about us. The Japanese had thought Ed and I were emissaries of President Roosevelt; they now suspected we were paid agents of Nanking! No one in his right mind would dare be an agent of the Soviet Union in those days, but this was suspected of us in some quarters. (In 1975, I discovered that the Comintern agent with the Communists, the German Otto Braun, had suspected both Ed and me of being American secret agents!) This might make a grand comic opera, but it did not seem comic then. Communists can just barely understand individualism. As for the Chinese, the whole idea of the individual was almost incomprehensible—you had to belong to some group or be paid for engaging in unusual activities. That newspapermen had the job of getting pure news, with no ulterior motive, was almost unimaginable to the Chinese. That is why so many foreigners have been arrested as spies in China and other Oriental nations. Individual initiative is too strange for them to grasp.

In Shensi, Governor Shao Li-tze was called to account, and the police and gendarmes were reorganized because Ed had kept his trip secret from them. (The next year I would have to pay for all this loss of face in Sian. I would have to make my escape alone through much the same cordon of police and Gestapo, but this time all fully alerted.)

When Ed's articles first appeared, Nanking branded them a hoax. Not until his photographs were published was this line of attack discontinued.

The big thing about Ed's trip to the Red areas was this: that the right wing in China as well as the left believed everything he said. He had total credibility. In this way, the trip became a part of Chinese history—helping to swing opinion toward a United Front against Japan.

All the lies and suspicions built up around the Chinese Communists fell down like the walls of Jericho at the trumpet blast of truth in a newspaper account. Ed's report even affected the dramatis personae, the Communists themselves, enhancing their self-image and most of all making them realize for the first time that all "imperialists" were not alike and that they might possibly be able to deal with one side against another, especially with Americans, and more especially with the *people* of America.

Had Ed been a Communist, his story would have had little value. He actually was a *reporter* telling it like it was. He disliked propaganda intensely. He liked his readers and thought of them first—that was his job in keeping the Watch on the Pacific. Ed was in love with his readers. In the McCarthy time, Ed was truly astounded and deeply hurt to be rejected, as it seemed then, by his *own readers*.

Ed actually was a typical American who spoke the language of his time and reached his public. He was the right man in the right place at the right time. He was free to form his own judgments, and he did so on the basis of observed facts, year by year. He was completely free of prejudice, with no ax to grind on any subject.

For two or three days after Ed's return home, he and I talked constantly while he smoked his Camels and drank his real Maxwell House coffee. Usually, Ed did not like to talk at all on any subject he was writing about. It killed the spontaneity, the fresh approach. Ed was ordinarily neither skeptical nor enthusiastic—he took facts in his stride. He was by no means unsophisticated, in the sense of suspending judgment and remaining unexcitable. He had no respect for anyone much, except Madame Sun Yat-sen.

Now he had discovered Mao Tse-tung, not only for himself but for the Chinese. This was real *terra incognita*. He had come face to face at last with the real China—and he realized it. Here was the natural leader of some 80 percent of the Chinese, a man who had already asserted himself in that role.

"Did you *like* him?" I demanded to know. "Was he friendly to you?"

Ed had a habit of raising his eyebrows with a smile to tease people. He rarely answered a direct question like that. And he was still formulating his conclusions.

"I was his first foreign newspaperman," Ed replied. "I didn't make any enemies that I know of."

Of course, he had got on famously with Mao Tse-tung and had liked him. But not till the next year did I discover that Ed had been a big success with the Communists, including Mao. In fact, he was probably the chief, if not the only, foreign friend Mao Tse-tung ever made.

Ed had no hero worship whatsoever for anybody. One thing he disliked intensely was the "our great leader" phrase then being used for Stalin, Hitler, Mussolini, and sundry others. He was glad the term was not yet etiquette for Mao. (In 1970, Ed asked Mao himself what he thought of the personality cult building up around him, and Mao said it was being overdone. This was widely quoted in China, and as a result the big statues began coming down all over the country.)

Nevertheless, the only photograph Ed ever put up that I know of was his own famous portrait of Mao Tse-tung, which is still used in China and for many years was the official photograph among the Communists. (The only other person he ever subsequently so honored was President Franklin D. Roosevelt; in his last election campaign, Ed put a big poster of F.D.R. on our front door in a solidly Republican town.)

The most important thing Ed had come back with was Mao Tse-tung's life story as told by himself, an astonishing prize to win from any Chinese. He had also got short life stories of Chou En-lai, P'eng Teh-huai, and several others. When I read them, I realized I had to make a similar trip at any cost, to get other biographical materials.

Ed asked me to cut down Mao's story and digest it for his book. He said he was going to rewrite some of it anyway, in his own words. I was horrified.

"But this is a classic. It's priceless," I protested. It would be the heart of Ed's book, the backbone. It gave Mao's whole background in perfect form. I argued that Ed shouldn't touch it, but should use every word as Mao had told it to him. "Why, this is like having George Washington at Valley Forge tell the story of the Revolution."

"You can't put a big indigestible lump like that in a book—it's never done. It will kill any sale the book may have."

"Never mind the sale. The reader can just skip over it if he likes. But it will *make* your book. Your book can be a classic, too, if it has the big story without too much temporary stuff in it."

Ed felt it would be just a waste of time for me to copy everything and ordered me to leave out "all these lists of names and places and armies. You can't publish a lot of Chinese names like that in a book."

Nevertheless, I sat down and copied every handwritten word exactly as told to Ed, lists of names and all. This was the inner history of the Communist movement, boring though it might be to some potential readers.

Ed and I had many arguments over including the whole story. I felt so strongly about it that I was afraid to go away on my own trip the following April, lest he cut most of it out in my absence. (That was the first thing I asked when I saw him again. He actually did publish nearly the whole story, with misgivings, but I think he did cut out many names.)

I agreed that it might almost kill the sale of the book—but on the other hand, I knew it would make the book of permanent value for years and years. Ed's idea was to communicate; mine was medicinal. I thought it was good for the reader to learn about Mao Tse-tung and his problems.

What busy, happy days we had writing up Ed's materials. How exciting it was when I brought back his photographs from Hartung's. Within half an hour I knew all of the individuals by name and face, and was sitting down to write long biographical captions from Ed's scattered notes. I wrote up most of what he brought back, and he rewrote it for the book. He gave me his original manuscript of Mao's autobiography as a present for doing the typing. (After the divorce, he demanded it back—and got it.)

The most urgent thing for Ed was to publish his interviews with Mao Tse-tung for their news value. It was the first time Mao had been quoted in the press. When the *China Weekly Review* published them, these ten pages shook the intellectual world of China.

Ed held a press conference at the American Embassy and his story was sent all over the world, then cabled back to China, where it stirred up big excitement.

A by-product of all this was that it was through Ed that Mao Tse-tung was introduced to the Soviet Union leaders, as well as to Europe and the Chinese. Before this, the Russians had totally underestimated the Chinese Communists and overestimated Chiang Kai-shek. They continued to do so, but not to the same silly degree. Their agent, Otto Braun, was giving them erroneous information; he had no experience in China and he personally hated Mao Tse-tung and his policies. The popular reception of Ed's story also gave the Soviet Union more hope of an alliance with America on the eve of World War II.

CHAPTER 26

The Sian Incident,
December 12, 1936

The Sian Incident came as a shock. The aftershock was an earthquake.

For six weeks after his return, Ed and I were in an entranced world of our own, talking and writing up his materials and sending them out. I took care of his mail so he could start writing *Red Star Over China* in his private building near the gatehouse at No. 13 K'uei Chia Ch'ang. I had been the chief publicist and public-relations director of the student movement for a year. Now I had a new project. I was handing out free of charge not only Ed's Northwest interviews but some of his photographs as well. Some of the free materials I sent to Randall Gould, editor of the American-owned *Shanghai Evening Post and Mercury*—an article on Chou En-lai, for instance, and a copy of a talk Ed gave at the Peking Union Church, where he was chairman of the program committee. Others I sent to J. B. Powell for the *China Weekly Review*. It was the material published in China that had the biggest effect, not only on Chinese but also on foreigners. These articles helped to pave the way for the United Front between the Communists and "liberals."

My love affair with China was reaching a high point. I loved the students, each and every one. I loved the whole Tungpei Army, each and every man. I was prepared to include old General Sung Cheh-yuan, the local Nineteenth Route Army, and any bandit leaders on the right side of the fence. I loved the teachers and missionaries who were avidly requesting Ed to make talks and show his movies, and who were all deeply concerned with his findings. They were dimly aware that the whole future of Westerners in China might depend on what kind of people these Communists were whom Ed had discovered.

Only a year before, as a forlorn hope, the Yenching students had desperately come out. Now all Peking—all North China—was closing ranks, not only against Japan but in an anti-Fascist front, even though official policy was to be only anti-Japanese. There had been a revolution in psychology and ideas among the armies and the intelligentsia. The December 9th movement had frightened the Japanese into holding back, but they still might occupy North China at any time. There was not one moment to lose. The world was moving fast. Austria, Hungary, and Yugoslavia were becoming quisling powers under the Nazis; the Spanish Republicans were losing. The Fascists were taking over in Europe. But in China we had the former Number 2 Fascist— Young Marshal Chang Hsueh-liang—completely on our anti-Fascist side. The Number 1 Fascist, Generalissimo Chiang Kai-shek, was still adamant, still refusing to allow resistance to Japan or any softening on the Reds.

On October 8, Chiang had received the Japanese ambassador favorably. And Japan's anti-Communist plan, which Chiang endorsed, would drag China into war on Japan's side if Japan and Russia clashed. On October 21, Chiang Kai-shek had flown to Sian to confer with Young Marshal Chang Hsueh-liang and others.

Newspaper headlines read: "Milan, November 1. Mussolini Seeks European Cooperation on Basis of German-Italian Agreement . . . Every illusion arising from the Wilsonian ideology must be pushed aside."

"Loyang, November 2. All traitors should be eliminated, especially the Communists, who, being well organized and well led by intellectual leaders, constitute a great menace to the nation, declared Chiang Kai-shek." (Until now these Communists had been referred to only as "Red Bandits.")

Chang Chao-lin's newspaper in Sian (where he and Sung Ling and Ch'en Han-p'o were influencing the Young Marshal and his officers) reported on November 11: "On the 26th inst., General Chiang Kai-shek gave a speech to the high officers which concluded: Enforce the suppression of bandits, defense is the talk of destroyers of the state. . . . At the 31st ult., the order for Communist suppression was given."

Chiang Kai-shek started moving his best army of three divisions into position under General Hu Chung-nan, who advanced eighty *li* into Red territory and fell into the usual Red trap. On November 18 and 21, he was defeated in surprise attacks.

On November 26, the Japanese-German anti-Communist pact was announced.

Chiang Kai-shek had gone to Sian to organize another anti-Red campaign. It was increasingly urgent to prevent this, and to close ranks against the Japanese.

December 12, 1936, was the date set for another student demonstration. Before daybreak the youth of Peking were leaving their dormitories in full demonstration attire—muffled in scarves and wearing heavily padded gowns. As they took to the streets, they were confident of the support of nearly all the students of China (except a small fringe of Fascists) and most of the nation, and they rejoiced in the secret delight of local authorities.

It was cold and frosty. I put on my blue suede beret, my red-white-and-blue scarf, and leopardskin coat. Ed and I got into a taxi to pick up Jim Bertram and Mac Fisher of the United Press. We had the usual trouble finding the demonstration. We located it by following student couriers on bicycles—you could distinguish them from ordinary bikers because their necks were bent down to the handlebars and their eyes were exultant, purposeful, as if they carried a message to Garcia.

"Are you cold?" Mac Fisher asked me. "You're trembling all over."

Nothing was further from our imaginings than any notion that at daybreak Generalissimo Chiang Kai-shek was, student style, climbing over a high wall at Lintung near Sian and making his frozen way, in nightshirt, up the hill nearby to hide.

We followed the students to Coal Hill near the Forbidden City, where the mayor addressed them sympathetically. In my regular article in the *China Weekly Review*, I wrote: "This demonstration is the most successful ever held in Peking." There were four thousand at Coal Hill; six thousand marched in the streets with little police interference. There had been a student demonstration in Sian on December 9— emphasizing the anniversary of last year's demonstration—and Chang Chao-lin sent us copies of the students' manifestos, which were distributed at the Peking demonstration on the twelfth. After the mass meeting at Coal Hill, they marched home with banners flying high, singing on the streets for the first time since 1927, I was told. They sang the new "Song of the Volunteers" of the Manchurian guerrillas, which had been an inspiration from the first during the December 9th affair. Chiang Kai-shek would have been no safer among these students than he was in Sian. The United Front was at high tide, rising higher every minute.

The day had been dizzily exhausting. But we had a dinner engagement with Jim Bertram and Ran and Louise Sailer. We found time to dress without keeping the party waiting too long. The Sailers' two pair of candid blue eyes were sparkling with joy. We waited for Jim. Presently he greeted the party, shaken out of his usual reserve.

"Have you heard? Chiang Kai-shek was killed by the Tungpei troops in Sian this morning."

Silence—total and unbelieving.

It was out of character for Chiang to walk straight into a tiger's trap. This was Chinese grand opera in the ancient tradition. It was too good a story to be true—as indeed it was not, not quite.

This was a once-in-a-lifetime moment. The tables were turned. Apparently, the vice-commander of all the armed forces of China had mutinied and arrested the commander in chief. The Number 2 "Fascist" had done a turnabout and captured the adamant Number 1 Fascist—dead or alive, no one knew for sure.

For the next day or two, telephone calls brought rumors and conjectures. No news was certain and no one would have believed it if it had been. The students in the dormitories were wild with jubilation—tempered by the thought that a new civil war might now be inevitable. The situation in Nanking was as dangerous and obscure as that in Sian. *Central News* reported on December 13 that Chang Hsueh-liang had mutinied and sent a telegram "demanding the overthrow of the government."

A student appeared (I think it was David Yui) asking for information and saying the Student Union demanded that war be declared on Japan at once and that representative government be established; they also denounced "any form or kind of civil war on any pretext whatsoever."

The streets were quiet. Not a sign of popular sentiment was evident. The Yenching students came to call. Hubert Liang came. The Tungpei people came.

One of the Tungpei people brought a volunteer from Manchuria. He told us there were 180,000 volunteers in Manchuria, with partisans—about 80,000 of them Reds. Some 50,000 volunteers had been killed since 1931, and about 8,500 Japanese. . . . "The dogs are trained to eat live people as punishment for anti-Japanese activity," he said.

At last the Tungpei people brought some exact information: Chiang Kai-shek had been arrested on December 12 at Lintung, near Sian, by Colonel Sun Ming-chiu, commander of the Young Marshal's bodyguard. All the Fascists in Sian were under arrest. The first individual shot was Chiang Kai-shek's ruthless and efficient nephew, Chiang Hsiao-hsien, who had been sent to Sian from Peking as head of the Third Gendarmes. Using ex-Communists in his gendarmes, he was the one chiefly responsible for destroying the Communist apparatus in North China by the end of 1935, as well as for executing without trial many innocent students.

The Young Marshal and General Yang Hu-ch'eng had been jointly responsible for the capture, and were trying to use "military persuasion" to force Chiang Kai-shek to accept the Young Marshal's eight demands. But Chiang refused to talk with them and demanded to be killed instead. He was a Confucianist to the backbone. "Face" was bred in his marrow.

The Young Marshal's eight demands were fully supported in Peking. Someone from the Tungpei People's Association had got the demands by private radio system, and they brought us a copy. They were:

Reorganize the Nanking government to include all parties.
Stop civil war and fight Japan immediately.
Release the patriotic leaders arrested in Shanghai.
Release all political prisoners.
Give freedom to organize for patriotic purposes.
Safeguard the freedom of the people to organize and to enjoy all political freedom.
Put the will of Sun Yat-sen into effect.
Call immediately a National Defense Conference.

The Tungpei people all agreed: Either you kill a tiger or he eats you. They knew that every one of them was a possible target for revenge—if Chang Hsueh-liang did not succeed. This was their moment of truth, building since September 1931. Every Tungpei man believed that if Chiang Kai-shek escaped, he would never forgive and would take revenge. (How right they were! The Young Marshal was still a prisoner on Taiwan over forty years later, not released until 1980.)

In the end, the only demands achieved, to speak of, were a temporary stop to the civil war during the fighting with Japan, though Chiang always kept his best troops to watch and blockade the Reds, and a release of prisoners was obtained after a time.

On the sixteenth of December the Soviet *Tass News* in mimeographed form was delivered to my husband's office. It was carried, still wet, by chit coolie to the half-dozen foreign correspondents in Peking, but it could not be mailed elsewhere until later. Ed was away, but David Yui came just as I was looking over the dispatches.

I read the *Tass News* with astonishment. My reaction was that the Russians had no information on the situation at all. I handed one page to David as I reread the other. David's hands trembled. His face drained pale as he read the unbelievable, false statements. He was stunned. I was afraid he would have a heart attack.

"They don't know anything." David's voice was low and hoarse with shock. "This is the Communist position in Sian they are attacking. This will harm the United Front."

The official government newspaper *Pravda* editorial was quoted:

The attempts to unite China . . . for a struggle against the foreign aggressor—such is the principal task which . . . confronts the Nanking Government. The forces of reaction inspired by the agents of the enemies of the Chinese people render stubborn resistance to these attempts. It is not accidental that the name of the well-known Japanese agent, Wang Ching-wei, is closely connected with the mutiny of Chang Hsueh-liang's troops. . . . Chang Hsueh-liang himself always conducted the policy of non-resistance to foreign intrusion. Now he . . . raises the banner allegedly of a struggle against Japan, while in reality he assists the dismemberment of the country and sows further chaos in China. . . . The Japanese incited and now incite the individual generals to come out against the Nanking Government. . . . The Japanese provocateurs won't be successful in covering up their traces. The Soviet Union remains true to its policy of strict non-intervention in the internal affairs of foreign states. The policy of the formation of "independent governments" and puppet states planted by the Japanese imperialists with an aim to seize Chinese territory is alien to the U.S.S.R. The wide masses of the Chinese people won't permit themselves to be deceived by the Japanese provocateurs and their mercenary agents. . . .

The above was dated *Moscow, December 14*. On the same date

the other Communist Party official paper, *Izvestia*, made a similar attack, with fantastic lies:

> In the past year took place a considerable rallying of all the forces of Chinese society around the Nanking government. . . . It is clear that whatever slogans and demands it uses for camouflage, it represents a danger not only for the Nanking Government but for the entire China as well. . . . The united popular front . . . should be regarded . . . not as a front against Nanking but as a front together with Nanking.

Izvestia then quoted an unspecified Japanese dispatch:

> "Chang Hsueh-liang's Government is supported by the U.S.S.R." . . . This obviously false information is circulated by Japanese sources.

David had been as astonished as the rest of us at the arrest of Chiang Kai-shek, but he knew the whole policy in Sian was carried out in consultation with the Red Army men, and that Chang Hsueh-liang conformed to their ideas exactly, except for this episode of arresting the Generalissimo. We did not then know who had engineered the arrest.

Well do I remember that moment of revelation when David and I looked at each other, speechless with horror. Not for the first time I thought, *I'm glad I'm not a Chinese*, as tears of pity came into my eyes for David and his beleaguered country, attacked from all sides, inside and out, with lies among other weapons. This kind of thing could turn public opinion in China, left, middle, and right, to anti-Soviet. It could turn Chang Hsueh-liang and the Tungpei Army against the Chinese Red Army. In Sian it would be beyond anybody's comprehension. The Fascists would be amused, but they also would never trust the U.S.S.R. (They never had.) It could even turn the Chinese Communists anti-Soviet—secretly, not openly.

David and I seemed to represent Chinese-American youth of the 1930s, leagued together by history. We were under attack by the Fascist powers and now by the U.S.S.R. as well. David was risking his life every day. For a year I had spent nearly all my time trying to help save China from Japan and from Fascist quislingism. We had never had any idea of implicating the U.S.S.R. in the "World Revolution" nor in the war against Japan. The whole idea was to mobilize China to defend itself, which could not be done without some democratic freedom. All we wanted was for the U.S.S.R. to stay out of Chinese affairs, just to let nature take its course. Now, the U.S.S.R. was suicidally attacking its friends, not its enemies.

I called the Tass correspondent on the phone. "Can you hold up getting these dispatches to the public for one day till I can get some information to you? Will you cable Moscow how mistaken they are and send them some facts?"

He said he could not consider such a thing; that he had no choice. I burst into tears and could not continue talking. I knew he might lose his job, but this seemed like a small thing compared to what was at stake (which became more apparent some thirty years later, when China and the Soviet Union were in a stance of near warfare against each other).

David had been listening in despair.

I hung up the phone and told David that he *had* to go to the Tass office and tell them the whole story, give them the Communist point of view.

"I can't do such a thing," he said. "We're not allowed ever to go there or to have anything at all to do with anyone from the Soviet Union. It's impossible."

"Nevertheless, it's got to be done. You'll have to sacrifice yourself, I guess. I'll go with you and take all the responsibility and tell them. I'm not a Communist and I'm an American—they ought to be ashamed to refuse to listen to me."

"You are right," said David, and requested a piece of paper to write a memorandum for them. There was not a minute to spare. The Tass chit coolie could be called back before the dispatches were given to the Chinese press—maybe. I handed David paper with carbons under it for the record. I kept a copy. For David to be expelled from the Communist party for breaking discipline seemed like nothing at such a moment.

I called the Number 1 boy to get a couple of rickshas, and I put on my leopardskin coat and my blue beret. Very firmly then, and forever after, I tied my red-white-and-blue scarf around my neck with the ends trailing out behind.

We arrived at the big Soviet Embassy compound. The Tass man received us, trying to be polite. He was young and obviously felt just as trapped as we, and just as puzzled. Briefly, I explained who David was and why he was there. David handed his memo over, and the Tass man took hold of it as if it were a stick of lighted dynamite.

In his memo David explained that five hundred students had left

Peking to go to Sian to create the democratic United Front there. He said, "Chiang Kai-shek played his last trick—to separate the Tungpei Army and cut its contacts with the Reds and to cut the United Front—then he meant to disband them. . . . If Chiang Kai-shek had not been arrested he would have used all forces to attack the Reds and destroy the Tungpei Army and to suppress the people's front. . . . It was a brilliant stroke to capture Chiang Kai-shek—it polarized all the pro- and anti-Japanese forces." His main point was that the cause of the Sian Incident was "Chiang Kai-shek's attempt to destroy the United Front."

David was not expelled from the party. On the contrary, he was subsequently sent as delegate to the Communist party conference in Yenan in 1937. While there, he made a point of calling on me on May 8 to explain that he agreed with Mao Tse-tung's policy as stated in *Chieh Fang*: "The central line is the struggle for democracy. . . . At present, the Communist party must unite all classes to fight Japan."

I had always thought the central line should be democracy; that was the mainspring of the December 9th movement. I would never have helped any students who were opposed to democracy, even if they had been for the war with Japan.

I hasten to add that I am not so small and childish as to continue to blame the U.S.S.R. I merely wonder what there is in the nature of "socialist ethics" and "socialist legality" that makes such situations possible. The Russians were in an even worse mess than the Chinese at this time. Only a few months later, the 1937 executions took place in Russia, and the story was told in China that the editor of either *Izvestia* or *Pravda* was one of those executed (all Chinese hoped so, even the rightists). It was stated that such persons were "traitors" who were actually working with the Nazis and the Japanese. Possibly one of them had thought up these fantastic concoctions to sabotage the Sian Incident. Later, when Yagoda, head of the Soviet secret police, was executed as an agent of the Nazis, the Chinese wondered if such intelligence men had not intentionally sabotaged the interests of the U.S.S.R. by lying about the Sian Incident—or else they themselves had believed lies told by or to their own sources.

The *Pravda-Izvestia* editorials did no one any good. They did generate a poison, in the minds of Chinese of all shades of thinking, that persisted into the 1960s, when the Soviet-Chinese hostility reached belligerent proportions. The Chinese Communists felt they suffered more from their "friends" than from their enemies.

We did not know at that time who or what it was that saved the life of Chiang Kai-shek. Mao Tse-tung had intended to hold a mass trial for him, with foregone conclusions. Not until late 1937, after my return from Yenan, did we learn the inside story, dug up by Ed in Shanghai and published in his *Random Notes on Red China*.*

Nothing that has happened in my lifetime has been as dramatic and strange as the Sian Incident—and it becomes more so with every new version. It reminds me of the classic Japanese film *Rashomon*, in which every observer of a murder saw it in a different way. Ed and I planned to write a book together on the subject of the Sian Incident, and on my own I actually did begin a few pages, intending perhaps an opera, perhaps a suspense movie.

If China has a "soul," it is immortalized in the Sian syndrome. It is impossible for anyone who has never tried to ascertain the facts about a historical event in China to imagine the difficulty of doing so—not to speak of the problems involved in publishing them. Sian remains one of the all-time challenges in Chinese puzzles.

At the time of the Sian Incident, not only did the liberal Chinese—as well as the Communists—have the greatest respect for the Soviet Union, but they did not want to admit any secret problems to outsiders, much less to break with the Soviets. The Communist discipline forced through after the Sian anticlimax was absolute. It shows the quality of Mao's leadership that he subordinated his own personal fury and pushed through the new line. Yet the scars of this traumatic experience will always remain in the Chinese psyche.

But it was not the Reds who had captured Chiang Kai-shek. This plan had been formulated by the Young Marshal's own three advisers, young non-Communist leftists—Colonel Sun Ming-chiu, Ying Teh-tien, and Miao Feng-shan. We learned the inside story from Miao in Hong Kong in September 1938. They led the young officers' group which wanted the Tungpei Army alliance with the Reds. The strange, enforced release of Chiang left them feeling betrayed by everyone, including Chou En-lai and the Communists. Miao had been dumbfounded when he read that the *Red Army Daily* called them left-infantilists influenced by "Trotskyists," which he said was not true.

* Harvard University Press, Cambridge, Mass., 1957.

Some of the young officers wanted to kill Chou En-lai for betraying them, but the Young Marshal's three advisers argued against it; they left Sian and were given protection by General P'eng Teh-huai.

This was the most unattractive thing about the Chinese Reds in 1937: In order to prevent a split in their party and to enforce discipline, they threatened to call anyone who opposed the release of Chiang Kai-shek or the settlement of the Sian Incident a "Trotskyist"—or in their word, a *Tu-lotsky-p'ai*. One can imagine the horror of Miao at having such an alien term thrown at him by the very Red Army people he had been trying to save from further attack by Chiang Kai-shek.

We first saw Miao Feng-shan about four days after the December 12 event. A Tungpei friend had secretly brought him to call. I can see Miao now in his foreign-style brimmed hat, black heavy overcoat with wide beaver collar, and lavender spats, his idea of a foreign bourgeois disguise. He was thin, nervous, sensitive, charged with tension and emotion, dedicated—even fanatical—and also likable and attractive. He told us he and his two young friends had been the prime movers of the Sian event, and that he had complete influence over the Young Marshal. He was a new and innocent convert to revolution.

Miao said he had to get to Sian immediately and wanted a foreigner to protect him on the way, as his life was in danger if he was discovered. He also wanted a newspaperman to send out the facts from Sian. Ed was a major hero in China by this time, but he was busy writing his book. Miao was in despair.

"Jim Bertram will go," I said instantly, hoping to make it up to Jim for refusing to let him accompany me on my trip to Sian. I thought Jim might be able to get to the Communist areas, as he so much wished to do.

Ed was not anxious for the *London Daily Herald* to be mixed up with Miao, but he agreed to let Jim go, though he had hardly any money to pay a correspondent. Miao was suspicious and insisted that I "guarantee" Jim, since I had suggested him.

I flew to the phone to locate Jim. He had to rush to catch the next train, with Miao posing as his secretary.

Jim told the story in his first book.* They had to go secretly, away from army posts. On Christmas Eve, the day before Chiang was released, they were still held up trying to cross the Yellow River at the temple to Emperor Yu. In this wild, Byronic spot, with high winter

---

* James Bertram, *Chrisis in China* (London: Macmillian, 1937).

winds howling, Jim read his precious Shakespeare in bed. A young lieutenant refused them a pass until Christmas Day. Miao didn't arrive in Sian until December 27, two days late.

The Tungpei armies and young people disappeared after this, ground up in the *tao-tieh* ogre jaws of history. Yet it was they who had forged the United Front in the beginning. I have always been against assassination, but I saw the provocations in 1936.

CHAPTER 27

Anticlimax at Christmas

During the days between the arrest of Chiang Kai-shek on December 12 and his release on Christmas Day, all kinds of Tungpei people called on us with information and misinformation. I died a thousand deaths every day worrying about what was happening or might happen to all the students and Tungpei people. Ed didn't get involved the way I did; he compartmentalized China affairs. He actually never worried, not even about himself. I made up for both of us.

Ed was not cynical, but he had lived in China long enough not to be surprised by anticlimax. It was considered axiomatic then that the Chinese would always compromise.

Sian was a lesson in *realpolitik*. You have to grow much taller than you are to gain perspective. Bigger than China was the potential alliance between the Soviet Union, Britain, and the United States on the eve of World War II. It was that historic necessity which governed the Sian denouement, nothing else—the need to use Chiang Kai-shek as a liaison. The Soviet Union would not want to jeopardize this over such a small thing as a few thousand Red troops isolated way out near the Great Wall and a few yelling students on the streets of Sian and Peking.

Agnes Smedley had got to Sian a day or so after Chiang's arrest and was sending out radio broadcasts of the facts. Over the wires from New York came a repudiation of her by the Communists, who did not want to be contaminated by the Sian affair. As she was not and never would be a Communist, this was gratuitous; it could never be explained to any kind of Chinese.

The American Communists always were and still are a mystery to the Chinese. In 1949, Anna Louise Strong, the pro-China writer, was arrested in Moscow as an "American spy," for the purpose of silencing her as a public nuisance. This was strange, but it was much stranger to

216

the Chinese that the American Communists refused to intervene in any way or to secure a hearing for her for the sake of simple justice.

The seeds of alienation between the Chinese and the Soviets and their Communist followers were sown along the road, beginning at least during the Sian Incident. Since Sian, I have felt that I understand China and the Chinese, but in 1936 I was thankful that China was not my personal or national problem. I learned a good lesson, which was to stay out of the water if you can't swim. I never wanted to be involved in any Communist party or situation. I was not tough and had no wish to become so. This does not mean that I failed to see the monumental achievements and special qualities of such people; only that it is not my way of doing things.

To me, the worst thing about the Chinese was that they were never taught not to tell lies, not even as children. Telling lies and deceiving people was one of the great arts of ancient China, part of the technique of rule and also of keeping face. The result was mistrust all along the line. It is a big revolution, not only in ethics but in tactics, for the Communists to adopt the Puritan ethic against telling lies. This was Mao Tse-tung's idea from the first. Under the Communists, the principle of "confession" is chiefly for the purpose of instilling a new ethic of being truthful, not only with others but with oneself. I do not myself happen to like this principle of confession—I am for privacy— but it is very healthful in China today.

I have always believed truth is on the right side. Lies only serve a bad cause. It is true that victories may be won temporarily, but this is not because of the lies alone but for other reasons as well. The truth never harmed a good cause or helped a bad one—not in the last ac- counting. You have to be able to trust information, to trust people.

I was surprised to find Ed becoming a social butterfly after his trip, though this is a natural reaction to danger, a letdown such as soldiers experience after a battle. He was being lionized. He even ac- quired two female admirers.

During the holidays we had been to a party with Harry and Betty Price, and at ten P.M. we four were in a taxi driving along the mall of the city wall to our house. Next morning the news came that our neighbor two doors away, Pamela Werner, had been murdered, proba- bly at exactly ten P.M. Her body was found near the wall where we had passed. Her heart had been cut out—probably after or at the time of death, for sale as "medicine." Or was it a warning, a form of terrorism?

Pamela was seventeen, just home from school in Tientsin for the few holidays. It would be hard to find a motive for her murder. She was last seen riding her bicycle along the mall, which is where I was well known to ride mine. Was it a case of mistaken identity? The Japanese and the Chinese Fascists had much to gain by frightening both Ed and me into leaving Peking.

I was already nervous with worry about dozens of my friends on whom the Fascists would surely take revenge after the forced release of Chiang Kai-shek. Pamela's murder was terrifying. Ed paid little attention to it; he went to parties all the same. But one evening I stayed home.

On this early evening, I received a visit from a Scotland Yard man from Tientsin who was investigating the murder. His face was pale green and he was shivering—not only from the cold.

He requested a brandy and was horrified to find that my husband had left me alone. "Don't you realize that the murderer has to be hiding somewhere, probably nearby?" he asked. He found our neighborhood spooky and didn't see how we could possibly live there.

I told him that it was precisely because our neighborhood was spooky that we felt safe there. The whole corner near the Fox Tower was supposed to be haunted. And besides, I was "alone" with fifteen servants; all four of the men armed with bigswords.

"There are no lights anywhere," he complained. "Anything could happen way out here in the dark." He implored me to pack up and leave immediately—to go anywhere rather than stay there. He considered Pamela's the most gruesome murder he'd ever heard of and speculated that the murderer was probably a maniac. "Or it could be something else," he said. "A warning to foreigners, to foreigners like you—or more especially, your husband. Or it could be mistaken identity."

We were sitting warm in front of the fireplace, but I also began to shiver.

I already knew, from a likable young "Fascist" Chinese who did my tailoring, that he and other local Fascists met on top of the city wall not far from our house at certain times of the moon to practice the T'ai Chi Chuan exercises done by the Boxers in 1900 as magic. Such primitive minds also believed in organ medicine, and could have cut out a murder victim's heart for such use. Of course, it was also true that the Japanese could pay such a person to kill anyone for no reason at all.

Ed came home late and he had been drinking too much, which

was all but unheard of. Always he felt himself the favored child of Providence—which he was. Always I worried ten times more about him than he ever did about himself. The murder of Pamela was nothing but a local incident to Ed. He really believed foreigners were still sacrosanct in China.

The mystery was never solved or even reasonably guessed at. I never really believed the Pamela Werner murder was directed against Ed or me, yet there was always a question.

As usual, I was working very hard. Even answering Ed's mail, so that he could write his book, was a big job now. *Life* magazine had bought seventy-three of his photographs, and *Asia* two, for which, to our surprise, they paid $50 gold apiece. The North American Newspaper Alliance was syndicating a series of his articles. *Asia* was publishing Mao Tse-tung's autobiography. In January, Ed was asked to be editor of a new magazine in New York called *Amerasia*, but he refused. Our book, *Living China*, was being reviewed favorably in England and America. I myself was being deluged with requests for articles, but I felt it was too urgent to get Ed's report and book out.

Though Reuters was attacking Jim Bertram as a "propagandist"—the only Britisher willing to try to find any facts at first hand—a big, big change was occurring, and Ed's report from the Northwest was the catalyst. The missionaries in China were intensely interested in the report and were asking Ed to give talks everywhere. One of them even said, "The Reds can march on Peking any day, so far as I am concerned."

Then, in the midst of all this activity, a true landmark appeared in the scenery—the missionaries had begun to wake up and decided to "join the club" in a new magazine project.

CHAPTER 28

We Start a New Magazine
Called *democracy*

It was a cold, windy January day in 1937. The Number 1 servant
brought in a calling card announcing J. Spencer Kennard, a name
totally unknown to us.

He had been given $1,000 gold by the Friends Service Commit-
tee to start a journal of applied Christian ethics, and wanted to use it to
reach the young people of China, he informed me, his eyes sparkling
with anticipation and fervor. He thought that Ed and I had more influence on them than any other foreigners in China. "No one else is
qualified to edit it," he said. He would give us the money and a free
hand on two conditions: that Edgar Snow's name appear as editor and
that the journal carry the subtitle A *Journal of Applied Christian
Ethics*.

"My husband's too busy now to do a bit of other work," I said,
"but I'll do it." I told him his arrival seemed like an act of God. If ever
a magazine was needed, it was just at that very moment in China. And
nobody had ever before offered us so much as $1 mex.

"Drop everything. He's offering you $1,000 gold," I wrote on
Kennard's calling card and sent it by the Number 1 servant to Ed's
garden den, where he growled happily at interruptions to his book—he
was enjoying this sudden fame.

Ed joined us in front of the glowing fireplace. His grin reached to
Kansas City when Kennard stated that Edgar Snow was the only channel through which Christian ethics could reach the youth of China.

"I have nothing against Christian ethics. I was brought up as an
altar boy," Ed laughed with delight. But, he said, he had not a minute
to spare. "I'm writing a book—supposed to be, anyway."

I said I'd do all the work if he'd just put his name on as editor and
let us publish chapters from the book. We'd have a scoop in every

issue. Also we could publish Jim Bertram's writing on the Sian Incident. What a spectacular opportunity!

"Excellent, excellent!" Kennard's intense eyes were approving. "There's no Christian ethic more important than telling the truth, especially to Quakers. Christ was crucified for it. It was Jesus himself who invented socialism. Read Acts, Two, of the Bible if you don't think so."

Ed choked on his tea and macaroons, and reached for a Camel.

We could use his name as editor, his photographs, anything that wasn't copyrighted elsewhere, Ed decided.

We all three shook hands.

"This thing is bigger than we are," I said. "We'll get all kinds of people involved. I'll be the managing editor, at least to organize it and get it going."

We all shook hands again, and after we took Kennard to the door, Ed turned to me and said, smiling, "Wonder what old Mao would think of this?"

When anything incredible happened, we used to use that phrase, in the kind of affectionate recognition of Mao Tse-tung that Americans use in referring to Lincoln as "old Abe." In our minds we imagined Mao Tse-tung in his cave wondering what to make of this type of thing and where he would place it in his new Marxist ideology.

It never entered my mind that I did not know how to start a magazine. I had been editor of grade school papers and co-editor of the high school yearbook; that was my editing experience. I was painfully aware that my "great book" would be yet further delayed. But I knew it was *dead right* to start the magazine; the moment of truth was at hand. Also I wanted a local outlet for my own writings; I had been making carbon copies for my small but avid following, and the sheer manual labor was exhausting.

Ed was not supposed to waste his time on any of it, but he refused to stay away from the long, argumentative meetings which actually did forge a new consensus. He was a real journalist—he loved even the smell of printer's ink and paste. Was not his father the owner of the Snow Printing Company which printed the *Kansas City Star*?

First, we telephoned Hubert S. Liang at Yenching University. He would become the moderator of our editorial board meetings. In the beginning there were only Liang, Kennard, the two Snows, and O. J. Todd, an American engineer who soon resigned as treasurer due to incompatibility with Hubert. Kennard's missionary recruit, whose name was Shaw, resigned when he found we were illiterate and intended to use no capital letters on our titles.

We mobilized the other December 9th sympathizers from Yenching: Harry Price, Ran Sailer, and Chang Tung-sung. Then Jim Bertram joined, on returning from Sian, and brought in Ida Pruitt, a missionary China-born and the first social worker in China. Jim lived in her vast three-courtyard palace, along with many Pekingese dogs and two adopted daughters. We each subscribed 150 Chinese dollars to the project, and Mr. Edwards, head of the YMCA, agreed to find a "guarantor" for us.

The board meetings debated every problem of human existence. We agreed on only one thing: free speech. The magazine was to be a forum which "recognized the taboos of neither Right nor Left," Ed wrote. "In two years, perhaps three, a mighty explosion is destined to shake the earth once more when all the arming forces of reaction . . . attempt to destroy the historic edifices of human freedom." We used grandiose language. We were dealing with grand ideas.

Ed and I decided on the name—*democracy*—but in those days the word was in ill repute. Even the missionaries were afraid it would cut us off from the students. It was also unfortunately true that no word remotely resembling this term existed in Chinese.

No sooner had the name been voted upon than Ran Sailer demanded a dictatorship: "Can't we have an understanding that you two *are* the paper . . . telling us where to get off, where you want us and where you don't, and all that . . .? If it goes that way you can raise my hundred and fifty dollars to three hundred."

As editor, I wrote for the first issue the policy article on "China and Democracy," saying: "It is in recognition of the great menace to civilization brought about by the temporary resurgence of all the forces of tyranny and despotism against which Democracy has fought its victorious battles in the past that we have ranged ourselves under this banner. . . . The special aspect of Democracy that interests us is . . . the discovery and dissemination of that deadly foe of reaction and invincible ally of freedom—the truth."

We had to think for ourselves. Democracy has many faces and many reincarnations in human history. One essential is the opportunity for upward mobility, the right to develop and improve. In China then, it meant either mobilizing the people or permitting them to mobilize against Japan. But Chiang Kai-shek was too weak and frightened to allow this. Of course, he knew it would be bound to get out of hand and threaten his regime.

Exactly what China needed in 1937 was an article by Yenching missionary president J. Leighton Stuart on democracy in China, side by side with one by Edgar Snow on Mao Tse-tung. That was what our first issue contained.

I had the first two issues of the bimonthly ready to start on April 1, yet the magazine did not appear until May. Except for Hubert Liang, I was the only one who truly loved this infant. But when I began organizing my own trip to the Communist areas in March, I had to turn the delicate child over to a total stranger to China. No one else would take this unpaid, dangerous job, and I had a hard time recruiting him.

I was holding Wednesday Nights in my sort-of-Madame-Récamier salon. Jim Bertram arrived one evening with an attractive young Englishman sporting a long cigarette holder. He sat back languidly, surveying me through a cloud of Virginia tobacco smoke as if I were something dragged out of a nineteenth-century missionary barrel. John Leaning was irreverent, witty, sophisticated, with an air of studied carelessness and a mischievous twinkle in his pale-blue eyes—in no way the type to inspire confidence in our missionary friends. (He and Kennard immediately became deadly enemies on all points of the compass.) John was visiting Peking for only a few days, and he was not much encumbered with capital. He had read Classics and Politics at Oxford and Princeton, worked for a year in Europe on *Fortune,* and been secretary to Sir Hugh Dalton, who was Undersecretary for Foreign Affairs in the Labour government and chief of the Labour party.

"I was an expert on unbalanced budgets," John explained.

"Capital! Just what we need in Peking," I said, wondering how to get him to join the club.

From talking so much with Chinese for several years, my approach in persuasion was to be clear, lucid, pellucid, repetitive, and emphatic, in basic English. I always sat on the edge of my chair bursting with gung ho Girl Scout enthusiasm, pumping this urgency into my audience. But John was not the Boy Scout type. I was never able to find anything he approved of. I was in no danger of being admired by him—which had been a problem with Jim Bertram. But I forgave John everything because he was so uncompromisingly anti-Fascist, and fresh from firsthand contact with Fascists, Nazis, and Franco followers. My idea was to put him in charge of all the anti-Fascist extra-China affairs, and to keep him strictly *out* of China affairs.

As I artfully led up to the subject of the magazine, John shrugged. "*Democracy*! You must be joking! You've missed too many boats."

It was unwise to bring up 1776, I realized with my crafty Chinese training. And the big bridge had yet to be crossed.

"The subtitle has to be A *Journal of Applied Christian Ethics*. That's the condition for getting Kennard's one thousand dollars gold."

"Oh, my God! This *is* Alice in Wonderland!" John actually stood up and paced the floor holding his head in his hands in merry ridicule. "O *frabjous* day!"

John refused at first to be contaminated by association with either title. Finally he compromised on the name but never would he allow the subtitle. The board voted to give it up and John agreed to stay, but only if we could pay his bare living expenses and rent a tiny Chinese house. But he did not want Kennard on the premises!

I kept to myself my opinion of a Great Labour Party Anti-Fascist who would quibble over trifles while Hitler was about to march over Europe, and Japan was ready to strike directly at us in a few weeks. Also in 1937, the Soviet Union was cutting off the heads of the old Bolsheviks instead of trying to change their minds by any despised "democracy."

John and I did have one thing in common. We both loved the verses of Ogden Nash. In the midst of failing to save China, I had not entirely lost my American sense of humor. Not only did John listen to my puns and non-sequitur witticisms, he even took his long cigarette holder out of his mouth and laughed. (He published some of my Nash imitations in our magazine, which also horrified Kennard.)

On March 25, I wrote to J. B. Powell in Shanghai: "Ed is in the hospital with a kidney stone—and I am rushed to death." I asked him to exchange ads with *democracy*.

On the very day my husband went to the hospital for an operation, the first proofs arrived from the printshop, a place where not a soul knew any English at all—they just copied down letter for letter. The dummy had to be made up immediately and returned. Neither John nor I had ever made up a dummy. I had expected Ed to supervise this first operation.

John came to our house. We spread the proofs out on the ballroom floor where once friends of the Prince of Wales had danced, and John presented an ultimatum:

"I don't want to live at Claridge's. I don't want any salary. But I do want privacy. I can't stand the sight of Kennard even once more. If you can't keep him off my premises, I'll have to leave Peking just as soon as this first issue is out."

I didn't say one word. Big salt tears dropped steadily into the library paste along with John's cigarette ashes as we scissored and pasted. I wept for John's cavalier blue-pencilling of my carefully diplomatic sentences that tried so hard to build our little anti-Fascist front among conflicting elements. I wept for China. I wept for the future of England, facing such Labour party fastidiousness while the boots of Hitler's Brown Shirts echoed through Europe. I wept for "The Story of Sian," Jim Bertram's contribution, as I handed it to John to paste up. As for Dr. Stuart's article, I pasted that up myself to keep John's selfish heathen hands off this holy writ. I couldn't even smile to see that John had included my Ogden Nash rhyme on "Dictator Ships":

In case of shipwreck you haven't even got a straw-vote to cling to
Though you may have a pretty brass band playing "Nearer My God to
    Thee" to sing to.

John couldn't possibly imagine why I should be upset. He had only been in China a few days.

We climbed into rickshas to rush the dummy to the printer in a *hutung* so dark and sinister that even our rickshamen thought it so. I had avoided going along the desolate mall where our neighbor Pamela Werner's body had been found a few weeks earlier. The night was black, gloomy, cold, and windy. We heard only the pad-pad of the rickshamen in the winding *hutungs*, lighted by their swinging lanterns. John looked apprehensive.

From the printshop, we unwound through more dark, narrow *hutungs* to see Ed at the hospital. John looked enviously at the white private room so brightly lighted—contemporary Rockefeller, not Victorian missionary.

Ed's operation was not entirely successful—the situation bothered him for some years.

When I saw John after Peking, it was in Hong Kong in 1938, where he was helping Madame Sun Yat-sen. Both of us were actually emaciated from dysentery and looked ten years older. "Have you read any Ogden Nash lately?" we echoed each other.

(John later married the daughter of an American China *mission-*

ary. In 1941, they helped me find our little house in Madison, Connecticut. I next saw them in San Francisco in 1945 when I was at the United Nations Conference as a correspondent. Still with his long cigarette holder, John was enjoying being chief of the British Information Services. I was told he was indignant at being a victim of McCarthyism. He went on to teach Greek and Latin at Wilbraham Academy in Connecticut.)

The last issue of *democracy* was captured on the presses by the Japanese when they attacked Peking on July 7, 1937. *democracy* was a brief flash of lightning on a dark horizon. Only six months after the magazine closed, the British consul in Shanghai was trying to get us to revive it. And in 1939, Kennard wrote from Szechuan: "Frank Price will join Hubert and myself" in reviving the magazine. Frank was Harry's brother and the missionary closest to Madame Chiang Kai-shek. We had come a long way since December 9.

Hubert Liang wrote to me in 1974:

> It was at 13 K'uei Chia Ch'ang that *democracy* was conceived. . . .
> Viewed in the context of the time and historical conditions it might have been one of the most important English periodicals ever put out in China. It was an immediate, sensational success, taking China's intellectual world by storm. . . . Many of its articles were translated and published in Chinese periodicals. . . . The Kuomintang took notice and protested against its pro-Communist leanings. . . . Even the arch-enemy of China, Matsuoka, then Japan's Director of the South Manchurian Railways, for purposes best known to himself, bought up 400 copies of the first issue of *democracy* to be sent back to Japan.

What happened to all those bright and argumentative people who started *democracy* with such high hopes?

Hubert Liang, who was a second-generation Protestant, taught English at the University of Nanking from 1954 to the present. He was the first of my old Chinese friends to write to me after the Nixon rapprochement in 1972. He spent nearly two years on a successful lecture tour in the United States before returning to China in 1982.

Kennard wrote to me from retirement in 1974; he was a Christian socialist and, I think, a Baptist missionary. He once wrote to me from Szechuan about 1939, asking me to come there to help revive *democracy.*

Harry and Betty Price ended up in Sevierville, Tennessee, still teaching. Harry celebrated his seventy-fifth birthday there in 1975 and I received an invitation.

Ran and Louise Sailer visited China in 1973 and talked with fifty of their old Chinese friends. They held a memorial service for Ran when he died a few years later.

Chang Tung-sung was one of the most influential intellectuals of China in the 1930s—he was my Hegel teacher. He founded his own party in 1931, the Kuo Chia Chu I Pai, and in 1944 was a founder of the China Democratic League, which allied with the Communists to form the 1949 government, under which he held high posts. During the Japanese occupation, he was a prisoner of the Japanese along with other Yenching professors, and was reported to have attempted suicide three times. Chang Tung-sung and his brother, Carson, were the chief social democrats of China; they once asked Ed and me to edit their national magazine—or me solo, if Ed couldn't—but we refused. Chang had edited Bergson's *Creative Evolution* in 1918 and was one of the few people in Peking I would talk with on philosophic problems.

In the 1930s, everyone wanted the Americans to act progressively in China—but only as individuals. The big problem then, as now, was that China should move into a form of socialism that was not anti-Western but could co-exist with the rest of the world.

PART THREE

YENAN

CHAPTER 29

Inside Red China—
My Trip to Yenan, 1937

When I left Peking for Yenan on April 21, 1937, I had no idea of the problems that would make it impossible for me to return until October 17—including the Japanese occupation of North China that began on July 7.

A whole new folklore and national mythology were born in the caves and hills of Yenan during the ten years following my visit there in 1937. A new religion was created around Mao Tse-tung, and the "Yenan spirit" became the theme of the Cultural Revolution of 1966, the purpose of which was to revive the classical revolutionary mystique. It was in Yenan that Mao Tse-tung studied and wrote his famous theses which are now scripture. Like a Delphic oracle, he drew the outline of the future—and was usually right. Visitors from all over the world make the pilgrimage to Yenan in the same way Westerners have for the past 2,500 years made the pilgrimage to Delphi at Mount Parnassus.

Except for nearby caves, the city of Yenan has disappeared, bombed to rubble in 1938–1939 by the Japanese, among other acts of total and unnecessary barbarism. The Chinese have rebuilt Yenan, though not as it was. But a photographic record of the old city exists in my more than three hundred photographs, taken in 1937, of the town, the Sung dynasty gates and the city wall, so massive for so tiny a city.

Yenan was set like a gem inside its wall and crown of hills. The city had pride of person, with ornately carved marble *p'ailous* arching the narrow streets, and brick houses inside the compound walls. Yenan stood sentinel for civilization, which elsewhere had survived in spirit only by hiding deep in ancient caves or behind mud walls that proclaimed the kowtowing abjection of total poverty. For hundreds of years, vast cavalry hordes from Central Asia had thundered through the narrow strategic valley on their way to conquest of China's Great

Northwest. Every hilltop bristled with battlements, where red-tasseled spears had held the fortress—and now descendants of those sentries handled rifles to guard the pass.

Yenan became as popular a subject for folk art as the Taoist heaven and its queen. The lazy, muddy Yen River still embraces the rebuilt town, and the *feng-shui* pagoda still stands on the hilltop. But the river is no longer a moat; over it a new bridge, as famous in China today as the one over the Yangtze, is arched against the floods. I suppose the old mound commemorating a long-ago matriarchal worship is still there, but the animistic Taoist nature-gods that once protected the gate of every dwelling have escaped into the troglodyte caves of remote ancestors.

It seems strange now that a young American woman should have become a part of the Yenan story. My book *Inside Red China* * was the first on Yenan, for many years the only one; and it is still the only book that personifies the old city and its special mystique. All over China young students read the translation and set out for the city, feeling confident that if an American girl could make her way there, so could they. In Yenan itself, my book was specified reading at the university, as was my husband's *Red Star Over China*, the setting for which was Pao-an; Yenan was not captured by the Communists until several months after Ed had left the Northwest.

The marvelous setting in history for the Yenan mystique takes some explaining. Mao Tse-tung and his column of southerners left Kiangsi in 1934 and, after a year and six thousand miles of the Long March, ended up right in the cradle of Chinese civilization, protected in a curve of the Great Wall, half encircling the remote upper reaches of the Yellow River. Yenan lies in a triangle with its apex at the most northerly Great Wall crossing of the Yellow River. (Pao-an, where the Long March paused along the way, was even more remote, thirty miles farther west in North Shensi, a place where life was barely sustainable.)

It was in Shensi, near Yenan, that the legendary First Emperor, or founder of China, had his being—or nonbeing. Huang Ti's tomb is the oldest known in China, dating back about five thousand years; the Great Wall itself was built around two thousand years ago. Huang Ti was followed by Yao, Shun, and Yu, who first tamed the floods on the

* Doubleday-Doran, New York, 1939; reprinted by Da Capo Press, Inc., New York, 1977; Da Capo Press paperback edition, 1979.

Yellow River. The fertile loess organic soil made human life possible in these desertlike areas.

One learns to think twice in North Shensi, where bare existence has had to hide in caves from the time of the saber-toothed tiger to the bombing planes of Japan and Chiang Kai-shek. Living in a cave, one is faced with eternity; one thinks long thoughts. The electrical currents in the organic earth come from deep sources, and if you have an ear to the ground, you can hear reverberating the sound waves of thousands of years.

Mao Tse-tung has said that he did not pick the route of the Long March or its destination. Greatness was thrust upon Yenan by necessity, not choice. Yet it was here, in the caves of the ancient civilization that Confucius tried to imitate, that Mao Tse-tung finally slew the old dragon of Confucianism—if it is truly slain yet. One does not have much respect for Confucius in a place where Chinese civilization was born, where it stagnated and died a living death for at least two thousand years past, with little but a cave to serve as monument.

CHAPTER 30

Sian

David Yui set the time for my trip to the Red armies. He told me that a Communist Party Congress would be held in Yenan early in May. He was going as a delegate, and I could go on the same train with him—pretending we didn't know each other. In Sian he would arrange with the Red Army liaison office for my trip to Yenan.

For the first time, far-flung Communist leaders would be together. I could interview them and add to the store of oral autobiography that Ed had begun in Pao-an. A few days later they would be hundreds of miles away, back at their military posts with enemy lines intervening. This opportunity might never come again, at least for me.

Fullsea Wang, who had practically taken up residence in our living room in silent observation of an American menage, volunteered to go as my interpreter. He wanted to do articles for his Tungpei newspaper in Peking. And David planned to ask Ch'en Han-p'o to be my liaison with the Red Army office in Sian. Ch'en was still editing the newspaper there, though our dear friend Chang Chao-lin had already had to escape from the Fascist takeover.

I had lost my eiderdown sleeping bag made from Gobi's favorite silk quilt on my first trip to Sian. I now took our two best camel's hair blankets to be made into a sleeping bag, which I would fold up in a big straw suitcase along with a camp cot.

At the last moment, Ed became silent and uncooperative. He refused to roll up my sleeping bag and complained about still being convalescent from the kidney-stone operation. He was not sorry to get me and all my multifarious and nefarious activities out of the house so that he could concentrate on writing his book. Yet, "I don't see what you've got to be so happy about," he grumbled.

Ed and Jim escorted me along the deserted mall to the station. Both were warned not to let anyone else know where I was going. I felt elated as I waved to them from the train steps.

On the two-day train trip, I ate *latzuchi* (chicken and peppers) and studied my list of words and phrases: louse, flea, bugs, donkey, make room clean, and similar useful concepts for the traveler.

From time to time I sent notes to my husband: "Chengchow, 9 P.M. I arrived without mishap. W. [Wang] was sick on the train. D. [David] was there all right. . . . It was certainly grand traveling first-class. I'll do it permanently from now on."

From Chengchow the Lung-hai Railway followed along the Yellow River to Tungkuan, the strategic pass for three provinces. Next was Sian, capital of the Northwest for over two thousand years of history and a Neolithic site long before that.

All the mutinous Tungpei troops had been forced to leave Sian before April 1 and were being shunted to oblivion along the railways, as Central Government troop trains arrived to watch them and replace them. The Young Marshal was still a prisoner of Chiang Kai-shek in his Nanking capital.

I had plenty of time to think about the anticlimax in Sian. After the release of Chiang Kai-shek on Christmas, Tungpei refugees had been scattered; as an entity they simply disappeared. The Fascists were just completing the takeover of Sian during the few days after my arrival.

I arrived at the modern Sian station at eight in the morning on April 23, and perforce had to go to the Sian Guest House, where all foreigners were required to stay, under police watch. Then—act of sheer idiocy—" . . . before the police arrived I left and Ch'en found a place in a Chinese family," I wrote to Ed on April 24, adding: "I am now freezing to death in an empty store room . . . hope I won't get pneumonia. It . . . is still raining today. The roads are terrible, so don't know when I can leave. . . . Yeh is coming to see me at eight."

Yeh Chien-ying was, with Chou En-lai, in charge of the Red Army's secret liaison office in Sian. Chang Wen-ping worked under them. (In 1974, Yeh became minister of defense of the Peking government, when his lifelong friend Chou was premier.)

My letter to Ed, written with blue fingers among sacks of grain, continued:

> Ch'en Han-p'o says the facts here are these: Sian is under absolute control of Ku Chu-tung, no freedom of press nor organization. Not one mass organization is left. Not a single Tungpei Army official person is left, only a few students. . . . And not only has Yang Hu-ch'eng no

power, but he is *forced* to leave for Europe in a few days, on the 28th. (This is still a secret.) Who will lead his troops is not known. Like Tungpei, they will now be under the Central Government. . . . Ku has four divisions here in Sian. . . . Yang has the two regiments agreed on for trimmings and no more. . . . Hu Chung-nan has remaining two divisions (he had four originally and two were completely destroyed . . . in fighting about two weeks ago.)

Hsu Hsiang-ch'ien, Red Army commander, had only 3,000 men in Ninghsia and lost 2,000. Badly defeated by the Mohammedans. . . . Of the 500 Vanguard students the Young Marshal had, all are in Pengpu with no work, except those who joined the Reds. . . . Sian is very desolate. . . . It's absolutely dead. Only two or three guests in the Guest House.

The interview with Mausie [Mao Tse-tung] was widely reprinted here. . . . I *urge* you to get the book out at all costs this spring and get it translated immediately . . . before a reaction sets in and it can't be read. . . . the whole atmosphere is very depressing . . . and a famine year ahead.

Ku Chu-tung was one of Chiang Kai-shek's most trusted officers, and Hu Chung-nan was his best officer, who, just two weeks before my arrival, had lost half his army to the Reds. From 1937 on, Hu commanded Chiang Kai-shek's best army of half a million men to blockade the Reds in the Northwest, instead of contributing in any way to the war against Japan. As for Yang Hu-ch'eng, he had been a partner with the Young Marshal in arresting Chiang Kai-shek and would pay for it now; he was murdered in prison eventually.

That evening, April 24, at eight, my first real Red Army man showed up (Ed's courier, Wang Ling, had been a railway worker, not a soldier). His real name was Chang Wen-ping, aged twenty-six, never married, tall, handsome, outgoing, engaging. There was something most un-Chinese about him, but I was too busy to figure out what this was until later. He explained to me that he was OGPU chief of intelligence in Sian. That explained his interest in me, but not his unusual personality.

As for Yeh Chien-ying, I do not remember talking with him—I think he only came in late to call on me for a few minutes. He looked so little like a Chinese that I thought he must be half foreign. He was a Cantonese and had been a top commander in the Canton Commune. Yeh obviously looked upon me as just another foreign journalist. He was then chief of staff at age thirty-four, one of the very few such "old" men in the Red armies. Yeh had known other foreigners, but for Chang Wen-ping I was probably the first foreign "friend," or even acquaintance.

Seated on damp bags of millet in the cold storeroom, Chang Wen-ping and I had an interesting talk. I could not believe that the Red Army men were like him; they weren't really. He was all but unique, a former Protestant YMCA member who had intended to be the Martin Luther of China until he turned his evangelical energies to Marxism.

Chang informed me that I could have left that morning on the secret Red Army truck, except for the rain; the roads were impassable. He told me to be ready at five the next morning, weather permitting, or on the first day the roads were usable.

Next morning, more than the weather did not permit. And I didn't see Chang Wen-ping until almost five months later, when I was sitting on a loess cliff outside Yenan watching some new arrivals and one of them ran to greet me. (In 1944, Chang was severely tortured and then executed in prison by the Kuomintang.)

Before five A.M. I was dressed and waiting in more of April's cruel rain. At seven a card was brought to me in the storehouse—Captain Ouyang's, of the Bureau of Public Safety. He examined my passport and noted that the visa was made out the previous year. No Sian visas for foreigners had been granted for 1937, he informed me. I could stay in the city only twenty-four hours without a proper visa.

I pointed out that the visa didn't expire until September 18, but Captain Ouyang held my passport in his immaculate white gloves with an air of anti-imperialist possession.

"Is that all?" I asked, and I gently but firmly and imperialistically retrieved my precious document from his grasp. The Chinese custom was to "hold" a visitor's passport for as long a time as they chose to prevent the visitor from leaving the city walls. And the ancient walls of Sian were high and capable. I had heard that my friend Victor Keene of the *New York Herald Tribune* had recently engaged in fisticuffs with a police captain who tried to take his passport.

Mine, Captain Ouyang conceded, was a special case. It was not only the visa. The Nanking government had ordered that no journalist could enter the military area around Sian, and therefore I would not be permitted to leave the city. I could not go to Sanyuan, for instance, because of what Captain Ouyang referred to as the bandit situation there. I understood this to mean that Sanyuan was the point of entry to the Red areas; it was a border town held by General Yang Hu-ch'eng, who was on good terms with the Reds.

Captain Ouyang went on to tell me that Nanking had sent a list of *verboten* foreign correspondents, the list headed by the name of Edgar Snow. He advised me to return to Peking immediately.

I grasped at a technicality. "My name isn't on the list, is it?"

"That's of no importance," said the captain. "You are the same as your husband. And you are doing newspaper work anyway."

I was now paying for my interview with the Young Marshal last year.

Our conversation was interrupted by the sound of some altercation outside the storeroom. Ch'en Han-p'o had come looking for me, and Captain Ouyang's four plainclothes police waiting at the gate had landed on him. I could hear Ch'en give them a false name and address to conceal his identity. This was worrisome, as he might be arrested for making a false statement to the police, though it was no crime for him to ask for me. But in China, terror of the police was so great that Ch'en was taking no chances on giving his real name.

Captain Ouyang decided to leave my passport with me—and something else as well: "I am giving you these four bodyguards to protect you while you are in Sian," he said. "Conditions here are very unsettled and it is not safe for foreigners."

Obviously, a new plan would have to be made. With all these "bodyguards," I could not continue to stay here, subjecting my kind hostess to constant official surveillance. I would have to go to the Sian Guest House and hope for a further message from Chang Wen-ping when the rains stopped. Under the eyes of the four plainclothesmen, I pretended that my sleeping bag and camp cot were just the normal furnishings of the storeroom, and left with Ch'en Han-p'o and only one suitcase.

Ch'en and I set out in rickshas, flanked by the four bodyguards, a miserable little procession in the unpropitious rain. At the Guest House, Ch'en left me. I didn't see him again in Sian. He was my only contact, my last hope of a liaison in arranging the trip. He sent me a postcard, "It is still raining," to indicate that nothing could be done. Later I learned the police had discovered his lie, and he had gone into hiding. (We met again on the road to Yenan, and he was there when I was—the last time I saw him in China until 1972. After 1949, Ch'en Han-p'o became one of the leading figures in journalism, though later attacked by Red Guards as "anti-party." We had a grand reunion at my home in Connecticut in 1980, when Ch'en came to this country as president of the Chinese Publishers' Association, for a book publishers' convention.)

The host of the Guest House, Mr. Chou, was slyly friendly, but he made it evident that he could lose his job and have to leave the city if he tried to help me. He was a leader of the YMCA and popular with all the foreigners who came to Sian. He arranged a special foreign-style breakfast for me, and wasted no time telling me to give up any plans to go to Yenan: "The trips that Leaf and Keene made to the Red districts have ruined your chances. A new chief of police was appointed a few days ago, and he is not going to let anybody else through, I can tell you."

Earl Leaf of the United Press had called on us just a few days before I left Peking. He had sneaked out of Sian at four o'clock one morning, spent a few days in Yenan, and returned before the police realized what had happened. Then, just a few days before my arrival, a young American photographer named Harry Dunham had secretly got to the Red Army front for a few hours and returned to Sian. And Victor Keene of the *New York Herald Tribune* had spent a few days in the Red areas just before Leaf.

Mr. Chou went on with his warning. The police would hold him responsible if I tried to escape; everybody in the hotel had been threatened. Orders had even been issued to every garage to refuse to rent me a car.

Not till I arrived in Sian had I any real idea of the delicacy of the situation there. Nothing more unwelcome and embarrassing could have been devised than the arrival of anyone named Snow, especially Snow *ux*, who was hardly worth an incident that might endanger the fragile thread of the United Front not yet in existence between the Reds and their Kuomintang enemies. Ed's trip the previous year had been secretly managed by the Tungpei Army, and was part of the high tide of liberalism climaxed by the Sian Incident. When that army was forced to leave Sian, the pendulum of reaction swung to the Fascist right again. My trip came just at the moment of maximum uncertainty and danger from the Fascists; no one had any idea of just how revengeful they would be for previous loss of face.

I was also informed that Edgar Snow would be in danger of secret assassination if he ever showed up in the Northwest again.

The Sian authorities were worried to death about me for two reasons: First, I might escape to Yenan, and second, I might *not*.

The grievances of the authorities were now visited upon me. I had to pay for all those who had preceded me in this unpopular expedition, all of whom had gone *secretly*. If I could ever find a way to get out of Sian, I would become the eighth foreigner (non-Oriental), the fifth journalist, and the second woman to break through the blockade of the inaccessible Chinese Communist Republic since it had been established in 1931—actually since the Red Army was founded in 1927.

Conspiracy

At the Sian Guest House, I told Mr. Chou wistfully—and not entirely untruthfully—that I'd like to go to some tourist places before I went dutifully back to Peking.

Mr. Chou gave me a room on the second floor, overlooking a balcony where one of my guards took up a post rather reminiscent of Romeo's. Soon their ranks had increased to seven: One was my personal bodyguard. Two more were plainclothes Blue Shirt Fascists, with criminal-looking faces, who terrified me—the local Gestapo; they were stationed at the doors on either side of the lounge. The others worked in shifts. Two mobile units went everywhere I did, and hurried to listen in on my phone calls, ready to interrogate all callers—none of whom called. Night guards seemed never to sleep. On April 26, I wrote to Ed:

> They seem to think I am going to fly away somehow. . . . It is very difficult for foreigners to come here now. The missionaries say it is impossible for them to come in without visas and can't get them, so many are very angry. There are about seven at Sanyuan including Upchurch. Some say there may be trouble when Yang leaves and his troops retreat again, but perhaps not. . . . The chief of the Bureau of Social Affairs said he received a wire asking me to be spied on—two days before I arrived. Who told the Peiping people, I wonder? Some of our loyal staff, I suppose. [I haven't yet figured out who that wire was from.] They are determined apparently to let no more foreigners go to any military districts—the United Front beautifully in process. The method is to make life so miserable they will be glad to get away alive. I have an awful feeling that some of these sapphire followers may start an "incident" with me as the object so as to prevent all further migrations of tourists and newspapermen. They control the whole city. All are here as before the 12/12. [The Chinese term for the Sian Incident of 1936 was 12/12, or twelfth of December.]

* * *

There was always the danger of an "accident" in China, though ordinarily foreigners, under the blessing of extraterritoriality, were not only safe but overly protected. I was more worried about Ed than myself, in case he decided to come. I had already written to him on April 25:

> Well, I have four detectives (Blue Shirts, too) in pairs following me. . . . They're sore. They know I am Edgar Snow's *frau* and don't like it, and they are furious about the three others who slipped out—just as I thought, I'm the victim. . . . Be sure to tell everybody I am in Shanghai. It's very important. I have no way to leave except to take the train back and whatnot as a camouflage. They want to prevent all foreigners from coming here now. If you come, you must do so with all preparations to leave immediately on arrival. They are gunning for you. The police chief today said you "are very bad," and so I need "special protection" as your wife. He is the same as Keene fought with. (You'd better *not* come, in fact. Everything will be done to cause you harm. It's not worth an accident. . . .) Nobody can come to see me nor I them. I am in a fix but I'm *not* going back this time under any circumstances. I'll write later on . . . or C. will if I have to escape in a hurry. Must hurry to mail this.

Mr. Chou informed me that Captain Ouyang, a squad of police, even the chief himself, had spent the night searching for me before they discovered my hiding place. They had searched the home of every missionary in Sian, and heaven only knows how many innocent Chinese households, as well as all cars and trucks leaving the city.

I sat in my room, my inescapable Romeo below, and faced the mountainous obstacles that loomed between me and the apparently forbidden city of Yenan. This was not the first time that a member of the Snow family had made life difficult for the established forces of Sian. Ed had been smuggled in and out of Sian the previous year, breaking the Red blockade just when Chiang Kai-shek's Gestapo was presumably on red alert for Chiang's arrival in the city. The police had been called to account when Edgar Snow was reported murdered in Kansu and Helen Snow murdered in Sinkiang. Governor Shao Li-tze had been held responsible. Much face had been lost. And now Sian's forbidden terrain was again positively niveous with Snow.

The other Snow bandit had had the Tungpei Army as his escort. Now "our" army was being railroaded off to Anhui, in retribution for their arrest of Chiang Kai-shek on December 12. General Yang had agreed to leave for Europe on April 28; his troops were expected to get out of hand any day, or at least to loot the Guest House as they had on December 12. The Fascist elements were hurrying back in a vengeful mood—and had complete control of the city.

I didn't know whom I could turn to for help. I felt absolutely alone. Who could risk going against a military order by smuggling me to Sanyuan? Ch'en Han-p'o was in hiding from the police. David Yui couldn't jeopardize his chances of getting through to his Yenan conference in May. Chang Wen-ping and the Red Army office were least of all able to help me, even if they had wanted to.

But I hadn't the slightest intention of not getting to Yenan. Who knew if a new civil war might not start at any time? I felt it was now or never. This might be my only opportunity for exploring the Red Republic.

There was one important point: I had to succeed *the first time*. I could not bungle any tentative tries. I was nervous and frightened, but resolute.

On my most unhappy day at the Guest House, Mr. Chou had an idea. He introduced me to the only potential young American knight-errant in Sian: the first cousin of our friend Janet Fitch Sewall, with the same big blue eyes, fair skin, and blond hair. They were YMCA cronies. I left his name, Kempton Fitch, out of *Inside Red China*, and I hesitate to mention it even now, though the McCarthy period is over. He was a scion of the chief missionary family in China which at one time had forty members there. Kempton's father, George Fitch, was head of the YMCA in China and one of Madame Chiang Kai-shek's best friends. Helping me could have cost Kempton his job in Sian (he was transferred soon after my escapade) and did cause him trouble in subsequent years. Without him I could not have got to Yenan.

Kempton already knew my whole story and advised me to return to Peking. This I adamantly refused to do. He then offered to escort me anywhere I wanted to go, except to my chosen destination; foreigners had to stick together, and he was not going to see any lady in distress with no one to protect her.

Flanked, as ever, by my bodyguards, we took a taxi to call on the missionaries. Before I could tell them what I had in mind—that they could help me get to Sanyuan to one of the missionaries there—they let me know that I had been enough trouble already: Captain Ouyang had gotten them all up in the night to search their houses for me, and besides, this infestation of journalists trying to get to the Red areas was making the missionary life extremely difficult. Some young people who had volunteered to work in the dangerous areas had been turned back by the police, who suspected them of being newspapermen in disguise. They said that missionaries were no longer allowed to travel when and where they wanted, and added that people doing "legitimate business" in the Northwest were having to pay for the "silly curiosity of transients."

I was hardly in a position to speak for the legitimacy of the journalistic business, but I did take the opportunity to ask them to subscribe to our magazine, *democracy*, and learn more about "applied Christian ethics" as defined in Peking, where Dr. J. Leighton Stuart and several other missionaries were working with us in an effort to bring democracy—including freedom of the press—to China, as well as trying to end the civil wars.

The missionaries said they would be glad to help me get back to Peking, but Sanyuan was definitely out.

Our taxi had been followed by a police car, whose occupants reported by telephone to headquarters at every stop. To our amusement, we found they were saying, "*We* are safe." They seemed to think an uprising in the city might be imminent and that they might be attacked by an armed bandit at any corner.

Kempton now had an altercation with the police captain, probably because he found this surveillance ridiculous and an insult to a "legitimate" foreign businessman—I do not remember the specifics. In any case, after our tour of the missionaries, Kempton was won over to my cause. He did not approve of it, but if I insisted on making the attempt, he was willing to do what he could to help me.

He was confirmed in this resolution by a visit to the Red Army office. They had become respectable and law-abiding. They told him they could not themselves help me get to Sanyuan; they were in the process of negotiating with Chiang Kai-shek, and though they disapproved of the order against foreign visits to their districts, they were not about to defy it. Nor could they afford to antagonize the police in any way just now; their delegates were coming in for the May conference and the police were watching, photographing, and keeping dossiers on arrivals suspected of being Communists. I was a special case for the police, and the Red Army office could not be responsible for all the trouble it would make if they helped me escape, but if once I could get there on my own, I would be welcome. They said they would secretly advise their office in Sanyuan to expect me, and gave Kempton the name and address.

Seeing that I was really alone, and not a Communist, Kempton decided to outwit the Sian authorities on my behalf.

There was only one person in Sian who could help, he informed me, and he was sick in the hospital. Effie Hill was a Swedish mechanic, another missionary's son, who had been in charge of Sven Hedin's trips. As Hedin was known to be pro-Nazi, Effie would not be suspected of helping an anti-Fascist. "He goes on all those archaeological tours around the Northwest to service the cars," Kempton said. "He's allowed to go anywhere."

He took me to see Effie, whom we found very ill. Effie did not hesitate to say he would do all in his power to help and only wished he were well enough to drive me to Sanyuan himself. He would have to hire someone to get hold of a general's car; anything less impressive might not be allowed out of the city gates. I offered him nearly all the money I had, which was not much. I think he said he could arrange it for about $150 mex.

I wrote to Ed on April 27: "Not a person will come to see me except a foreigner, Fitch. . . . What an incredibly horrible country. If I can't continue my project here I can't see any reason for staying around. Extraterritoriality is an excellent institution. . . . I'll send you a wire when I leave but don't wait at the station long. Will decide in a day or so I think . . . after trying every known expedient with a little help here and there. They're surely watching English mail now."

I wrote again on the twenty-eighth: "Still no excitement. . . . A definite reaction set in two weeks ago with the Central Government taking over everything. . . . The Communists are going to be very sorry they sacrificed their two allies. Yang has only about 15,000 men left I hear now. He's completely ruined and all his following. I feel very miserable tonight but no use to worry about things beyond my control. How're Ginger and Gobi? I wish Ginger were here to sink his teeth into my unwanted friends. Be sure to get your book out immediately and don't waste any more time because I'm leaving China after this experience."

This was almost word for word what Ed had written to me from Sian on the eve of his own trip. He had realized he might be giving up everything for a chimera.

I had no wish to risk my life or health in unnecessary adventures. I only wanted to get to Yenan to write down history and to get back safely. I was by nature the quiet, gentle type—except for my tongue—and my only particular courage was the moral kind. To my Galahad,

Kempton Fitch, I presented a mystery—a small, feminine, baby-faced sort, not at all the kind of girl to be trying to make a trip into the Communist bandit areas. But though I was far from the physical type to carry out these man-size projects, I was possessed of will and determination enough for two.

Coming back from the visit to Effie, I knew I now had not one friend, but two. Effie's mischievous Viking smile had brought the northern lights to my bleak horizon. We made a plan: Effie was to get a driver and a general's car, which would not be stopped at the city gates when they opened at dawn. I had to elude my guards at the Guest House and meet Kempton, who would escort me to the rendezvous with the driver of the car and then make himself scarce. It was important that we leave in time to have three hours in which to run the blockade to Sanyuan; we knew that as soon as the police discovered I was gone, they would not only set out in pursuit, but could telephone ahead to any of the Central Government garrisons on the way to stop me. We set the date: the evening of the twenty-ninth and morning of the thirtieth, I think, but I cannot remember for certain; it may have been the twenty-eighth to twenty-ninth.

I had been performing a few diversionary maneuvers in advance: I had exchanged my second-floor room at the Guest House for one on the first floor that had a back window overlooking the rear of the walled compound. I had also been "oversleeping" regularly, so that no one would start looking for me if I didn't appear at an early hour.

I gave out the impression that I had given up my idea of traveling to the Red areas and would soon return chastened to Peking from the unfair city of Sian. I sent Ed a telegram which I hoped he would know was a phony: EXPECT LEAVE TOMORROW. MEET AT TRAIN. But I told Captain Ouyang that first I wanted to see Lintung, where Chiang Kai-shek had been captured on December 12. My good conduct had almost made me a trusty prisoner, and my bodyguards seemed to be enjoying their job now. I had even taken them to see an American movie called *Spy No. 13*. Perhaps they gained some professional tips.

Captain Ouyang agreed to the Lintung expedition—after all, I was leaving, and besides, what harm could we come to? But just in case, he gave elaborate instructions for coping with any emergency to both the chauffeur and my two armed bodyguards.

We had a pleasant picnic at Lintung, all of us climbing up to the cliff to read the big characters being carved on the rock to commemorate Chiang Kai-shek's narrow escape from death. I was now myself a prisoner on the same spot and had much more sympathy for the Generalissimo. We skirted the mountain tomb of Emperor Ch'in Shih Huang-ti and returned happily to the Guest House. (In 1978, I spent a day with a television crew at this tomb, where six thousand terra-cotta warriors, buried to protect the emperor over two thousand years ago, were being excavated. This site is now one of the most exciting archaeological digs in the world for tourists.)

CHAPTER 32

A Narrow Escape

There was only one other visitor besides me in the Guest House to-night. The ordinarily bustling hotel was silent, almost desolate. Only the omnipresent guards were in evidence. I was more frightened and nervous than ever, and even more resolute. For nearly a week I had been getting by on insufficient sleep and inadequate food. It had not occurred to me to bring sleeping pills, nor did I think to take up drinking to break the tension of those days.

The thing that was worrying me most was that our plan called for me to hide in the luggage compartment of the car. I simply could not bring myself to do it. Although I had never had claustrophobia before, this prospect had caused me sleepless nights. Not only did I fear suffocation from gas fumes, but there was not a doubt in my mind that the driver would leave the luggage compartment locked if he found it dangerous to open it. I was sure I would be found dead from unknown causes—and the driver would say he did not know I was in the trunk.

Now, this was the night. At precisely 12:45 A.M., I should see a lighted cigarette glowing at the top of the compound wall. This would be my signal to jump out of my rear window and go to the spot where there was a pile of dirt high enough to enable me to scale the wall. It was the spot where Shao Yuan-chung had been killed trying to escape Yang Hu-ch'eng's troops on December 12.

Kempton Fitch would be waiting outside the wall and would take me to a house where the car would pick me up when the city gates opened at four A.M. The car belonged to a general—Yang Hu-ch'eng himself, I thought; the driver was a Yang man not averse to sniping at the Generalissimo's followers. We would head full-tilt for Sanyuan, avoiding the main road, which was heavily garrisoned by Chiang Kai-shek's troops. Sanyuan was Yang's garrison. We had the address of the Red Army office there, and could count on them to accept delivery and forwarding responsibility for the Snow parcel.

248

I expected that my usual night shift of guards would be on both sides of the lobby and in the room opposite mine, with the door open. I also expected that the night-duty Guest House staff would be on watch, as always. What I did not expect was the news I received at eight that evening: Martial law had been declared in Sian. General Yang was due to leave the city, and his two remaining Sian-based regiments were expected to riot, or at least to repeat their December 12 looting of the Guest House. There were soldiers patrolling the very wall I was to climb over. If any unexpected figure emerged from the night, they were free to fire on sight, and it was unlikely that they would be able to distinguish a sacrosanct foreigner in the dark.

An even more crushing blow was to discover that Mr. Chou, hoping to preserve his few remaining unlooted woolen blankets, had assigned squads of hotel servants to patrol the grounds inside the compound at fifteen-minute intervals throughout the night.

It looked hopeless. But I knew I had to go through with the attempt tonight. I suspected that Kempton and Effie doubted I would measure up to my own role in the drama. Surely they wouldn't take a second chance on me.

I did not realize it then, but it was the very circumstance I most feared that made my escape possible: martial law. Surprise is after all the chief advantage in guerrilla warfare. Who would dream that I would attempt a getaway on such a night? At any rate, our escape plan had not taken into account any need for last-minute communication among our little band of conspirators. I had no choice but to make the try.

At 12:30 I put on as many layers of clothing as I could under my tan camel's hair slacks and matching camel's hair coat which I had had specially made for my inglorious expedition the year before. I pulled on my ancient and honorable blue suede beret and tucked all my curls under it. I had worn this beret when I had my photograph taken for the newspapers before leaving the States in 1931; I had worn it in the student demonstrations, and in Sian the year before. It was a talisman.

Like a truant schoolgirl seeking to escape detection at bed check, I arranged pillows and blankets into a person-shaped mound in the bed, so that I might seem to be sleeping late the next morning and thus delay pursuit. I loaded my handbag with the bare essentials for my expedition: a Waterman fountain pen with a very fine point (which I dearly loved and still possess), lipstick, powder, cold cream, a couple of handkerchiefs, and all my money in a thin roll of paper bills—there wasn't much left and this worried me—and slung the bag securely over my shoulder. I put on my Crookes' lens sunglasses (I am still wearing them), and sat tensely at the window looking at the moonlight outside.

The appointed hour of 12:45 came. I should see the glow of a cigarette on the compound wall. Nothing. I could hardly breathe from disappointment. But I couldn't stay here watching in the window. I had timed the patrol of the servants, and soon they would be coming around again. I took a last cautious reconnaissance of the ground below the window—the last thing I needed was a sprained ankle—and jumped down. The twenty-yard space between the hotel and the wall was bright with treacherous moonlight: I was sure my shadow would give me away as I sprinted across the seemingly endless open stretch to the shadowed sanctuary beside the wall. I crept along it. Still no welcoming cigarette gleam.

In the corner was the pile of dirt and concrete where Shao Yuan-chung had been killed trying to escape over the wall. I clambered up and peered over. The arc light in the main street revealed a special patrol of ten gendarmes. Looking the other way, I could make out the helmets of the soldiers at the end of the wall. I slid back down and hid in the deep shadows of the dirt pile, observing the servants' house patrol.

After some forty minutes, I was forced to the conclusion that the unforeseen exigencies of martial law had prevented Kempton from keeping our rendezvous. There was no way I could climb over the wall unseen or back into the high window of my room. I was out in the open, on my own, and down to desperation measures. As soon as the next inside patrol was out of sight around the corner of the building, I made a run for it, skirting the open spaces of the hotel compound, running afoul of a tangle of barbed wire, hating my moon-cast shadow, which seemed enormous, determined to give me away.

Miraculously unseen by anyone in the Guest House, I got to the entrance walk by the front gate. Now it was time for a change of tactics. On the theory that the best defense is a good offense, I marched up and tried the handle of the big iron gate. Another miracle—unlocked, it turned beneath my hand. Boldly I stepped out and faced the guards.

"Where are you going?" they demanded.

Assuming the stance of a typical imperialistic foreigner in China,

I replied (in Chinese, of course), "I want to return to my home. Are there any rickshas around?"

Still another miracle: A solitary ricksha came down the street. With a peremptory *"Yang-chê, lai, lai!"* I got into it and, in a loud voice for the benefit of the police, directed the rickshaman to a false address in the general neighborhood of our agreed-upon meeting place. I do not know how to explain the fact that the police at the gate did not stop me. Perhaps no one had given them orders to detain any foreign women. Perhaps they hadn't realized I was a foreigner in the gate's dark shadow. Perhaps they were new at their posts. Most likely, my special guards inside the Guest House considered themselves exclusively in charge of me and had not even told the gate guards about me—it would entail some loss of face to suggest I might evade them. And then again, no one would be likely to think I would try to escape through the increased security measures of martial law.

My ricksha bowled along through streets deserted by all save police patrols. My heart skipped a beat every time I saw a policeman, but they stopped me only once.

"I am a foreigner. I am going home," I said. It was sufficient explanation. Nobody in China at that time found it surprising that a foreigner would wander about, even at a most unlikely hour, circumventing martial law and order.

Through some appalling error of omission, I did not have the exact address (if it did have a number) of the house I was supposed to go to. I did not know the name of the house owner or of the driver. It had been gnawing at me ever since I had sat in my window watching—hoping—for the signal glow of Kempton's cigarette. Without him to guide me, all that I knew was that our "safe house" lay a certain number of blocks beyond the Drum Tower, past a big red-painted gate, which wasn't the place but would serve as a guidepost to a subsequent side street, which wasn't the place either, but where there were big *un*painted gates, which . . .

I had never before been so aware that all Chinese streets are positively *measled* with big red gates. My only hope was that in China everyone usually knows where any foreigner is. I meant to keep asking until I found someone who had seen Kempton Fitch at a house in the neighborhood, hoping against hope all the while that the alarm had not yet gone up at the Guest House and sent my bodyguards in hot pursuit of me.

And then the final miracle occurred: A bicycle shot by me. I could not make out the rider, nor could he see me with the hood of the ricksha down, but just before the bicycle passed on out of earshot, I instinctively called out, "Hi!"

At the sound of my voice, Kempton literally fell off his bicycle in surprise. His astonished grin was as wide as that elusive red gate as he came up to me. "Did you actually make it? Congratulations!" He had been unable to get near the compound wall because of the soldiers on patrol, and had thought I wouldn't dare try to escape that night. He had waited on the street for about twenty minutes. Then he had heard a shot, and assumed I wouldn't dare try the wall. In fact, he had feared the shot might have been directed at me. He had decided to give up for the night and was just going home to bed when I called out.

"The shot was not fired at me, I am happy to say," I said, with a grin even wider than his own. For a minute we looked at each other, smiling foolishly. Then he got back on his bicycle and waved me on with an elegant sweep of his arm. "This way!" he said.

We were very near our destination. I paid off the rickshaman at the wrong gate, so that later he would not be able to report the right one to the authorities, and walked to the appointed house. A car stood in the compound, and Kempton introduced me to the driver. We solemnly shook hands. He was an older man with a nervous manner— definitely peculiar. I certainly would never allow this man to lock me into any luggage compartment.

For the next few hours, as we waited for dawn and the opening of the city gates, the slightest street noise sent me ducking behind a sofa, lest I should be found by pursuing police. Then, just before sunrise, the driver left the room. We expected his imminent return, but in half an hour there was still no sign of him. We searched the house. We searched the compound. He had simply disappeared.

Kempton suddenly struck himself on the forehead. "I might have expected this," he said. "Do you know what he said to me last night? He calmly remarked, 'You know, I always feel very brave and fearless at night, but I never seem to have any courage left in the morning.' He smokes opium at night, that's why!"

Well, isn't there some saying about the darkness just before the dawn? We were organizing a search party of nearby opium parlors when the prodigal returned, eyes suspiciously bright, posture down-right swashbuckling.

There was not a minute to lose. Before the opium courage had a chance to wear off, Kempton put a man's hat on me and swaddled me to the nose in a quilt. With my slacks and dark glasses, we hoped I would be taken for a tubercular boy going home to his missionary parents at the Sanyuan mission.

Our plan called for Kempton to bow out at this stage. But the Chinese driver showed ominous signs of refusing to go unless he came with us. I would not ask him to, but Kempton decided to come along—an act of pure chivalry.

Reasonably secure in the knowledge that no mere sentry had the right to stop a general, we set out in our general's car. Flaunting our military license, we sped straight through the gates, and with consummate hauteur, scattered a squad of soldiers repairing the road outside.

"I wouldn't have stopped even if the sentries had fired," the driver said, but it may have been the opium speaking.

We bumped along a road intended for camel caravans from Mongolia, not for illegitimate wayfarers on wheels. But this seldom-traveled route avoided the town of Hsienyang and the main posts of the Central Army. More than once I feared we wouldn't get out of the mud, and though it was almost fun crossing the flooded Wei River on a raft, it was no fun at all when several times we encountered Central Army officers and troops. The presence of Kempton Fitch saved the day; nobody questioned his right to tour the countryside if he liked, although he did not tell anyone who he was. He had lived long enough in China to know exactly how to handle unwelcome inquiries.

Oh, little town of Sanyuan, how beautiful you looked to me on that spring morning of 1937. Only a couple of hours later than planned, we arrived in this neutral territory between the Kuomintang and the Reds, held by the native Seventeenth Route Shensi Army. Kempton refused to leave until he had delivered me safely to the office of the Red Army. We had the address, a godown near one of the city gates, where we were to ask for a Mr. Wang. But we were beginning to give up hope of ever locating it when we stumbled right into it, almost onto the point of a bayonet held by a young sentry in a red-starred cap. Kempton had little time to spend in negotiation; he simply expropriated the cap and dashed to the car, confiscated souvenir in hand, to get back to Sian before his absence should be discovered. The sentry did not know whether to laugh or to shoot at this example of imperialist highway robbery.

When I next saw Kempton, it was in 1945 in New York. He told me they had made a mad dash for Sian, and he had got into the company's compound—he was the head of Standard Oil in Sian—in time to pretend he was oversleeping. Captain Ouyang got on the phone, Kempton told me. "He said he was coming to see me, so I got into bed and rang the bell for the servant as usual. When he came, he was white as a sheet and hopping mad. He had got hell at headquarters and he came back four times to see me. He said your escape was the last straw absolutely. They had done everything to keep you from going. He returned three days later, also. . . .

"Someone said you were trailed all the way from Peking," he added. "All gendarmes and police had instructions, Captain Ouyang said, and he informed me I would have to leave town. They had found some evidence on the car and had been told that foreigners had been seen. Three days later the company announced that I had been transferred to Changsha. I left Sian a month or so later, about July, and went through Hsuchowfu after it was bombed. The opium driver got into trouble later but got out of it. Only the three of us were involved. Chou, the [hotel] manager, was worried to death, not knowing if you were alive or dead or what would happen to him. Two of the guards were put into prison for six months. All the missionaries' houses were searched and every other likely place."

A certain element of Providence is discernible in this tale of how I became one of the legends of the Sian Guest House and Mr. Chou's favorite heroine—but not until long after.

In the McCarthy time, two FBI men came to call on me with a copy of *Inside Red China*. Although the book gave no names of my two Galahads, the FBI men asked if I knew of any disloyalty to the United States on the part of Kempton Fitch. I refused to tell them who had helped me to escape, and they did not insist. I informed them I was sure Kempton Fitch had no subversive ideas. I knew that Kempton—and his father—had made no secret of the story, but even so, I would never have given his name, as a matter of principle. He not only had no sympathy for any Communists, but even had none for me in making my trip. It was just that his self-respect as a gentleman was at stake. He was as much a prisoner of his conscience as I was of the gendarmes. Effie Hill was the same. He had not the remotest interest in Communists, but he could not resist helping an American girl alone against the whole wide world.

I had sense enough to write a letter from Sanyuan to Captain Ouyang, telling him I was taking a trip for a few weeks and not to worry about me; I was safe. Kempton wrote to my husband on May 1 about my safe arrival "after more or less strenuous experiences," and added: "It would no doubt amuse you if I could give you even a slight idea of how burned up the local so-called secret service are here . . . from what I hear here, it would be a very easy matter to have you assassinated by a Blue Shirt. . . . Political opinions aside, a lone American always sticks up for another lone American, and it seems that a young man always assists a lady in distress, so far be it from me to stray from the path of custom."

Later on in 1937 I learned more: My luggage was detained at the Guest House. The authorities thought I might have left Sian by railroad and then doubled back across country—which was what I had originally thought of doing—and they had telephoned to posts as far as Tungkuan on the Lung-hai Railway trying to trace me. The chief of police again felt called upon to reorganize his department, again because of the Snows, but it had never occurred to me that two of my bodyguards would be reorganized right into prison.

Everybody imaginable was put on the lookout for my return, which could pose a problem in the future more important and even less easily solvable than my original escape—how to get back through Sian without suffering confiscation of my films and notebooks. There was not a soul in the world to whom I would entrust all my notebooks, though I did later send some films by someone leaving Yenan for Peking, and Ed got them just in time to put eleven photos in *Red Star Over China*.

One aspect of the whole affair that caused other people worry was that the Fascist Blue Shirts were known to be fond of kidnaping and assassinating undesirable Chinese. This type of thing had been going on in Sian regularly for the past year. The Sian officials at first suspected this might have happened to me, that I had been secretly done away with. Mr. Chou had been really afraid of this, and it was also one reason that Kemptom Fitch stayed always by my side. Everyone warned me that Ed must never come to Sian again or he might suffer such a fate. No records were kept of the Chinese who disappeared when the Fascists took revenge on them, and there was a point beyond which the Fascist Chinese found even sacrosanct foreigners unendurable.

On May 2, I wrote to Ed from Yunyang:

Here I am in P'eng Teh-huai's headquarters near Sanyuan. Yesterday was May Day and they had a big demonstration. The Red Army is incredible. They are so young you can't believe it. I had a terrible time trying to get here but arrived successfully. Today I am going to see Ho Lung and then to Yenan. I have only a minute in which to write this. Fullsea Wang is all right and Ch'en Han-p'o had to escape from Sian and is also here with me. I have been too busy and tired to think since I came here. I feel swell, not sick at all. Had to leave all my things at the hotel when I climbed out of the window. I'm certainly happy to be here. It's quite an accomplishment now. . . .

On May 3, Ed still didn't know I had made it through to Sanyuan. He wrote a cryptic letter, saying, "Maybe you'll be seeing Jim before you finish your holiday." Jim and Ed were trying to get their books done. They had no idea of what I was undergoing—we could not trust straightforward truth to the probably censored mails—but both were considering coming to my rescue if necessary. Ed's letter ended: "Do you think I could possibly help any if I came up to see you, or do you think it would just decoy the germs from you to me? That would be good, if possible. Ah, I love you so."

CHAPTER 33

Arrival at the Red Front

I had been almost ten days in the getting there, but at last, on April 30, 1937, I was in Red Star country. Ch'en Han-p'o was there, and the contact in Sanyuan, "Mr. Wang," had telephoned the nearby Red Army headquarters of General P'eng Teh-huai of my arrival. The general had sent a Dodge touring car for me, a gift to him from the Young Marshal along with two others and twelve trucks. The driver said, "I came with the car"; he had been one of the Young Marshal's chauffeurs, and he told me that many Tungpei people had joined the Red Army.

At the Front Political Headquarters, I was greeted with a smiling embrace by a sweet, pretty, gentle girl named Li Po-chao, whose room I would share. With a shy grin, a little boy in uniform brought me a welcome basin of hot water. I had heard from Ed about the troop of *hsiao kuei*, "little devils," mostly orphans aged about eight to fifteen who served as orderlies to the army.

At twenty-six, Li Po-chao was a favorite playwright among the Reds. She was director of the Front Theater and was married to the chairman of the Front Political Department. She told me the story of the Long March; she had crossed the terrible bogs of the Grasslands three times. "The Propaganda Department tried to amuse the men with dances, songs, and slogans, in order to keep their spirits up and encourage them," she said simply. "At night we made fires along the riverbanks and had recreations. The scene was very beautiful. Each night we checked up to see how many had been killed. . . . None of the thirty women with Mao Tse-tung's troops died on the Long March, but on the contrary, it improved their health. Those who had been weak are now strong."

But Li Po-chao, like many in the Red armies, had tuberculosis.

Every morning she coughed blood. (Nevertheless, she was still alive in the 1980s, after a long history of ups and downs.)

I was taken to a large ancestral hall to talk with Lu Ting-yi, head of the Front Agitprop Department, a gentle, intellectual-looking man in thick glasses. Lu was thirty and had been an active Communist twelve years. In charge of press relations, he had been Ed's guide the year before, and welcomed me in excellent English.

Ed had left his camera with him so that Lu might take some photographs of the legendary heads of the Red armies and send them on to Ed. Lu explained that he was still learning to use the camera and so far had gotten only one shot that pleased him. "I have had many enlargements made to give to friends to hang in their rooms," he said, and proudly displayed a picture of a branch of plum blossoms! I was to see many a copy of Lu's plum-blossom masterpiece on the walls of the Red officers.

The other picture that went everywhere with Lu Ting-yi was a tattered photograph cut from a magazine. "It isn't my baby," he explained, "but it looks exactly like him. I don't know what happened to mine—my wife was executed in Fukien nine years ago."

My first two acquaintances were singularly appealing and eminently civilized. These were my kind of people, I thought, and I wondered how they managed to survive the rigor of their daily lives with their gentleness and sweetness apparently intact. From this moment I felt no fear or uncertainty about my strange environment.

Li Po-chao advised me to wear the jacket and cap of the Red Army uniform as well as my dark glasses, till I got to Yenan, so as to be less conspicuous while traveling. Uniforms were regulation among the women of the Red armies. Li Po-chao had a tailor make up a slate-blue jacket and red-starred cap for me within two hours, but my legs remained out of uniform in my comfortable wide blue slacks, which I much preferred to the regulation army puttees.

At the front General P'eng Teh-huai gave me several interviews. Except with the "little devils," who worshiped him, P'eng was gruff, businesslike, impersonal to the last degree. He was known among the Reds as the most puritanical and Spartan of them all, a John Lilburne type. Oliver Cromwell was much less the Puritan than P'eng, who rigidly opposed the least sign of loose morality, and had an aversion to women. As a natural result of such an attitude, women found him most attractive. Ting Ling, the writer famous for her anarchist views on free love, set her cap for P'eng—who rejected all her wiles.

P'eng was the deputy commander in chief of the Red armies from before the time I met him in 1937 until 1958, when he was purged as minister of defense and his post was taken by Marshal Lin Piao. It was said P'eng was eliminated from power as a pro-Soviet "rightist" who opposed the communes. In 1949, Lu Ting-yi became chief of the influential Communist Party Propaganda Department, but in 1966 he was removed from power, though later "rehabilitated." (He had been a friend in Peking of Anna Louise Strong, the famous American author, who spent her last years in Peking and died there in 1970.) Ting Ling, China's most important woman novelist since the 1930s, was exiled as a "rightist" at about the same time as her nonadmirer, P'eng Teh-huai. (P'eng died, but Ting Ling lived to be at the top of the heap once more in the 1980s.)

Most of the Reds who first welcomed me in 1937 were purged during the 1966 Cultural Revolution, since they were the pro-Soviet element. It is said that revolutions destroy their own children, the way they did in France and the Soviet Union. Yet in China no "Old Bolshevik" has been executed, as they were in the Soviet Union in 1937 when I was in Yenan. The Chinese Communists have appeared more civilized in this respect than the French and Russians in their revolutions, and more capable of disciplined leadership. They still retain the ancient Chinese respect for and fear of words and ideas, however, and have not emerged from the stage where orthodoxy is a chief weapon of control and power, as it is in all primitive societies.

CHAPTER 34

A Room in the Old Walled City

Our truck heaved to a stop outside the Sung gates of Yenan. Bound for the Red Academy there, the thirteen young university students who had been singing the "Budyenny March" as they jounced about with the luggage in the back, jumped to the ground. All of us were covered with mantles of gold velvet—the fine loess dust blown down from the Gobi Desert. We shook it off in a cloud of glory.

Our old December 9th friend Huang Hua greeted Ch'en Han-p'o and Fullsea Wang, whom we had met en route (along with my cot abandoned in Sian). Huang Hua was in charge of the arriving "students." David Yui was there, too, to make a report on North China at the secret Communist Party Congress. (When David called on me later, I found that he was surprised at having been profoundly influenced by Mao Tse-tung and his speeches.)

Huang Hua took me to see Po Ku, the commissioner of Foreign Affairs, one of the opposition to Mao Tse-tung. Po Ku escorted me to the Foreign Affairs compound, to a small room of my own, with paper windows and a heavy blue padded curtain for a door. A carved square table near the window held a candle and my special teapot. Two chairs and two benches made up the rest of the furnishings, except for the built-in bedroom in one corner, hung with blue cloth for privacy. This was a *k'ang*, or raised platform of brick, where I put my canvas cot and sleeping bag. The legs of my cot sat in four cigarette tins filled with kerosene, which did discourage crawling insects, though it seemed to have little deterrent effect on the high-jumping fleas.

The brick floor was inhabited by both competitive and communist insect life, despite the lime dust with which I covered the cracks. I put my leather saddle shoes up high every night and shook them out every morning, looking for scorpions and centipedes as well as lice and fleas. Overhead the ceiling was of sagging white cloth, and rats ran back and forth on the rafters all night, shaking the golden dust down as they raced. Under my bed was a rat trap, and when it caught one, I waked the whole compound with my screams. This was the pure, organic life—without pesticides, without chemicals, without machinery.

It is not the rat but the flea that carries the black plague—and northern Shensi was one of the few places on earth where that killer disease was still endemic. My floor was covered with fleas, all gregarious and fond of foreigners. The Chinese were not immune, but generations of exposure had created a mighty army of antibodies in their blood to protect them from disease. I never forgot that the black plague had once destroyed half the population of Christendom, and had brought into fashion in Europe a concern for cleanliness that did not seem as yet, some centuries later, to have reached China. Though my own compound thankfully suffered no plague that summer, there was one case of typhoid, one severe case of dysentery, along with plenty of the common everyday variety, and my personal bodyguard had advanced tuberculosis. TB was so common that little attention was paid to it. Probably everybody in Yenan had dysentery, but the Chinese seemed usually not much bothered by it.

Of the four foreigners in Yenan, I acquired dysentery after less than a month. The Comintern agent, Li Teh—the German Otto Braun—had had a bad case of it for two or three years. Dr. George Hatem, the Reds' first foreign doctor, known as Hai Teh, was thin to blueness and thought he had tuberculosis; he was only twenty-seven. Agnes Smedley, the American writer and activist, in her mid-forties, had a long history of being ill in sanitariums much of the time with a bad heart and stomach problems. In midsummer she hurt her back when she was thrown from a horse, and spent much of her time in bed in her cave on the hill after that, depressed and unable to work.

Except during her black spells, Agnes Smedley had a special charm, even wit and humor. I used to climb the hill to her cave in Yenan just for the pleasure of hearing her refer to Chiang Kai-shek as "that feudal bastard." The Yenan line had become so saccharine on that subject, in the hope of justifying the release of Chiang the past December, that it was almost unbearable. I don't think it even occurred to Miss Smedley to hold in her temper or not to speak her mind. She enjoyed her explosions and they helped her to survive.

During the four months I spent in Yenan, I gathered enough

material for four books, plus parts of other books. I was too busy, too fascinated, to notice how weak I was becoming from dysentery. The acute stage passed, controlled by eating as little as possible. At night I gnawed on steamed biscuits when I was too hungry to sleep.

We were all starving for our own type of food. What was the World Revolution compared with a can of American peaches? I lived chiefly on rice, *man-t'ou* boiled biscuits, bismuth, and dysentery pills called Yatren. Dr. Hatem used to announce his arrival under my paper window by singing, "Arise, ye prisoner of starvation."

I was surprised by the attitude of the three other foreigners living in Yenan. Always, in China, isolated Westerners were desperate for new acquaintances, even for a few hours of talk. But though Dr. Hatem tried to be nice to me and to Li Teh, neither man was even on speaking terms with Miss Smedley. They said she had "told lies" about them, which she may have done during one of her occasional periods of psychiatric difficulty, but they were totally unforgiving.

I was in no den of Christians. I shouldn't have expected "Marxists" to be, but still, I was shocked. On one occasion I cried and cried till, to shut me up, Dr. Hatem was finally forced to climb up to Agnes's cave with me to look at her injured back—but neither spoke to the other except for medical questions. Miss Smedley made a Christian out of me during the summer—there was no other way to get along with her, or for me to grow big enough to overlook all these psychological and sociological shocks.

Apart from his private war with Agnes Smedley, Dr. Hatem was normal, charming, witty, and likable, with a sense of humor. He always "stayed out of messes," a good rule for foreigners in China. (He married a Chinese, had children, and became "sinicized completely," as he told me when we talked in 1972.)

Just as I was making my first acquaintance with this type of Westerner, so were Mao Tse-tung and the Chinese. Mao and Li Teh were at war politically and detested each other. Li Teh, whose real name, Otto Braun, was unknown in Yenan, was blond, blue-eyed, in his mid-forties. The Comintern agent's ideas were opposite to Mao's in all ways. (As late as 1965, he was still attacking Mao from East Berlin, where he died in August 1973.) Li Teh barked at me viciously when I dared ask him some complicated and contradictory question. I realized then that he did not understand China, but thought of it only in terms of the European experience. Mao was amused when I asked him the same questions and was eager to explain.

I well realized that Li Teh was sick with dysentery, and edgy and disagreeable due to so much hostility around him. I also knew he could not talk with an outside reporter like me for many reasons. But I was mystified by the way he treated me as if I had a contagious disease. It seemed amusing to me when I learned the underlying reason, which was not until 1975 when an American student who read Braun's 1974 book, published in German, sent me a letter saying: "I thought you might like to know what he had to say about you and Edgar Snow. He did not trust you. He was convinced you were American secret agents. Your information was simply too good. For this reason he avoided contact with you while you were in Yenan. He could never be sure if your aims were purely journalistic or not. . . . He was a very mistrustful man."

Even less than Li Teh understood enterprising American journalists did he understand China and the Chinese—and he knew it. Yet Mao Tse-tung had an accurate picture of the whole situation. It was also amusing that Mao thawed out and became friendly with me when he was told Li Teh disliked me and argued with me.

I can understand how Li Teh came to be so paranoid, but what a lot of harm he did to future relations between China and the West! *I'd hate to be taking orders from anybody in the Comintern like Li Teh,* I thought.

It is possible that 1937 was the critical breaking point for the so-called World Revolution and for the Comintern. While the few foreigners in Yenan were caught in a sticky web of contradictions, in the Soviet Union the old Bolsheviks were actually executing each other, for reasons both paranoid and real.

Even then I realized that the human being cannot survive too much of the danger and intellectual tension required in political work. There is a breaking point. Those geared to the destructive phase of revolution may be unable to shift gears to the constructive work required after revolution succeeds. And so they turn and rend each other, as Jonathan Swift put it, "for want of enemies." Revolution devours its own parents as well as its own children.

Both Li Teh and Agnes Smedley had reached the breaking point. I did not want to become like these foreigners. I was out of my element. I didn't belong among these tough, hard, aggressive characters; nor did I belong among the Chinese. Where did I belong? There was a special place for me, right on the cusp of change, between two worlds, between two eras, between the old and the new. This strategic place was more sensitive and difficult than most. I was not and am not afraid of changing the world, but through influencing other people, not in the open confrontations that are soul-destroying, poison to the human personality. My husband and I played much the same role, except that he reached out to the big public, while I worked quietly through other people, behind the scenes.

CHAPTER 35

Mao Tse-tung, Chu Teh, and Chou En-lai

I was still groggy from the hard trip by truck over the roads to Yenan when my new bodyguard announced on my first morning that Chairman Mao Tse-tung and General Chu Teh were in the courtyard to pay me a call of welcome. I could not decide whether to freshen my lipstick—my one lifeline to Western civilization—or to take it off altogether. And so I did neither.

We shook hands, Chu Teh with the "Yenan grip," which became the custom all over China, where bowing had been traditional and handshakes, particularly between the sexes, almost unheard of. The grip was two-handed the second time around (as when Chu Teh formally welcomed me back to China in the Great Hall of the People in 1972). My husband had not met Chu Teh and his armies, so I had no preconceived idea of what I would meet. My first impression was shared by every foreigner who met him: He was instantly *simpatico*. You could trust this man. You felt his universal humanity and friendliness toward the whole human race.

He was a true folk hero. From the moment she met him Agnes Smedley considered him her best friend on earth, and after she left Yenan, she went first to Sian and then to Chu Teh's headquarters in the Shansi mountains. She identified with him so much that in writing his biography later she put herself into the portrait. He was possibly the only person she ever actually *trusted* in her whole life, though she also came to admire Evans Carlson—partly because he, too, identified with Chu Teh from the first minute and thought of him as a "warm and generous friend." Knowing Chu Teh justified for both of them all the long years they had spent in China groping for identification, or at least some communication, with the "real" Chinese.

It is of special importance that these two grass-roots Americans had to travel to the remote mountains of China to find a people's leader they could admire, respect, and identify with, as Carlson admired his friend President Roosevelt, though in an entirely different way. Had Carlson disliked Chu Teh, Agnes would have hated Carlson violently.

Gung Ho-ism for the American Marine Corps in World War II was conceived the minute Evans met Chu Teh—and at the same time that, in Shanghai, Ed and I and New Zealander Rewi Alley were inventing the cooperatives from which the name *gung ho* derived. For all of us, the feeling sprang from identification with the *people*, particularly those who worked with their hands, the *producers*. Chu Teh represented the good earth of China to us all. He was *good*, and one knew it instinctively. He was the child of a remote Szechuan village who had to seek out his own learning, and did so, even as far as Europe. He was a Hakka, which helps explain a great deal: The Hakkas are an ethnic Chinese group who never allowed foot-binding, and who cottoned to Christianity early on. The Hakkas near Canton started the T'aip'ing Rebellion of the 1850s, and were among the first Communist rebels. (The writer Han Suyin wrote that she is part Hakka, "with Chu Teh." So also were Teng Hsiao-p'ing and Yeh Chien-ying.)

Most of all, Chu Teh was not blindly anti-Western, but open-minded, open-hearted, honest, and fair.

It is highly significant that we Americans recognized Chu Teh's quality—and that a German like Li Teh despised it, as he also despised Mao Tse-tung and all other folk figures. The Chinese, in turn, recognized that we Americans represented what was good, trusted us and liked us, while they hated Li Teh. This was part of the old, continuing bond of Chinese-American friendship, which has never existed to anything like such an extent among any other nationalities.

In his old age in Peking as chief of state, Chu Teh was called "the old gentleman" by foreigners like Rewi Alley. That was what he represented to us: all the gentlemanly qualities so precious to our Western traditions. In my own mind, even before Rewi used the term to me, I had always thought of Chu Teh as what the Chinese called a *chün tzŭ*, or "perfect gentleman."

Both Chu Teh and his wife, K'ang K'e-ching, made a big point of commending me for bravery, though courage was no news in Yenan, but Mao Tse-tung was never personal in that way at all. Chu Teh welcomed all foreigners in his special way. In 1972, James Endicott told me that a missionary had once saved Chu Teh's life in Szechuan, which perhaps helps to explain his unusual attitude. I wish some other foreigner had saved Mao's life—who knows how much influence this would have had on international relations?

Chu Teh and Mao Tse-tung were counterparts of one whole, so much so that some people in China thought "Chu-Mao" was one person. Mao was the brains, the theorist, the "chairman." Chu Teh was the heart, the army, and by all instincts a leader of men, of human material. Both were made of superior stuff, which enabled them to be still at the head of the People's Republic in their eighties and nineties.

When Mao Tse-tung shook hands to welcome me to Yenan in that ancient brick courtyard, he was casual, cool, and questioning. *He is a Chinese*, was my first thought, *and Chu Teh is not*. Chu Teh went the extra mile without noticing it, but Mao Tse-tung stayed within his own province, on his own terms, in a kind of sly sovereignty.

Chu Teh put his hands in his sleeves as he sat modestly behind the battered table and kept his cap on his crew-cut head. Mao Tse-tung pulled his chair away from the table and took off his limp red-starred cap, letting a shock of plentiful black hair fall around his ears. He crossed his remarkably beautiful, powerful, and aristocratic hands over each other, and looked up at me quizzically, even with good-natured humor. These hands showed real power. They were not at all like the usual hands of an intellectual in China, nor were they like those of the working class. Mao was unusually tall and well-built for a Chinese, and his hands were appropriate to his physique.

There was nothing harmless about Mao Tse-tung. He was well-bred, but inside he was made of steel, of hard resistance, of tough tissue—the kind of tissue the Boxers thought they had by magic, and bared their solar plexuses to foreign bullets. Agnes Smedley told me she thought Mao sinister and feminine, and hated him on first sight. She had a hard time overcoming this feeling and reverted to it at the end of her stay in Yenan, when she told me she was afraid of him. But I liked him and felt a rapport with him, as Ed had from the first.

Neither Agnes Smedley nor Evans Carlson had the least understanding of Mao Tse-tung for some reason. Evans wrote of him as "a humble, kindly, lonely genius, striving here in the darkness of the night to find a peaceful . . . way of life for the people." *

Of all the things Mao Tse-tung was *not*, Evans had the list—except that he *was* a genius. That was obvious to everyone, and proba-

* Evans Carlson, *Twin Stars of China* (Dodd, Mead & Company, New York, 1940), p. 170.

bly had been clear to Mao and his friends since his boyhood. Evans judged people by the Christian yardstick, which got in the way of his clarity of vision. To him, humility was a beautiful thing, especially in a commander in chief.

It was probable that I already knew more about Mao Tse-tung's life than anyone else except my husband—because Mao had never before told his life story to anyone. "I typed up your autobiography as soon as my husband got back to Peking," I told Mao. "It is a very great classic. It will influence everyone who reads it. I decided then that I would have to visit your areas at any cost. My husband wants me to get the last chapter from you."

Mao Tse-tung chuckled in his habitual way and nodded affably.

Because Mao had opened up to Edgar Snow the year before, all doors were open to me as well. Chu Teh brought his generals to call during the few days they were at the party congress in May. (Only one important leader did not pay a call on me—Lin Piao, who was evidently more anti-foreign than the others.) For my books, especially *The Chinese Communists,* I collected thirty-four brief autobiographies and held many other interviews—all because Mao had set the example. Mao Tse-tung was the arbiter in everything, from etiquette to foreign policy.

During the summer I had a special relationship with Mao, though not as close as Ed's had been the year before. I sent him a long list of questions and we had several interviews. He was much interested in my questions, many of which asked for explanations of what seemed to be contradictions. He would chuckle audibly and say, "Some things in China are very strange, you see." He would sometimes turn in his chair and ask: "And what is your opinion?" This made me uneasy. I realized later that he genuinely wanted to know what such a foreigner thought.

During this summer Mao Tse-tung was formulating and adjusting some important new theses, tentatively presenting them in lectures in K'ang Ta University in Yenan. He knew I had studied Hegel, but I could not accept the large Marxist simplicities without real explanation. He was willing to try to clarify things for me—he enjoyed an intellectual challenge—and agreed to write with me a booklet on revolution in China. What a scoop that would have been! Just to be nice, on the American Fourth of July he gave me a first interview on "the nature of revolution in China." But Japan attacked China on July 7, and Mao turned me over to Wu Liang-p'ing, his right-hand man, and Lo Fu, the official historian, for the rest.

During 1937, Mao Tse-tung first presented his lecture "On Contradiction" at the university; this was after he had read my long list of questions and agreed to tackle the explanations for non-Marxists. The main answer he gave me was this: that you cannot understand revolution in China through formal logic, but only in terms of contradiction. I was prepared to accept this thesis, though I never liked the terminology, which tried to fix the old Western Marxist labels on a different Chinese content. And I am sure the German Li Teh and the Soviet Union could never accept such an idea or even understand its logic. I never expected, however, that the contradictions that bothered me in 1937 would actually lead to armed confrontation in the 1970s between China and the Soviet Union and its satellite Marxists, even though Li Teh and Mao were in opposition that summer.

The beginning of wisdom is to recognize that contradictions *exist*; that this is the nature of truth, which is always two-faced. The problem is to be able to perceive the contradiction at its point of change—and to act in the right direction. This was the special genius of Mao Tse-tung. He tried up to the age of forty-two at least (at Tsunyi in 1935 during the Long March, when he took over supreme command by necessity) to understand and to follow the theories and theses of Soviet Marxists. In 1937, he was still anxious to support the Soviet Union's position, even to the point of releasing his old enemy Chiang Kai-shek to serve as a rallying point for foreign support against Japan and the Axis. But there was a point of self-annihilation beyond which he could not follow. That was the point of real suicide for revolution in China. Mao always waited for this contradiction to reach that breaking point; then he had to reassert his own leadership and shift course (the Chinese called him the "Great Helmsman"). This happened in 1927, in 1935, to some extent in 1938, and then in the 1940s when civil war resumed. Finally, in 1966 he invented the Cultural Revolution to revive the revolutionary quality of the Communist movement.

Mao was never a dogmatist. If he had been, much in China would have been different. He was flexible, willing to change and learn, and most of all, patient—up to that breaking point. He waited for the nadir, then took action on the upturn of the wheel, not too soon, not too late. He led history by following it.

The Communist Congress lasted from May 1 to May 15, 1937,

and when the Central Committee met in August, Mao Tse-tung's living authority was established permanently, except for a hiatus before 1966. On August 13, 1937, I had an interview with Mao at which he gave me the Communist party's ten points for "saving China," particularly from the present threat of Japan. The main thrust was to "give the people the freedom of patriotic activity and the freedom to arm themselves."

To avoid antagonizing the weak and frightened Kuomintang, the ten points included no economic program; the United Front was so fragile that nothing permanent could be proposed, not even simple economic mobilization of the population.

At the end Mao stood up and pounded the table; his face grew red and his eyes flashed lightning. If with the cooperation of the Nanking government these ten points could be realized, "We can strike down Japanese imperialism; *if not, China will perish!*" He repeated the last phrase angrily.

"I feel exactly the same way." I stood up and nodded. "China has to *mobilize* in any way possible or China will perish. Any kind of organization is better than none."

That was my chief conclusion during my Yenan summer: The population had to be mobilized for action in every possible way—which was one way of saying "democracy." (Mao came up later with the key phrase "the *new* democracy," and Ed and I wished we had added that small but important word to the title of our magazine.) I learned that the Communists could organize the people—with nothing whatever to offer them materially, only a fraternity of spiritual power or, as they put it, to "live and die together." Whole armies of teenagers would volunteer—all Red soldiers were unpaid volunteers—and be destroyed. But then new armies would arise. In the loess soil of Yenan, where human life subsisted though vegetable and animal life could barely survive, an awakening of spiritual power was occurring that fed on starvation and danger. The youth of China were in revolt against all the dreadful sickness and helplessness of the past. From beginning to end Mao Tse-tung's revolution was a youth movement, and its *élan vital* always included women.

Mao Tse-tung became deified in his old age for various reasons. He came to personify the "New China," with both its aspirations and its limitations. He was a complicated person with a dialectical mind, and Western categories do not describe him and his career, except at the risk of beclouding more than clarifying. He was the most optimistic person of his entire era, yet he was also cynical and did not trust fools gladly, if at all. He was more open to outside influences than any man of his age in China—and yet he sifted out the chaff from the grain with marvelous dexterity and an instinct for true value.

Mao Tse-tung was a folk figure, writ large. He was China, writ small. He personified the 80 percent of his country that was the village Chinese. The other 20 percent feared him, but in the end recognized his authority and more or less went along with the deification as long as Mao was alive. Mao more resembled Abraham Lincoln than he did any other Westerner, even to being of tall, large presence, grand in natural simplicity. He had the same insatiable desire for learning; even in the 1970s he was studying English to set an example for the people.

The term for Mao Tse-tung is *big*—in every way. Always he established the broad outlines of policy and theory and left the details to administrative people. As a person he was never petty or mean or vengeful, a revolutionary thing in China. He was a winner, and he enjoyed the process of winning, which he accomplished mostly by winning over the minds of others. He never had any rival executed, so far as is known, which was a considerable step up in civilized behavior over the French and Soviet revolutions. In 1937, when the Old Bolsheviks were executing each other, Mao granted freedom to two of his deadly enemies—who continued to try to destroy him up to the end. One was the Comintern agent Li Teh. The other was Chang Kuo-t'ao, who was teaching at K'ang Ta University when I was there; he was allowed to leave Yenan, and he went to Chiang Kai-shek's headquarters, hailing him as the only "true leader."

The key to The Thought of Mao Tse-tung, as the Chinese call it, is that "revolution can change anything." This is not idealism; Mao meant action, not only ideas. He was a radical, root and branch, like the Cromwellians. In 1971, Mao described himself as left of center, and always he moved toward the mainstream to guide the ship of state.

Maoism is a method of change, of revolution; a thesis, not a set blueprint for reconstruction. It is a bridge, by which pre-industrial nations such as those in Asia and Africa may pass lightly over feudalism, as well as capitalism, and seize the weapon of socialism to develop and become strong. Even as a boy in Changsha, Mao realized that socialism was a powerful weapon and tool for development. His method was not to wait for new tools and machinery to change the mode of production, but to engage in armed revolution. His armed local peasants protected the other peasants while they changed the economy and society by act of conscious will, not by waiting for economic determinism to come from outside.

Like all forms of socialism, this type contains within itself its limitations and remnants of the past. It does not take account of the nuclear age, perhaps does not even understand the nature of fallout, which could poison the whole environment.

In the triumvirate of China's long revolution, if Mao Tse-tung was the head and Chu Teh the heart, Chou En-lai was the executive hand.

The first news I had of Chou En-lai was on my arrival in Yenan in May. I was told that "one week before you arrived, a truck with Chou En-lai and Mao Tse-tung's chief of staff was fired on and ten Reds were killed instantly and several wounded who later died. This was only fifteen *li* [five miles] from Yenan. Chou and the chief of staff and one newspaperman escaped with one other man, by a miracle— they ran to cover. Only four escaped injury." This was the truck I had hoped to take from Sian to Yenan but missed, only one week before.

In June of 1936, Chou had ridden out to welcome Ed, and they were good friends ever after. I did not see Chou until June of 1937, as he had gone to Sian, but we had several talks thereafter.

Born in 1899 to a mandarin family, Chou En-lai's experience spanned two revolutions and the transformation of the old clan-familism. The marriage of Chou and his wife, Teng Ying-ch'ao, was the national model of the modern marriage. In 1920, while a student in France, he was a founder of the Chinese Communist Youth League and visited London, Germany, and Moscow. In 1924, he was deputy director of Whampoa Academy under Chiang Kai-shek and became the model for the young cadets of the 1925–1927 revolution. When the revolt failed, he escaped to the Soviet Union, but returned to Kiangsi. From there he embarked on the Long March, during which he made an alliance with Mao Tse-tung at Tsunyi that continued a long time.

In 1949, Chou En-lai became premier of the People's Republic and kept working, it is said, when he was hospitalized for stress, over-work, a heart condition, and cancer. His style, like that of Mao Tse-tung, was extremely Chinese—yet it was also the opposite of Mao's. Chou was a born diplomat and all his life functioned as such, internally and externally. "Chou En-lai-ism" was based on liaison, on finding common ground, the tie that binds. He held the reins of power from the first as if he were using a gyroscope as a chariot seat, always in the middle but moving from side to side.

While Mao Tse-tung liked to stir up volcanoes in the earthbound minds of men, Chou En-lai came along like an engineer to organize the pieces, with the most meticulous attention to detail, superskilled in the art of dealing with the "Chinese" situation. No ancient mandarin could ever have outfoxed Chou. Maoism is the art of the impossible; Chou En-lai-ism the art of the possible. Mao was a statesman. So was Chou, but he was also a natural politician. Chou was a master of teamwork, and was chief of liaison for the United Front with the Kuomintang.

It was always said that Chou En-lai lived a charmed life, that no one else had so many unsuccessful attempts made on his life. Even in the 1960s, thousands of ultra-leftist Red Guards surrounded his office, demanding the secret files of the Communist Central Committee, but Chou talked them into leaving. In 1967, when Chou discovered that a mob of Red Guards was attacking the British *chargé d'affaires'* office, he went there and furiously ordered them to "go home and stay there."

Chou En-lai was not a folk figure like Mao. He represented what the Chinese call students, and was the patron of the intelligentsia. His career started in the May 4th movement of 1919 in Tientsin at the Christian Nankai Middle School; he was more of a treaty-port type than the Chu-Mao pair, more polished and sophisticated. He was actually a "military scholar," as the Chinese call such men. Yet always, at least on the surface, he let Mao Tse-tung preempt the field of theory.

It was not surprising that an East-West thaw was possible during Chou En-lai's active time as premier. Chou was big, liberal, generous, highly civilized, charming, outgoing, and open.

(I did not ask to see either Mao Tse-tung or Chou En-lai on my trip to China in 1972, though doubtless I should have. I was told later that Mao would have liked to see me, but one does not take liberties with Mao Tse-tung and I was afraid he might say no. After I left Peking, two special couriers brought letters to me from both leaders, inviting me for a return visit. Chou En-lai said he regretted not seeing me, but meantime, he had asked his wife to take care of my visit, and said I could stay as long as I liked and go anywhere I wanted in China. His wife, Teng Ying-ch'ao, joined with Chu Teh and his wife, K'ang K'e-ching, to receive me in the Great Hall of the People, where the two women had a dinner for me afterward.)

CHAPTER 36

Four Months
in Yenan

I had intended to stay in Yenan for only a month or so, but in June I heard from my husband in Peking that he was arranging for several traveling Americans to visit Yenan, expecting them to protect me on my way back. He knew how worried I was about carrying my films and notebooks. On June 22, Owen Lattimore, T. A. Bisson, and Philip and Agnes Jaffe arrived in a car driven by Effie Hill, now restored to health, who had helped to arrange my escape from Sian. They stayed a day and left on the twenty-third.

But I couldn't go back with them; they had gotten through the Sian blockade on the pretext that they were merely tourists off to visit a famous mountain, and if they suddenly produced me on their return, they would be in real trouble in Sian, they figured. Even worse, Effie's tiny car was already overcrowded. So I had to entrust to them some of my films and precious notebooks to give to Ed—I was afraid these would be confiscated by the Sian police if *I* carried them back—while I myself was marooned.

I planned to take the first Red Army truck going to Sian, but none came. The roads and bridges between the two cities were washed out in heavy downpours for weeks and remained so until fall, so I was stranded in Yenan until September.

Still, there was much to see and do, and many people to talk to. During the summer I made many appointments and asked thousands of questions. I interviewed at least sixty-five persons and had long or short talks with various people. Nobody except Chang Wen-ping, my evangelical friend from Sian, tried to influence me at all. Quite the contrary. Nobody intruded on me, nor did they go out of their way to help me either. I was on my own the whole four months. The Chinese thought the other foreigners were taking care of me—but the foreigners were much too concerned with their own problems to pay attention to me and mine.

For safety, Agnes Smedley and I were asked to wear army uniform whenever we ventured outside our compounds. I loved wearing pants all the time. This was real liberation. Foreign women in China almost never wore pants then, except for outdoor travel, at which time we usually wore jodhpurs. Yenan was 100 percent trousered. This was a big thing for the new students, who, male and female, had always worn gowns. A gown was the mark of the student and of the aristocracy in China, while the working class, villagers, and common people, male and female, had always worn baggy trousers—pantaloons in fact. The revolutionary men had adopted the "Chungshan" uniform when Sun Yat-sen invented it in the 1920s. Communist men and women still wear it today—and their pants are much less baggy than ever before in the history of China.

Among the Communists, you could hardly tell the men from the women except that the women generally had longer haircuts. The Yenan natives stood with mouths open observing these strangers. All the native women had bound feet, and the feet of some girl children were still being bound. Local peasants still often wore queues and had pompons on their string sandals.

I was not the best kind of visitor for Yenan, though I was willing to adapt to my environment *almost* the whole way. I refused to give up lipstick, however, though I tried to make sure it was not noticeable. I was sick and I felt sicker without it. Makeup was taboo. The only other woman who used it for hundreds of square miles around was a pretty, talented actress recently from Peking, Wu Kuang-wei, interpreter for Agnes Smedley. (Never in her life had Agnes worn makeup—her style was Early Woman Suffrage.)

Immodesty for either male or female was also taboo, and still is. For a female to try to be attractive as such was considered "politically unreliable." Romantic entanglements had to be avoided in this Puritan, Spartan army, which sacrificed everything for the Revolution.

The chief Communist characteristic was puritanism in all ways, and this is still true of the New China. Outside visitors got the feeling that they were in a Boy Scout or YMCA camp. (This same code is still being taught in the New China, especially to schoolchildren, though without any religion other than Maoism.) Male and female could travel in the same groups, but they never touched each other physically at all, not even in handing things to one another, and they were usually segregated into sections. That was why this mobile revolution was possible, and why women could participate, traveling with the Red armies without the least problem. Discipline was 100 percent, not only in the armies but among political people, too.

At first, the penalty for rape was death, and this problem did not exist at all, Chu Teh told me. Extreme Puritan modesty and strict morality were part of the program for winning over the population. Raising the status of women was fiercely defended by the Communists and was a key to their success. This meant special protection not only against rape—or disrespect of any kind—but also in the home and at work, where women had been chattels. A new, nuclear marriage was being instituted, and puritanism was the only effective framework for it.

In Yenan the philosophy of puritanism, stoicism, and spartanism was absolute. Except that a tiny few smoked cigarettes, beginning with Mao Tse-tung himself and his best woman friend, Miss Tsai Ch'ang. (She was the top woman Communist from 1927 to 1966, when Mao's wife, Ch'iang Ch'ing, took over this role.) Today in China, cigarettes are prevalent everywhere—a tremendous waste, as tobacco growing destroys the soil. One reason so many smoke now is in imitation of Chairman Mao, who lived to be over eighty. Yet in other things, Mao was a strong physical culturist, as were Chu Teh and nearly all the male leaders. Mao's slogan was always "plain living and hard work," with no waste—except for cigarettes.

Of course, in Yenan the Red Army had no wine, or even *tea*; they drank hot water. They were all volunteers, without salary. They acquired merit by sacrificing as much as possible. And they enjoyed every minute of it, with group emulation and identification.

They took immense pride in their uniforms, particularly in wrapping their puttees. Men patched and darned and washed, but no ironing existed for wrinkles. Everyone dreamed of wearing a fountain pen in his pocket, even if it wasn't a working model, and tried hard to capture one.

The soldiers loved everything *mo-teng*, or "modern." For sports and drill, many of them wore white athletic shorts with red stripes or other designs. One of the more ubiquitous designs was of a fat little animal that looked for all the world like a sort of middle-aged Mickey Mouse. I asked a soldier what it represented.

"It's a Mickey Mouse," he said.

* * *

An entry in my notebooks reads: "The flies are thick. My interpreter has a cold and trachoma and is very weak but nice. He has no place to stay so he eats here and has only a pallet at the Dramatics School."

My interpreter did not have an easy time of it. When I started a friendly conversation with a bodyguard in my best Peking Chinese, the embarrassed guard instructed my interpreter to tell me that he didn't understand English! Though I told him that I had no trouble communicating with my Peking houseboys, who spoke not a word of English, I don't think he was ever convinced that it was a form of Chinese and not English that we tried to share that summer.

Language was a real challenge for the Red armies, as the soldiers came from all over China and spoke many different dialects, some of them completely unintelligible to a fellow soldier from a different province. (This was a universal problem in that vast country; the Chinese Women's Club in Shanghai had been forced to settle on English as the one tongue its members all had in common.) The effort of constant mental translation evidently sharpened the language skills of the Red soldiers, for they all came to understand each other, though each continued to speak his own dialect. *My* Chinese certainly improved over the summer, to the point that I could at least understand much of what was said to me, though I still needed an interpreter to translate what I wanted to say.

In addition to an interpreter, Agnes Smedley and I each had an armed bodyguard at all times, as all the important Communists also did. My personal bodyguard was Teng Ming-yuan, who had such a hard time understanding my Chinese. He was eighteen and looked younger, with rosy cheeks and fair skin, and was hardly as big as the huge Mauser pistol he carried. He had been in the Red Army for four years and, as an "intellectual," was something of a pet among the six bodyguards who lived in our compound.

Commander of this squad was Tsao Hsing-tsun, whom I privately nicknamed Porthos for his resemblance to that robust Musketeer. Once when I had been on an interview across the river, a heavy downpour threatened flood, and the ferryman refused to return me to the opposite shore. The river was rising fast, and it looked as if I would be marooned for as long as a week. Porthos commandeered a white horse from an officer—who had just made it across the river clinging in the water to the horse's tail. My Musketeer forced the nervous horse back across the river, threw me across his saddle like young Lochinvar, set out through the floodwaters for a third time, and deposited me wet but safe on the far bank. Ever after, Porthos was my hero.

A new and popular activity among the Red Army was singing. Everyone sang at the least opportunity and at the top of his or her lungs. "Dixie" was the favorite in Yenan, with new Chinese words. The whole valley echoed to song, especially just before suppertime during the beautiful sunsets. Across the wall in my compound, a group of Christians made Sunday melodious. Perhaps it was the missionaries who first introduced European-style mass singing to China.

Of all things, the Chinese have most loved the theater, and still do. From the beginning, plays were essential to the Communist revolution, not only as propaganda but as a means to win the population by entertainment. When the Communists reached a new village, first the play was put on. Then the big speech was made to gather converts. Even the young Chinese children are natural actors and appear to have not the least shyness or stage fright. All Chinese seem to love public speaking, too, with no sign of embarrassment. These are still the chief entertainments of China: speeches, meetings, singing, and the theater.

Here was where I failed to measure up. I flatly refused to sing or dance in public, or even to make a speech, though one or more of these performances was expected of all visitors, especially foreigners. Agnes enjoyed performing. But I was petrified at the mere idea of making such an unmitigated idiot of myself. I have no voice at all, and I have refused to make public speeches since high school, where I spoke too much.

General Chu Teh took me to my first night at the Yenan theater. He introduced me and I stood up to bow, but refused to walk up on the stage. I simply couldn't. The whole audience began to clap and demand a speech or song or dance. Chu Teh finally realized that I was really terrified and announced: "Mrs. Snow has a sore throat and she says she never sings or makes speeches anywhere, anyway." This did not make me popular with many in Yenan. (Nor could Mao Tse-tung get me to make a speech or sing.)

I never in my life wanted to be an actor—though I always wanted to write plays—and I dread nothing more than public appearances, which I scarcely ever make. I also dislike quarreling and intramural battles among political people, though I enjoy all kinds of private discussions.

Strangely enough, I discovered that the women of Yenan ap-

proved of my modesty and shyness in public. They warmed up immediately. I soon made friends with most of them. During the summer
Po Ku's wife, Liu Ch'un-hsien, was especially friendly to me, along
with Chu Teh's Amazon wife, K'ang K'e-ching. Liu Ch'un-hsien had
been in charge of the separate column of thirty women during the
Long March. It took her a while to approve of me; first she had to find
out what my ideas were on the status of women. The women were
well-organized in defense of their ideas. Only Ting Ling and Agnes
Smedley dared to disagree with them, especially over the issue of free
love versus marriage, and they were ostracized.

The women simply did not understand Miss Smedley at all, and
only Ting Ling and Chu Teh had any sympathy for her, though she
was desperately in need of help. None of the Chinese appeared to be
the least bit neurotic either. Except for Miss Smedley and Li Teh and
the Korean, Kim San, everyone seemed happy in Yenan.

The most important phenomenon of all was the truly unbelievable *esprit de corps* of the armies and their political leaders that existed
at the front. The "rear" was considered to be dreary and full of politick-
ing, intrigue, and backbiting by comparison. Evans Carlson later told
me he was astonished at the difference. At the front he was received by
Chu Teh and the officers and soldiers in such a way that he gave up
the rest of his life to trying to understand and promote this morale in
America and its Marine Corps. The gung ho spirit was revolutionary
élan, made up of the pure in heart facing self-sacrifice for a purpose.
Then, wonder of wonders, I myself became part of this *esprit de corps*;
during the ten-day trip when I left Yenan for Sian with the young Red
soldiers, though every night I was so exhausted I could hardly crawl
into my camp cot, still, every day I actually forgot how sick I was.

This is spiritual power of a high type and intensity—and for it to
occur in ancient, changeless China is not easy to understand. To say
that it is because the Chinese are alike, like a swarm of bees, does not
explain how it was that I caught some of the mystique, as did my
husband, Evans Carlson, Rewi Alley, and other visitors.

Ting Ling also felt the mystique and tried to explain it to me:
"The Red Army is a new type you cannot find anywhere else in China.
They have never known anything but revolution. Nothing unhappy
comes to mind—they care only for the difficulty of the work. They are
all very young and when I came here I began to feel as young as they
are. Before I came, I couldn't sleep, but now I sleep soundly and am
becoming fat. The simple life is good."

CHAPTER 37

Ten Days on the Road

Peking and Tientsin were occupied by Japan during the first week in August, and fighting began at Shanghai on August 13, 1937. On August 16, the U.S. Legation ordered the evacuation of American women and children from China. Railways were bombed and cut. Ports were closed. Yenan got word of the big events, but details, such as how one might travel, were clouded. I felt stranded, and I was ill. The first thing I had to do was to get to Sian and find accurate facts. But still it rained and rained.

As an alternative, I consulted Mao Tse-tung about becoming an amateur war correspondent at the Shansi front. I told him I had observed the 1932 war in Shanghai, and he had heard the story of my escape from Sian, but nonetheless he looked at me with considerable misgiving in his eyes. I had weighed only 108 pounds on arrival. Now I looked ten years older and more than ten pounds lighter.

"I will write a letter of credential for you to Teng Hsiao-p'ing at the front," Mao decided, shaking the black mane out of his eyes as he wrote the letter in his own hand.

(By the time I arrived at the front, Teng and his army had marched on. But in 1979, Vice-Premier Teng Hsiao-p'ing was the guest of honor at an official "normalization of U.S.-China relations" reception in Washington, D.C., and I at last, forty-two years later, handed him Mao's letter. Teng was already becoming, of course, the chief power in China, masterminding the anti-Mao changes.)

"Hsiao Ching-kuang will take care of everything here," Mao went on. "We welcome Mr. Snow to visit us again at any time."

Hsiao was a big, muscular officer with apple-red cheeks, in command of the rear military area. (In the 1970s, he was still in the top echelons in Peking.) He shook his head in disbelief at my mission and annihilated my poor, frail little bodyguard with one withering glance.

Hsiao said he would get the best bodyguard available to take care of me, as well as a pony to ride and two mules to carry the baggage. "You can go with the first possible contingent," he said. "An armed escort is necessary, of course, for this group."

Agnes Smedley called on me. Her back had not substantially improved, and no one had any idea how bad the injury was. X rays seemed imperative. Mao Tse-tung had peremptorily ordered her, as a troublemaker, out of Yenan. She had already handed me her few small treasures with instructions for their disposal, bequeathing her silk stockings to me personally. (I still have them.)

Miss Smedley's sense of private property tended toward confiscation.

"Do you need that suitcase?" she wanted to know. "Let me have it."

Then and there she handed it graciously to her bodyguard, as a gift, while my bodyguard watched in astounded reproach. "Why didn't *you* give it to *me*?" he later complained.

"How much money do you have?" Agnes next demanded.

"Hardly any," I said. "Maybe a hundred dollars or so for my whole trip."

"Give it to me," she commanded. "You can borrow some here but I can't." Her best friends, Chu Teh and Miss Ting Ling, had marched to the front with the armies in August.

I handed over my hundred dollars, feeling as guilty of riches as a fat bourgeoise on the way to the guillotine.

Who would I borrow from? I decided on Chou En-lai as the most understanding person. Cash was more than scarce in the Red capital, and I borrowed only the smallest amount necessary.

Though communication between Yenan and the outside world was slight, Ed managed to get a radiogram through to me from Tientsin on September 6: YOU CAN STILL RETURN VIA TSINGTAO BUT URGENT YOU LEAVE IMMEDIATELY OR CANNOT RETURN THIS YEAR. By a stroke of great good fortune, the rains stopped, and a Red Army group who had been awaiting a break in the weather to set out for Sian scheduled our departure for the morning of the seventh.

I received a formal visit of farewell from Li Teh, who had scarcely spoken a civil word to me all summer. He handed me a thin black mirror from Germany which he had brought to the Red areas in 1933 and had carried on the Long March. He also gave me a dagger that had been captured with its owner, the highest-ranking Kuomintang officer ever taken in the South, and had been given to Li Teh as an honor.

"These are my only treasures," Li Teh said, and his voice was tremulous with emotion. "I hope you understand how difficult my situation is here. I want you to have them to remember me by."

I was overwhelmed by this unexpected show of sensitivity. "Of course I understand," I said, and told him that he had helped to make a real Christian saint out of me, instead of teaching me Marxism as he should have. I felt that in a way Li Teh knew that he, and through him the Comintern he worked for, were defeated in China. He was passing the torch on to America. (In 1972, I sent the dagger to Chou En-lai for the Revolutionary Museum in Peking. "We will not mention Li Teh's name," they said, "but it will be taken care of anyway.")

Dr. Hatem also appeared to bid me good-bye. He gave me a palimpsest, an old Tibetan book that, for lack of paper, had been written over with Communist propaganda on the Long March. "I like you more than you think," he said cryptically in farewell.

"I *hope* so," I replied.

As Hsiao Ching-kuang had promised, the OGPU (security and intelligence) sent their prize bodyguard to take over from Teng Ming-yuan, who was dispatched to a sanitarium with an advanced case of tuberculosis. It had not occurred to me that his pink cheeks were a symptom—nor that he was coughing into my tea all summer.

My new bodyguard was named Ko Sun-hua. He was not only a hero of the Long March from Kiangsi but a *p'ai-chang*, a sergeant, emanating natural authority and command. On first arrival in my courtyard, Ko Sun-hua looked me over with undisguised alarm. He would probably have liked to check my arm to see if I had any muscles at all. Ko Sun-hua, aged twenty-three, even stood up to Chief of Staff Hsiao Ching-kuang. He demanded a new Mauser and examined the horse and mules critically, making sure we got the best. (The OGPU picked such men for training to become high officers. I wish I knew what has happened to Ko Sun-hua.)

That the grueling twelve-day, 250-mile trip from Yenan to Sian turned out to be a great experience was in no small part due to Ko Sun-hua. I left everything to him to manage—even Agnes Smedley.

When the morning of September 7 dawned, I was so deathly sick I could hardly get out of bed. But I *had to make the trip*. It was the first, perhaps the last opportunity for a long time.

Most of the bridges were still out, and we had to ford the rivers. My horse, apparently well aware of my weakened condition, tossed me off his back in the middle of our first river crossing and headed back for his Yenan stable, taking one of the mules with him. By the time Ko Sun-hua had got the animals and their two *mafoos* (grooms) under control, the rest of our traveling companions were way ahead of us. Half a dozen Red soldiers had to backtrack to guard the tardy group, with much loss of face for Ko Sun-hua—but I noticed it had no effect upon his sound masculine ego.

Exclusive of the armed escort and *mafoos*, our caravan consisted of about thirty, at least three of whom were the wives of Red leaders— Chu Teh, Hsiao Keh, and Po Ku. Hsiao Keh's wife had her baby with her. Chu Teh's wife was determined to get to the fighting front, though women were not allowed there. Several Red officers in our group were on their way to the front, too, and we marched more than twenty miles a day in an effort to catch up with the army before it left for battle.

The *mafoos* and animals were local *Shenpei* (northern Shensi) and not inclined to take orders from any southerner from Kiangsi, especially when they could hardly understand his dialect—and, of course, did not wish to. Thus for the trip I became an interpreter between the southern Red soldiers and the local volunteers and villagers. I taught my pure Hait'ien Mandarin speech to Ko Sun-hua along the way, and we carried on long conversations in a few dozen basic words—chiefly Marxist.

Miss Smedley was part of the entourage in a stretcher with five bearers, plus her bodyguard and her *hsiao-kuei*, or boy orderly. Neither of them was much use, and she treated them like children— which they rather liked, as it enabled them to shirk responsibility.

The first moment Miss Smedley got a glimpse of my muscular, healthy new bodyguard, her eyes brightened and she took a second look. I well knew what was in her mind. All during the trip she coveted her neighbor's manservant, but there was a limit to the Christian Girl Scoutism I had practiced all summer trying to be friends with this irascible, complicated person, who was charming one minute and impossible the next. My suitcase and my hundred dollars she might have, but my bodyguard? Not until the last mile to Sian had been traversed. I figured she would confiscate Ko Sun-hua the minute I left Sian. She did. But while he was still *my* bodyguard, I teased him about being exchanged for Miss Smedley's hopeless one. Though Ko Sun-hua was a serious, responsible young man, with not much sense of humor, he could produce a half smile at the teasing.

(When I said farewell to a visibly unhappy Ko Sun-hua at the Sian station later, I teased him for the last time: "I'm not sure whether you hate to see me leave or whether you're afraid of Miss Smedley.")

Miss Smedley also coveted my horse and, except for my body-guard's firm action, would have taken it away from me most of the trip. I let her ride it part of the time, but at other times Ko Sun-hua insisted that I ride. Of course, Agnes loved this protective characteristic and coveted him the more.

You can imagine the confiscatory gleam in her flashing blue eyes (she looked like Bette Davis in her queen of England roles) when she discovered that Ko Sun-hua was a 1932 veteran and had been a squad commander in the 1st Company of Cheng Ken's 1st Division of the First Red Army Corps, the elite corps of all the armies, which had never been defeated. He had been on the banks of the Ta-t'u River at the most famous crossing of the Long March, and he knew that I looked upon him as a legendary Long March hero.

Ko Sun-hua never sang, but soon several of his friends added themselves to our group, and we all developed a warm rapport. As we crossed the hills, all of them, even the dour Ko, picked bluebells, larkspur, daisies, and other wild flowers to deck my saddle. And they sang. The southerners were homesick for the green fields of their native South, which they expected never again to see.

Every day Agnes thawed out a little more and finally reentered the human race after her spell of hostility. We stayed in the same peasants' huts, or stables or schoolhouses, and my bodyguard took charge of everyone, including, when I asked him to, firm command over Agnes and her entourage. I was no psychiatric nurse—but Ko Sun-hua was. Psychologically, he took the place of her protector, Chu Teh, until she was able to rejoin that guardian. Later, she wrote: "Each day my admiration for him increases. . . . When out of patience with other men, I think of Kuo Shen-hua."* Except for Mao Tse-tung, I never heard of anyone else who could command Agnes Smedley save our mutual bodyguard. She felt secure with him and did as he ordered—sometimes.

---

*Agnes Smedley, *China Fights Back* (London: Victor Gollancz, 1938), p. 95. Her spelling for Ko Sun-hua looks more Mandarin than mine in print—but on the march, my Kiangsi accent was impeccable when I called the sergeant.

After the first terrible day of the trip, a sort of revival set in. When the human body reaches a maximum point of stress and exhaustion, it often experiences a second wind. Adrenaline flows, and cortisone, and all the lifesaving substances the body secretes to save itself in a real emergency. I decided to enjoy the journey—and I actually found it delightful, despite my exhaustion.

We slogged through mud, walked or rode over twenty miles a day. Each day before dawn we set out on an empty stomach, stopped for our first meal in a village at about eleven, and ate our second (and final) meal when we stopped for the night in another town. My body-guard ate only millet, but for me he made an egg custard with water, and boiled squash every night. Sometimes we were able to purchase from the villagers some parched corn or a few hard pears.

All our food, and that of everyone in the Red armies, was always paid for. No tents were used; the soldiers were always billeted in deserted buildings or with local families. They paid their hosts for even a few minutes' use of a stove, and always left their quarters as neat and clean as they had found them—or even cleaner. No matter how hungry he was on his meager millet diet, no one would dream of raiding an orchard or garden in passing. This almost unbelievable respect for private property, particularly astonishing in a Communist movement, was a great factor in winning and keeping popular support; even merchants and landlords welcomed the Reds passing through.

At Yao-hsien, where we bedded down in a stable among every conceivable form of insect life, I thought I had contracted the black plague or typhus, which is carried by body lice. My temperature shot up, and the room reeled around me. I was convinced that I was dying, but Dr. George Hatem, who fortunately was with the army there, was able to reassure me. Evidently the few cigarettes I had borrowed from a *mafoo* had been doped with opium, a practice of the Japanese that effectively increased sales among the North China population—and perhaps decreased resistance to the invaders as well.

At Sanyuan we learned that the army of Liu Pei-ch'eng was beginning a night march for the Shansi front from their headquarters in Yun-yang. I did not want to miss meeting this famous commander, and also I had my letter from Mao Tse-tung to deliver to Teng Hsiao-p'ing. So, before dawn, Po Ku's wife, Liu Chien-hsien, and I were in hired rickshas on our way to Yun-yang, with only our two bodyguards for protection. When we reached headquarters four hours later, great was the angry consternation there. We had blithely crossed a dangerous bandit no-man's-land, and Po Ku's wife would have been a valuable prize for ransom, not to speak of Edgar Snow's. And we had missed Liu and Teng by only a few hours; the last detachment of the Eighth Route Army (as this branch of the Red Army was now called under the United Front) had left during the night.

We stayed overnight in Yun-yang and were sent back the next morning to Sanyuan with a military escort. A truck with another armed escort was to take us from Sanyuan to Sian, with a special pass to get me through those gates I had so illicitly passed five months before.

CHAPTER 38

Reunion in Sian

My chief worry about returning to Sian had been that my notebooks and films might be confiscated, either there or at any other point in my travels. To contain them I had made a sort of life belt with pockets, and I wore it around my waist under my coat whenever the going looked dangerous.

Once we had left the Communist areas, it was very important *not* to wear the Red Army uniform that we had worn for safety during the summer. Agnes Smedley had worn loose black slacks and a white blouse and jacket, foreign-style, for most of our ten-day excursion. However, the morning we left Sanyuan she put on full army gear, including belt and cap, to make a dramatic entrance. Our escort commander was furious and ordered her back into civilian togs. But she did not obey. Agnes was by nature a real actress—and she knew when an entrance could be made.

We boarded our official Eighth Route Army truck and entered Sian on September 18—the date my Sian visa expired. We went straight to the Red Army office, where, among others, I met Chou En-lai's wife, Teng Ying-ch'ao, for the first time. Just a few days earlier, she told me as she invited me to share her small room, Ed had helped her escape from Peking. (In my subsequent visits to China, in both 1972 and 1978, she and K'ang K'e-ching, Chu Teh's wife, received me at formal banquets in Peking, a far cry from the cramped quarters and Spartan fare we had shared in 1937.)

The next morning, September 19, I headed for the Guest House. My visa for Sian had expired the day before. I was in the city illegally. However, Sian had changed, fortunately. The United Front was now operating—a little. At the Sian Guest House, Mr. Chou was delighted to see me. He telephoned Captain Ouyang for me, to ask him to help ship me out of town. Though that had once been Captain Ouyang's overriding priority, this time he didn't even come to see me. Three spies did show up for my "protection," in time to spend three hours with me, and Agnes and Ko Sun-hua in a bomb cellar when Japanese planes approached within twenty miles of the airport. It was evident that the story of my previous escape was well-known in Sian; and their attitude toward me was not without a certain sly admiration.

My bodyguard was uneasy and worried. I informed Mr. Chou that Ko was a hero of the Long March, and even the three spies viewed him with professional interest. He was wearing a too-small student uniform and nobody ever looked less like a student. He had the usual Communist assurance that the future belonged to him, that he was worth a hundred enemy soldiers—which was the official Red reckoning of the proper combat ratio.

After the abortive air-raid scare, I registered for my old room at the Guest House and showed Ko the window I had jumped out of in April.

"And this is American imperialism," I announced proudly, showing him the beautiful modern plumbing with white porcelain equipment. He studied the strange water faucets. "We invented all these scientific marvels. We take a bath every day."

At that Ko looked unbelieving. For ten days none of us had so much as undressed at night, though we did brush our teeth and sometimes used a hot washcloth on our faces. In North China, water was precious. Bathing was sponge-style, out of the same washbasins the armies also used to prepare and serve food.

Continuing Ko's introduction to the wonders of modern civilization, I took him (and my three spies) to his first movie. Ko was spellbound, speechless. The film, of Suiyuan, had been taken by Newsreel Wong, Ed's old Shanghai friend who had made a newsreel of me in 1932.

My problem was how to get out of Sian. When I learned that the railway to Tsingtao on the coast was still open, I gave up my plan of becoming a war correspondent and snatched at this hope of escape. Because the railway was regularly being bombed, I would need a special pass from the governor of Shensi to get on a troop train.

The Eighth Route Army arranged for this; and on my thirtieth birthday, September 21, 1937, Mr. Chou and Ko Sun-hua took me to the railway station. Two of my old "bodyguards" from the April days came along to join the three new ones—they had to report that I actually *did* get on this train.

"Someday the Sian Guest House will be looked upon as a center of romantic adventures," Mr. Chou predicted. "You are my favorite story." (In 1983, Peter Chou wrote me from Australia, asking my help in getting his niece, resident in Peking, into a United States university. It is a Chou family tradition now to recount the story of how he introduced me to Kempton Fitch, the only possible way I could have got to Yenan then—as Mr. Chou was well aware.)

Ko Sun-hua stood at the bottom of the train steps, silent, with his head downcast. He was swallowing hard. He kept his head averted so the spies would not notice the tears that rolled down his honest, suntanned face.

The Great Wall between China and the rest of the world seemed very far away. Here was the scrutable Chinese man in tears, as if leaving his dearest relative. This was grass-roots Chinese-American friendship. Never would I do anything to break this special relationship, woven of such a few, fragile threads in a world where merciless swords cut at international understanding and natural human identities.

It was eleven o'clock when the special express whistled its long, long note of departure. As I waved from the steps of the train, the knot of spies, who had kept their backs to me until now, turned to look. They all blushed and bowed, smiling in embarrassment.

But they were not rid of me yet. . . .

About seven hours later, in the early evening, the troop train stopped at Tungkuan, known to travelers as the most sinister city in all China. It was Chiang Kai-shek's military and strategic headquarters for the whole Northwest of China. Where the half-mile-wide Yellow River, flowing south, bent at an angle to the east, two other rivers drained into it near the bend: the Lo and my old friend the Wei from near Sian. The city stood on a bluff about eighty feet above the Yellow River. It had been a walled-in fortress from time immemorial.

There, Chinese were searched and often disappeared, not only those suspected of being Communists but other kinds. I knew there had been an order in April to apprehend me if I got to Tungkuan and tried to circle around to the Red areas. And now, like the most terrible nightmare coming true, four military gendarmes and some police burst into my compartment, grabbed my luggage, and pulled me struggling off the train. Never have I been more frightened.

"Why? Why?" I asked piteously.

They didn't know why, or wouldn't tell me. All they would say was that they had received a telephone call from Sian.

Daring to touch me or my luggage was most un-Chinese behavior, and hence doubly terrifying. They refused even to look at my special pass from the governor. Tungkuan was the Gestapo Fascist security headquarters. I was wearing my life belt of notebooks and films under my coat. Were they planning to force me to give information about the Reds? Would I simply disappear in Tungkuan, with *anyone* blamed for it?

For half an hour an armed escort took me in a ricksha through a labyrinth of dark, desolate streets. Tungkuan was under martial law; four times we were stopped and my passport examined.

We finally arrived not at some secret Gestapo outpost but at the China Travel Service Guest House. The manager put in a telephone call to Sian and handed me the phone. The voice in my ear was garbled but oh so welcome: "Jim and I came here to Sian to find you. We just missed by four hours. Take the next train back here. I haven't heard a word about you for weeks and weeks. Are you all right?"

I was just able to prevail on my heart to get out of my throat and down where it belonged so I could speak: "I'm simply petrified. Yes, I'll be on the next train." A reprieve from terror, the best birthday present I could have received. Threading the dark maze back to the railway station to get the first train for Sian, my armed escort no longer seemed sinister.

On the station platform, several Chinese gathered around me. Foreigners seldom stopped at Tungkuan, but all over China, Americans were usually greeted with eager warmth. This time it was different. One man brandished a newspaper threateningly and said, "It says here that President Roosevelt refuses to help China." Never before had I felt *any* anti-Americanism in China.

My train arrived in Sian at 2:00 A.M., and Ed and Jim Bertram were waiting, with a police guard, to take me to the Guest House, where they were staying.

Ed commented on my condition: "You don't look much like the canary that swallowed the cat."

"You look like a missionary in that blue Chinese student gown— quite picturesque," Jim contributed.

"What's happened to both your books?" I wanted to know.

"Both finished and safe with the publishers," Ed reported. "I came to find you as soon as I got the last chapter off in the mail."

"Of course you're going to Yenan," I said to Jim. "You'll be the first British national in the Communist areas."

At the Guest House, Mr. Chou was waiting up for me with his best YMCA smile. "I'm putting you in your same old room—my favorite room now," he said, bursting over with the drama of the situation. He offered us some Tsingtao beer.

"This calls for some of Li Teh's brandy," Ed decided. Jim fetched a bottle from his luggage. "You can tell him I bought a bottle for him when you get to Yenan," Ed said.

Mr. Chou hurried to produce some water glasses.

Ed proposed a toast. "To canaries and missionaries," he said.

But Jim frowned. "Why don't we say something epic, something to remember this by?"

"To Sian," I said. "And to Mr. Chou, who introduced me to Kempton Fitch, who introduced me to Effie Hill, without which I'd never have got to Yenan. And to the Sian Guest House, where we all three have cooked up so many nefarious plans."

As we drank Li Teh's brandy, I promised Mr. Chou that someday I would write a comic opera about him and the Sian Guest House. "You can translate it into Chinese," I told him.

In his second book, Jim wrote: "We saw the Snows off next day at the railway station, to the infinite relief of the Special Police, who still followed our every move. Peg's guard . . . was profoundly affected by this second parting." *

Ko Sun-hua was waiting when we appeared in the hotel lobby next day, his face alight with anticipation. He took hold of Ed's hand, begged him to go to the Red front to report on the "real war," and applied for the post of Ed's bodyguard forthwith.

Ed explained that the *London Daily Herald* had ordered him to go immediately to Shanghai, where the major war against the Japanese was in progress.

"Chairman Mao will be disappointed," said Ko Sun-hua, marshaling his arguments. Why did Ed think there wouldn't be a big war in the Northwest? "We'll have the first victory. My division has never been defeated—no, not once—and it never will be, not by anyone."

---

* *Unconquered*, published in 1939 by the John Day Company, New York, was about Jim's trip to the Red armies and to Yenan. "Peg" was my nickname. The blue gown he referred to is now in the Metropolitan Museum in New York, along with the string sandals I wore in Yenan.

He brought up another point: "Mrs. Snow has a special pass from Mao Tse-tung—in his own handwriting, too."

Two days later, on September 24, Ko Sun-hua's division in which he was sergeant, the famous never-defeated 1st Division, under the leadership of Cheng Ken scored the first Chinese victory against Japan, at Pinghsingkuan in nearby Shansi. All China was astonished—except the Ko Sun-huas. They expected it.

Ko Sun-hua had not even hesitated to order Edgar Snow to the Red front, the best way he knew how. Ko Sun-hua epitomized what became known in the 1960s as "the Yenan spirit," which Mao Tse-iung then tried to recapture for both army and civilians. Sergeant Ko never questioned that "revolution can change anything," or that his 1st Division was invincible. Greater yet was his open natural friendliness toward Westerners and their scientific advances. Ed and Jim both recognized immediately that a special East-West rapport was embodied in this serious youth, just as Agnes saw a young Chu Teh in him.

The X rays of Agnes's back had indicated no serious injury, and she planned now to go to the Red front. We said good-bye to her, and to Jim, and to all our other friends in Sian, and on September 23, we took the eleven o'clock train for Tsingtao on the coast. At the station my bodyguard pumped Ed's hand enough to prime a whole new Chinese-American entente—which Ko was trying to establish with the other Snow, hoping we would both come back.

In his fourth book, *The Battle for Asia*, my husband (who usually referred to me in his books by my pen name, thought up by him from the Greek *nym*, meaning "name," and Wales, because I was part Welsh) wrote of our Sian reunion and of that train trip:

> It may seem trivial to dwell on the fate of one wife in a country where they come in pairs or better, but Nym was the only one I had. . . . There was perhaps a design in the accidental timing of my arrival in Sian. At Hsuchow we got off to change trains . . . it had been heavily attacked; 85 Japanese planes had bombed various cities of the Lunghai and Tsinpu railways. I asked about the wrecked train I had seen not far from the city; many passengers were killed. Nym would have been on it if I had not called her back from Tungkuan. *

In Tsingtao we went to the Edgewater Beach Hotel for a few days of rest and good food and swimming. We were the only guests at the

* Edgar Snow, *The Battle for Asia* (New York: Random House, 1941).

hotel, as I remember it, but no Germans were leaving this special area, which they had long dominated.

My voice was still husky from nervousness and stress. Ed also needed a vacation, after being in the war in Peking and working hard on *Red Star Over China*. We rode in horse carts, ate ice cream sundaes at Jimmy's, and enjoyed the beautiful city—but who knew when Japan would attack here?

Ed went on to Shanghai to cover the war. On October 12, I boarded the *Yochow* for Tientsin, crammed with refugees as all coastal ships were—some prosperous Chinese just rode back and forth, treating the ships as if they were hotels.

My old diary reads: "October 13, Chefoo. Seven U.S. destroyers at Weihaiwei and one Jap plane. Had six cruisers outside the bay. Would not let the Chinese ships out."

At Tientsin I took time to look at the city. The Japanese had bombed and destroyed Nankai University on July 29.

I had to pass the Japanese inspection ports twice in Tientsin and again in Peking, which they had occupied on August 11. All Chinese were carefully, and rudely, searched. But the Japanese dared not touch any American then for fear of involving us in the war. Still, I always worried about my life belt of notebooks and films under my coat. Most of all I feared for my notes on the Korean whom I wrote about in *Song of Ariran*. The Japanese would have seized those notes without question had they suspected such valuable information was available.

I was homesick for Peking, the ancient city without courage and without fear. On October 17, the mournfully whistling train passed the outer walls at Yungtingmen. Then the Temple of Heaven came into view, and the Fox Tower, my old friend on the Tartar wall, and Ch'ien Men, the big main gate where Ed and I had photographed the students confronting the Chinese police.

Japan now occupied this dead city, haunted by old ghosts of forgotten glory. But only twelve years later, Mao Tse-tung would be standing on Tienanmen saying, "China has stood up." I was not surprised.

PART FOUR

GUNG HO

CHAPTER 39

Farewell to
Peking

At the German Hospital they found I had not only the dreaded amebic dysentery but four other kinds as well. Their special treatment for dysentery included a picture of Hitler on the wall of my room. I could only hope the doctors and nurses would not take revenge on me for my war against the Axis.

C. M. MacDonald, correspondent of *The Times* of London, was leaving for Shanghai, and when I got out of the hospital, his new wife asked me to stay with her. The servants despised MacDonald's wife and were sure she must have been a chambermaid because she made her own bed and expertly cleaned the bedroom herself. (Later, when she followed her husband to Shanghai, their new baby's crib got shrapnel through its mosquito netting. Then Mac was on the *Panay* when the Japanese attacked it on the Yangtze. She left for England permanently. She had hated China and everything about it.)

At first, I couldn't sleep at all and I was jumpy and nervous. It turned out that the tonic given to me by the doctor had strychnine in it. Once I gave that up, the recuperation began. But though supposedly cured of the cause, I had painful abscesses and was continuing treatment for them.

I had been away almost seven months. Stacks of letters awaited me, with requests for articles and books. The reviews that had collected of our anthology, *Living China*, were lyrical.

At that moment, one could buy marvelous things for almost nothing. It was hard to resist and I did buy a big gold-colored camel's hair rug. (I later had to sell it in another starving time.) It was time to leave Peking, to join Ed in Shanghai. Our servants sadly packed up the files and some books—forty boxes' worth.

As with thin, trembling arms I packed my trusty old friends from the closet at No. 13, I remembered the healthy, happy American girl of twenty-three who had arrived with these few beautiful evening gowns six years before, weighing more than twenty pounds over her present one hundred. I still didn't *want* to be a martyr. I was too busy to think about myself much, and had been so since 1935. I had been pulled away from myself by a cyclonic wind and carried into another world not intended to be my own, like Dorothy in *The Wizard of Oz*, my first favorite book.

I was painfully aware that I had not yet even written my first book. This time I would write it at any cost.

CHAPTER 40

Gung Ho: We Start the Industrial Cooperatives

I left Peking and Tientsin on November 21, 1937. In a few days I stood at the window of a Butterfield & Swire coastal steamer, as six years before I had stood on the deck of the S.S. *President Lincoln* looking out at the busy and prosperous Whangpoo harbor. What a different scene met my eyes today.

There were miles of devastation along the Whangpoo River. Japanese freighters were already loading looted machinery and scrap iron for the home islands. Shanghai was still burning; the Chinese had resisted from August 13 to November 9. I was in time to witness on December 3 the solemn, tense victory parade of Japanese troops on Nanking Road, where once I had ridden in my ricksha to my job at the American Consulate General. No tea dances were being held now on Admiral H. E. Yarnell's flagship *Augusta*. The foreign Asiatic fleets were still on the Whangpoo, but Japan had occupied the entire Chinese part of Shanghai. (Not for another four years would Japan take the foreign settlements, at the time of Pearl Harbor.) Without opposition, Japanese troops were marching the two hundred miles to China's capital, Nanking, occupying it on December 12 with atrocities hard to believe.

Waiting for me at the customs jetty, their coat collars turned up against a bitter wind, were my husband and J. B. Powell. I didn't want to hand Ed the luggage manifest, but I had to. He whistled with horror. "You've got nearly forty boxes of useless stuff here. Who's going to pay all the transportation and storage on this junk?" How he hated luggage! He actually traveled with half what he needed and was always half-prepared for whatever came up.

"It's only your files and my files, some books—no furniture."

As J. B. Powell and I waited, I asked him how it would be possible for the Chinese to fight without any machinery.

"Seventy percent of China's industrial plant was in Shanghai and Wusih," he said, "and most of the rest is in Hankow on the Yangtze."

In a taxi we three drove through suffocating crowds of refugees in all stages of disease and rags. "There must be six hundred thousand factory workers unemployed and dying on the streets," J.B. said. He was heading some Red Cross projects, and they were swamped. "Ridiculous even to think of soup kitchens for this relief problem. The Settlement has at least a million and a half refugees altogether."

Ed remarked that almost no machinery had been moved to safety in time by the Chinese, and asked J.B., who was a close friend of Kuomintang leaders, if there wasn't some way to get the government to evacuate some before the Japanese got every scrap of it.

"It's never been done that way in China yet," came the seasoned reply.

At dinner with J.B. in the American Club where he stayed, I was briefed on some details of the fall of Shanghai. J.B. had been watching from the roof of the club when hundreds of people had been killed nearby as Chinese pilots bombed by mistake. Blood ran in the gutters.

Ed had rented an apartment at the Medhurst on Bubbling Well. It was there that a project was hatched, during many long discussions with many people, that I would be able to look back upon as my small but long-term contribution to history: the gung ho industrial cooperatives.

One early December Sunday, Ed took me to lunch with Rewi Alley at his place—roast beef, with walnuts for dessert. Ed had met him briefly on the railroad while reporting on the dreadful famine in the Northwest about 1929, but I had never seen this powerful muscular dynamo before. I liked Rewi instantly. He had sandy hair and blue eyes as deep as the ocean off the continental shelf. Most of all, I was delighted to look at a foreigner who was healthy and athletic after so many years in the East. However, he had arrived in 1927, and the massacres of that year had left a permanent scar on his psyche, as had his terrible experiences during World War I with the New Zealand Army.

Rewi was charming, shy, quiet, well-bred, lonely, and quite isolated, though he had adopted two Chinese orphan boys at the time of the famine. His sense of humor had been arrested, and he was God's angry man, volcanically alive with all kinds of frustrated indignation.

"I'd like to get behind a machine gun," he announced, crushing walnuts with his fingers.

Rewi personified the best in British civilization—Irish-English poetic sensitivity, physical culture, sports, love of nature and hiking, most of all the Puritan ethic—not only the work ethic but also the conscience, as well as the identification with honest, working people. He was a natural socialist, in other words, with healthy instincts and emotions. He had all the good qualities of the Boy Scout tradition, the British soldier code of total courage and sense of duty, and he had respect for every human being. Well, no—he had a blind spot when it came to "intellectuals," who refused to work with their hands. He never did get along with them, especially not the frail Chinese type who lived by "face."

Of all things, Rewi detested "face." Never would he get dressed up, not even for his talks with Madame Chiang Kai-shek—which became something of a detriment to his gung ho work. (The Communists finally did get him into long pants for formal receptions after 1949.)

Rewi had leadership qualities, but he also had humility and did not mind taking orders, which he had learned to do in the army in his teens. This was part of his "socialist" characteristic. (In 1960, he finally joined the New Zealand Communist party, meantime becoming somewhat sinicized and fitting into his China environment. He still makes his residence in China—at the former Italian Embassy in Peking. He has been one of the all-time travelers in China, hiking and taking any means of transportation to the most remote places.)

Rewi already had a following among the YWCA secretaries in China, all of whom represented Western social conscience. When Ida Pruitt met Rewi in 1938, she decided to devote the rest of her life to being his girl Friday. Rewi was the only man she or any such Western social worker had ever met who came up to their ideal of what a Western man in China should be.

At our regular Sunday lunches, Rewi and Ed at first spent most of their indignation criticizing and blaming Chiang Kai-shek for everything. They were furious that machinery had not been evacuated before Japan could get hold of it, either for Japanese use or strategically to destroy the industrial base of China. Ed and Rewi wanted Big Industry to function.

My point of view was not the same. I didn't believe in criticizing unless I had something better to offer. Why waste time blaming Chiang Kai-shek or anyone else for the Chinese situation? It was clear that Rewi was expending valuable energy that could better be put into production. But what could he do? What could anyone do in the dreadful, hopeless mess? Our three minds should be able to think of something practical. Rewi was a natural mover of mountains—and I was a natural prime mover of people like Rewi. Something had to click.

Rewi was the factory inspector of the International Settlement. As soon as the Japanese allowed, he took me around in his official car to see the devastation of the industrial areas. After one such trip in 1938, Rewi recorded, I "stood over" him and said: "'Now look here, Rewi, what China wants today is industry everywhere . . . a movement for industry. . . . I tell you, Rewi, you say you like China, you ought to drop this job . . . and get out and do something that will be useful at this time. The Chinese are made for cooperation.' This she said and much more . . . 'Let's put it all down and make a word picture of what could be done.'"*

After one of these inspection trips, I wrote the first article about Indusco, as our organization was eventually called, for Powell's *China Weekly Review*. The title was "Japan's Vampire Policy," and it got J.B. concerned.†

The original idea germinating in my mind was inspired by the British consul, John Alexander, after a dinner party. I was surprised to find him enthusiastic about cooperatives in Scandinavia, as opposed to Marxist ideas of socialism. We did not discuss industry or the Chinese problem at the dinner, but John had given me a new concept when he said, "Cooperatives are a democratic base in any kind of society— capitalist, socialist, communist, or what have you. There's no argument against them, for anything can be built on such a base."

Wasn't that exactly what China needed? I wondered later, reviewing the discussion in my mind. Why not combine industry with cooperatives? As soon as this concept came to me, I was sure it was *dead right*, imperative; nothing could shake my conviction. But I had no example to point to nor any language to use; and at first, neither Ed nor Rewi was willing to accept the vague idea, new as we thought it was, though we imagined such cooperatives must exist somewhere.

* Rewi Alley, *Two Years of Indusco* (Hong Kong, 1940).
† This was picked up by *Reader's Digest*, September 1938.

Not for some time did we find a book in Shanghai that described what I had in mind. It was by C. F. Strickland and I have lost the title, but in 1938 in May we reprinted some of it in our first booklet, *Chinese Industrial Cooperatives:*

"The Co-Partners Society . . . in which the labourers themselves own and manage the factory . . . Production through distributive societies which employ wage-earners is the more usual method of northern Europe, while the co-partners' workshop of secrecy . . . is not cooperative. Publicity is essential to cooperation. . . ." *

Ed was always open-minded and not afraid of original ideas, but Rewi was not only cautious but already committed to what he thought was "Marxism" of the orthodox Soviet variety. None of us wanted to be called "social democrats," which was then a term of utmost contempt. At that time, in Germany the conflict between Marxists and social democrats was so great that Hitler came to power because of this suicidal division.

We all three knew how rotten and useless the existing cooperatives in China were; the missionaries had got them going, and some were being used against the Communists in Kiangsi. But I had got hold of the key—*producers'* cooperatives were not the same as the others. A change in the *mode of production* was the Marxist key to a change in the social structure, not a change in distribution or credit. The village needed the industrial revolution—why not bring it about by cooperatives?

(A bigger objection was not then clear to us—but it is now one of the principal causes of hostility between the Soviet Union and China. *Small* production breeds capitalism rather than leading to socialism— this is the Soviet theory. This may be true, but even so, no alternative existed in China. The Communists were then opposed to any kind of collective production as being premature. They had only state industry and private industry, with no plan to industrialize China except to imitate the Soviet Union. My husband wrote a letter to Mao Tse-tung, asking if he would allow the industrial cooperatives in his areas and the reply was yes. This was the chief form of industrial production in Red areas until after 1949.

* A detailed account appears in Nym Wales's *The Beginnings of the Industrial Cooperatives in China*, Scholarly Press, 1961. In my book *China Builds for Democracy*, 1941, may be found the constitution and by-laws, which were checked by the League of Nations.

Mao Tse-tung's idea has been aptly stated as "walking on two legs," building both big and small industry. But the Soviet Union never approved of the cooperatives in China and does not now like the fifty thousand in India, where the idea of Big Industry was pursued also.)

In a 1982 speech at the tenth-anniversary memorial of the death of Edgar Snow, Rewi Alley remembered: "It seemed to us that in 1937 the big problem was how to develop enough economic strength in the interland for the resistance to carry on. . . . Peg, Ed's then wife, said, 'There must be a people's movement for production, and the only way to get that is to have the people organize and manage themselves, linking their production units up together. Industrial Cooperatives are the answer!' Ed agreed and enlarged on the possibilities. I went home, and altered the plan I had made, in accordance with their ideas."

Rewi and his Chinese engineer friends in Shanghai drew up the technical plan. This was revised until the blueprint was suitable for any Asian village or any underdeveloped country. (By 1947, Indusco had been copied in India, Burma, Japan, and elsewhere. Jawaharlal Nehru begged Rewi to come to India to get the work going, but Rewi never wanted to leave China.)

Rewi was the indispensable man. He went out into the villages and got the work moving by sheer force of effort and personality, though constantly harassed and sabotaged by the opposition. The creation of these cooperative industries is one of the most astonishing accomplishments in any pre-industrial country.

The first Chinese I turned to in 1938 were two YWCA secretaries, Chang Hsu-yi and K'ung P'u-sheng. They found the only expert on cooperatives in Shanghai, Lu Kuang-mien, who got the first cooperative started—of blacksmiths. In the back of my mind was a productive notion: that all the Protestants in China jolly well ought to get to work at the grass-roots level for the first time to compensate for their educations and for foreign help. By the same token, all the missionaries owed it to China, and to their homeside financial supporters for a century, to get behind a viable self-help project for the *first time*. These groups did help. I never heard of even the most reactionary missionary who opposed the gung ho cooperatives, though they did not give them much help. They preferred to keep their students in school, instead of getting into production and helping to "save China," as the phrase was then.

The first Committee for the Promotion of Industrial Cooperatives in China was formed on April 3, 1938, at a dinner in the King Kong Restaurant in Shanghai. Hubert Liang was chairman and John Alexander was secretary. Hubert brought the three leading bankers of Shanghai, including Hsu Hsing-loh (who, while carrying our plan to Hankow a short time later, was killed in a plane crash, some thought not accidentally). Hubert also brought Miss Huang Ting-chu, a clubwoman. I brought our publisher, Hu Yu-tze (who became head of Peking's publishing work in 1949). With Rewi and Ed, eleven were present. The eleventh was Lu Kuang-mien, the cooperative expert introduced to me by K'ung P'u-sheng.

John Alexander had to be incognito at our meetings. He had been away on a trip after our first dinner, and we did not see him again until March, when there was a confidential meeting on March 18. The minutes read: "Edgar Snow and Helen Snow had suggested and in collaboration with Rewi Alley had worked out a skeleton plan for the establishment of cooperatives in China. . . . Alexander had been consulted and asked to help . . . Alexander volunteered to get the support of the American and British cooperative movements."

As in the case of our magazine, the Indusco meetings were forging a united front of divergent elements, reaching out for a *modus vivendi* to mobilize economic resources as best we could.

However, no wheel would have turned except for the British ambassador, Sir Archibald Clark-Kerr, who was asked to help get Chiang Kai-shek's government to allow the Indusco work to be started. He got Madame Chiang Kai-shek and her sister Madame H. H. Kung behind the project. In Hong Kong, the third Soong sister, Madame Sun Yat-sen, had been asked earlier to give her approval to our project. She was the liaison for left-wing and liberal causes then.

As for the government, all roads led to the Soong dynasty. Dr. H. H. Kung, the premier, became nominal head, forced into this by his wife, Eling, and her sister Madame Chiang Kai-shek, who burst into tears when at first Kung refused. Five million Chinese dollars were set aside from relief funds, but it was doled out so slowly that the Chinese Industrial Cooperative (C.I.C.) movement was almost strangled.

Indusco was the only project the entire Soong dynasty agreed on. Madame Sun Yat-sen, for example, was a good friend of Edgar Snow, but Madame Chiang Kai-shek detested him. Madame Sun influenced her favorite brother, T. V. Soong, to support it—but he was at odds with his brother-in-law Dr. H. H. Kung! Behind the scenes, T. V. Soong was helpful to Indusco and also assisted left-wing causes. He was at the time the most important banker in China.

By June 15, 1938, we were meeting at the Bankers' Club and J. B. Powell had joined, along with one of Rewi's YWCA friends, Talitha Gerlach. (Like Rewi, Talitha still lives happily in China, where she helped Madame Sun Yat-sen, and has become somewhat sinicized.)

Meantime, W. H. Auden and Christopher Isherwood were guests of Ambassador Clark-Kerr, on a trip to write their book *Journey to a War.* We introduced Rewi to them, and they tried to get the ambassador into a more active stance, helping Indusco. But the chief influence on Clark-Kerr was Ed and his new book, John Alexander told me years later.

Rewi had arrived in Hankow as chief adviser to the C.I.C. by July 1938, flanked by his Chinese engineers, known as the "Bailie boys" because Rewi and all of them had been influenced by the late Joseph Bailie, a missionary.

At the end of the first year, 1,284 industrial cooperatives were functioning with 15,625 members.

By September 1938, I had written my first book, *Inside Red China,** which had been taken off my typewriter to be secretly translated by Hu Yu-tze's underground National Salvation group, along with Ed's just published *Red Star Over China.* I had also written for Hu a book called *Lives of Revolution,* including some of the thirty-four autobiographies I had written down in Yenan, plus another book, *Women in China.*

I had been trying to get the Fourth Marines in Shanghai to carry out sanitation work in the YWCA refugee camps to cut down the cholera problem, and to influence the girl factory workers to go to the interior.

But my best energy and creative ability went into thinking up ways and means of getting the industrial cooperatives going, and pumping such energy into getting people to work on the project. The

---

*Published by Doubleday, Doran & Company, New York, 1939, it was a *succès d'estime.* The front-page review in the *New York Herald Tribune* said: "She has a gift for travel narrative, that gift for ballasting humorous and colorful anecdotal narrative with solid information, upon which the French came near having a monopoly and which is extremely rare among Anglo-Saxons." *Esquire* wrote: "*Inside Red China* has drama, color, excitement, and new material, which ought to make it a best seller."

gung ho project had a life of its own, an independent entity. No matter how many times it was given up as impossible and hopeless, it rose again like the giant Antaeus.

Ed wrote a foreword for my book *China Builds for Democracy* for the first Hong Kong edition, 1940:

> A little less than three years ago, Nym Wales . . . accompanied me to dine with a good friend in Shanghai. . . . Our host, a cooperative enthusiast, advanced the idea that the world should be organized on a cooperative basis as a means of making democracy work and of avoiding wars. Nym Wales did not agree with him . . . But a couple of days later, I heard Nym speaking very well of some of the cooperative ideas. . . . She was advocating refugee producers cooperatives in China; to put an end to soup kitchens and non-productive refugee camps. . . . She saw also in one brilliant glimpse into the future the tremendous social and economic importance which such a movement could ultimately acquire in building a better post-war China.
>
> "Industrial Cooperation," as realized today in hundreds of busy self-supporting workshops throughout China, was thus first of all the brain child of Nym Wales. It was she who first interested Rewi Alley in the possibilities of industrial cooperatives. . . . This fact is generously acknowledged by Mr. Alley (new chief technical advisor to Chinese Industrial Cooperatives). . . . Chiefly owing to Nym Wales' prodding, Alley and his Bailie engineers worked out the technical details of this scheme which has become such an important pattern of economic and social change in China. But for the soundness of her original concept, and the genius of her faith and enthusiasm, the movement might never have come into being at all. . . . her own role in the creative thinking which launched this great movement . . . inspired [others] . . . by the example of her own tireless and unselfish labor and devotion.

CHAPTER 41

Hong Kong

About June 1938, Ed went to Hong Kong from Shanghai, and thence to the interior to do newspaper work and gather material for his next book, *The Battle for Asia*. After the fall of Nanking in December 1937, the Chinese government had escaped to the interior, first to Hankow, then later to Chungking far up the Yangtze River. When Hankow in its turn fell to the Japanese in the fall of 1938, Ed returned to Hong Kong for a rest. I repacked the forty boxes to join him there for swimming and sun at the Repulse Bay Hotel.

Since 1936, we had both been stretching our efforts far beyond our capacities—or at least I had; Ed never quite reached that point. He was down to about 125 pounds from his usual 165, and I was still under 100 pounds. Yet we were still intoxicated with a sense of power and achievement, living on something beyond physical strength. We had our feet on bedrock—we were *right* and we knew it. We had been certain of that since the Sian Incident. And this certainty held a power to influence others.

It was another comic scene when my Butterfield & Swire coastal steamer docked in the Hong Kong harbor and Ed and John Leaning appeared, both emaciated and pale, but with triumphant burning eyes in the darkish circles.

"For the love of Pete, what has she got in the shape of luggage now?" Ed exclaimed.

My roomboy was carrying by the top handle a marvelous invention of mine—two bamboo bookcases or cabinets with priceless miniature trees anchored in the compartments.

"This maple changes color in the fall," I explained. "This grove of tiny bamboos is rare. This gnarled pine tree is ninety years old. It's a real collection. These are going in the taxi with me to the hotel."

How I loved miniature gardens and trees! My houses had always been full of them.

Ed grimaced. "Where's the luggage manifest? I told you to get rid of half those forty boxes from Peking."

"You can keep your cruel, destructive, dilettante claws off that," I announced. "From now on, I'll take care of them myself—and at my own expense, too. No more arguing."

I handed the manifest to a godown warehouseman waiting at my elbow, and took the receipt from him, bedding it down in my handbag emphatically.

(When we finally left China, I accompanied the forty boxes on the ship in December of 1940. I had developed an exaggerated sense of the value of files and information, because they had been so hard to find. We actually had risked our lives to gather some of these files.)

The few days at the Repulse Bay Hotel in all that humid heat were among the high points of our marriage. Both our books were on the way to becoming classics for the Chinese, influencing a whole generation of liberal and middle-way youth. Hu Yu-tze took them to Singapore and Indonesia, where they had the same effect on the young Chinese there. All the long, difficult years for Ed since 1929, and for me since 1931, seemed justified. We looked at each other with approval, even amusement, like starving refugees finding each other on a Himalayan lost horizon.

The two grand-dowager widows of the Kuomintang were in Hong Kong, Madame Sun Yat-sen and Madame Liao Chung-k'ai, with the latter's two children—Cynthia, and Liao Cheng-chih, whom I had first met in Yenan bedridden from dysentery. (When I later talked with Liao in 1972, he was in charge of the rapprochement with Japan. And the two widows were given the most honored posts for women in the 1949 government. Madame Sun was the first woman to be elected vice-chairman of any national government, and on her deathbed in 1982 was made honorary chairman of the People's Republic and joined the Communist party. I was one of a dozen foreigners on her funeral committee.)

I identified with Madame Sun Yat-sen, more or less, and I felt she was the one person in China who understood and appreciated my work and my situation. We both protected and clung to our femininity as our inner being and strength. It was in token of this that she gave me a turquoise pin and a dark-red Chinese-style dress, along with material for another dress. I had not seen Madame Sun since the bright, untarnished days of golden youth, overflowing with vitality and the mindless generosity of my early twenties. She looked with alarm at the frail, exhausted shadow I had become and advised me on my health. I had just turned thirty-one in September.

I have never lost this special identification with Madame Sun. All options were open to us both, yet we chose the lonely, thorny pilgrim's path. But Madame Sun had something I never had: the Chinese power of survival, by which you always reserve enough of your energy for your own survival and never go to extremes. Madame Sun never lost her sharp sense of humor or irony. She was a natural politician; she enjoyed the art. (I last saw her in 1978 at lunch in her palace in Peking's Forbidden City.)

Madame Sun's China Defence League was the center of left-wing activity in Hong Kong, raising funds for the Communist areas. Helping her was the attractive wife of the port doctor, Hilda Selwyn-Clarke, a Labour party socialist. Hilda had not learned the art of "dealing with the Chinese" and was being blocked at every turn, for mysterious reasons.

"How do you do it?" she asked me anxiously.

"Never break the surface. By not trying, all things are done," I said. "In China, you can never mend a piece of broken porcelain."

To our total astonishment, *Red Star Over China* was a best seller. Only one vote, that of Heywood Broun, kept it from being the Book-of-the-Month Club selection. What might we not have done with that $75,000! Also to the surprise of everyone, especially the Chinese, the American Communists attacked the book and banned it from their bookstores. Two or three sentences implied errors on the part of the Comintern. Ed never recovered from this picayune orthodoxy. It seemed too childish and petty to him perspiring on the front lines of history, while these academic quibblers had never lifted a finger to help history along. We did not then quite realize that this was an indirect attack on Mao Tse-tung, from whom Ed had got his information.

In the end I concluded that the Marxists of the Soviet Union following had never understood China and the Chinese at any time, certainly not since 1927.

We were both too busy learning and reporting on the facts of China to understand much of the big ideological impulses then sweeping over Europe. Only the year before, the old Bolsheviks in the Soviet Union were executing each other, and later the Comintern would be dissolved. The Munich Pact between the Soviets and Hitler would also be signed. In the back of our minds, which had been stretched by the immensities of China, was the premonition of the 20 million Russians who would die in World War II.

These were big things, dark things, like ancient dragons emerging out of prehistoric caves in an irrational world. When next I was in China, in 1972, the Soviet Union had a million troops on China's frontier and the two nations had been hostile since 1960, hardly even noticing that nuclear warfare threatened everyone alike.

On the beach at Repulse Bay, Ed kept staring at me.

"Why, your face has changed shape," he marveled. "You don't look like yourself. Don't you feel well? You have an ethereal look, as if you're not long for this world. Think I'll just take a picture of you."

"Why waste the money?" I brought up the old phrase he had always used when I stood pitifully beside some historic landmark, hoping vainly to have my presence there commemorated on film.

"Do you remember the photograph I took of you that day in Hangchow when we first met? The time the coolie looked up and said, 'Ding hao!' to me with his thumb up? That was when I decided I couldn't live without you and that you'd be a big success with the Chinese. Well, you have been, but what a price to pay!"

"What makes you think you look any better than I do?" I inquired. I proposed that the next thing on the agenda should be for both of us to take a long rest somewhere. There were too many demands in China.

"We'll go to the mountains in the Philippines," Ed decided. "I'm dog-tired. I've just let down this minute. I feel like a walking corpse. We can play golf in Baguio."

"I'm too tired even to pack up," I observed.

Yet every morning, from some unknown source of energy, I received enough new vitality to get through another day. Power and success flowed back to us both from the positive and negative conflicts of history.

CHAPTER 42

A Time for
Planting Mustard Seeds

America's golden child lazed pleasantly in tropical warmth, all ma-
ñana and cockfighting. No thought of harm from the Japanese clouded
the blue sky. Except among the one hundred thousand overseas Chinese, there was an undeclared pro-Japanese siesta in the Philippines,
while the poor peasants contributed to charity for Franco in all the
Catholic churches.

At the pier to meet our ship was the Filipino editor of the *Manila
Bulletin* and his wife, friends of J. B. Powell. I think his name was
Escoda. His wife told us we just had time to get dressed for a ball at
Malacañan Palace, in honor of some German royalty who were stop-
ping over with the Quezons. "I've brought Philippine costumes for you
both," she said.

"But my wife has brought forty boxes and twenty trees with her,"
Ed announced with distaste. "I'd like to leave all of it on the ship. And
she brought a big rug along."

The editor requested the luggage manifest, and introduced a
bodega warehouse agent who would take care of everything. But he
said, "You have to leave all trees and vegetables and flowers in quarantine at customs."

"What about husbands?" I asked. "Mine has distemper—the
worst kind."

At a small hotel, we were pinned into the costumes and were on
our way to a banquet within a few minutes, with leis of jasmine and
tuberoses around our necks. My diaphanous dress had a train. What
fun it was to get into a ballgown again after several austere years.

This was the first time Ed had been received as a big celebrity. He
loved it. He even allowed his photograph to be taken with his wife.
Oh, what delirious fun it was to dance a Viennese waltz again!

*　　*　　*

The Chinese had a large reception for us, which seemed surprising. We now discovered a new type of Chinese: the wealthy, self-made, overseas emigrant, who had started with nothing and gotten control of trade and part of the economy of underdeveloped places like the Philippines.

About 8.5 million overseas Chinese were listed as part of the population of China, nearly all (8.2 million) in Asia—mostly in Thailand, Malaya, the Dutch East Indies, and Hong Kong. The idea of Indusco, as productive self-help, struck a responsive chord with them. For generations, overseas Chinese had been sending help to their families at home, a bottomless pit of poverty. In the four years before 1940, over two billion Chinese dollars was sent to families in China. Relief money to China from the overseas Chinese ran to about seventy million Chinese dollars a month.

Sun Yat-sen had been financed chiefly by overseas Chinese, and the Kuomintang was strict that no aid should be funneled to China except through government channels, yet everyone knew that Indusco relief funds would disappear in such hostile and sticky hands. (It was nothing less than a minor revolution when the top Philippine Chinese and the bankers decided later, in 1939, to send several hundred thousand dollars to Indusco, and asked Ed to go to Hong Kong to form an international committee to handle funds. They insisted on having T. V. Soong on the committee, though he was the enemy of H. H. Kung, nominal head of Indusco. Ed detested committees, but he had no way out. The Philippine Chinese did not trust anyone else; nor did T. V. Soong—or even Rewi Alley. T. V. Soong sent his wife and children to Baguio for me to introduce around, and they attended Indusco meetings to raise funds.)

Just as a vacuum had existed in China before we came along with the Indusco idea, so was there one in the Philippines. We were drawn into it immediately, getting hardly a week of respite from endless demands.

Meantime, we had just missed Rewi in Hong Kong. He wrote from there: "You should get Peg up to Chengtu to put some guts into the student body that hangs out in those quarters. Suppose she does a tour via Yunnan to Chengtu, and you go to meet her . . ."

That I was working far beyond my capacities already was of no concern to Rewi, who never had any understanding of physical weakness, or any other kind.

On October 3, Rewi sent us the first Indusco badge and wrote: "If it ever gets going, it is going to take a lot of stopping."

He did not have enough money to get hold of two trucks and was using his own cash for emergencies. The only money Rewi had for unspecified purposes was what we were raising in the Philippines. These funds were sent to Rewi personally through Madame Sun Yat-sen and T. V. Soong. The Chinese Women's Relief Association sent the first $20,000 on October 27, 1938, about a month after our arrival in Manila, an advance on a $140,000 amount voted by them. (All monies are in Chinese currency, unless otherwise noted. We figured we could put a member to work in a cooperative for about U.S. $7 each. Exchange then was rising over the five-to-one ratio that had prevailed before the Japanese attack.)

On November 5, 1938, an additional $60,000 was sent, ear-marked by the overseas Chinese to start an Indusco center for the Communist New Fourth Army in Anhui; they were actively fighting Japan, so this was urgent. Ed had talked about Indusco with its famous commander, Han Ying, in Hankow.

We thought nothing of giving orders to poor Rewi to bridge the dormant civil-war situation and to move instantly across China to do it. We had the formula for the United Front to win the war, the only one. And it was working!

By November 7, Mrs. Dee C. Chuan's Chinese Women's Relief Association had sent $120,000 to Indusco. It was this contribution that saved Rewi and the project, and frightened the Chungking govern-ment into allowing Indusco to continue. It hit Chungking like a stroke of lightning, and the government was furious. They were wild with anxiety about this revolt in the Philippines. The consul general in Manila was changed (not without the approval of local Chinese), and two emissaries were sent to the islands to repair the damage we had done, mostly unintentionally.

Chungking insisted that no money be sent except through the government and Madame Chiang Kai-shek. This was complied with temporarily, and from January to March 1939, $209,106.90 was sent to Chungking.

We were only trying to save Indusco from infanticide, but no more brilliant a political stroke could have been devised than this re-cruiting of patriotic overseas Chinese. Philippine support saved the whole project, and Rewi as well, just at the strangulation point. It also made possible giving help to Mao Tse-tung's areas by way of Indusco, which was the most important influence in the long run.

There was a major contradiction involved in the support of Indusco by the overseas Chinese: Cooperatives in the Philippines could ruin Chinese business interests, which were tied in with American products. The Filipinos began to want cooperatives, chiefly of a consumer nature, principally as a means of taking retail trade out of the hands of the Chinese. I had to talk fast to explain that *producers'* cooperatives were of value to everybody, while the consumer-credit type of cooperative was not, especially where a front *against* Japanese goods was needed, not a channel for selling them.

The islands were within three years of being occupied by Japan. But Manila was asleep. (A year before Pearl Harbor, Ed and I warned our friends to leave, but they only laughed at us. At a luncheon with General Douglas MacArthur and the High Commissioner, Francis B. Sayre, both laughingly ridiculed the idea that Japan would ever attack the Philippines or Singapore. They had no idea that Japan was not controlled by its diplomats and civilians, but by a medieval, samurai, fanatical army of kamikazes. Ed and I had studied past history for the purpose of foreseeing the future, and we recognized that Japan had a war machine without brakes.)

Not until the Indusco committee was formed in the Philippines were the Chinese integrated socially into the Establishment there. The top Americans supported us, and the committee was the first ever to have a mixture of Filipinos, overseas Chinese, and Westerners, right, left, and middle. The overseas Chinese were grateful and amazed.

Most of the work and diplomacy was handled by Polly Babcock, former American YWCA secretary, married to W. R. Babcock, an American importer and exporter. In Baguio, Mr. and Mrs. E. E. Crouter formed the committee and supported all our projects and Rewi 100 percent, as the Babcocks did.

The dean of all the overseas Chinese in Southeast Asia at that time was Dee C. Chuan, known as "the lumber king," who as a penniless orphan had been adopted by a merchant. Though he was ill most of the time, we made friends with him and his wife. He decided to sponsor overseas help for the industrial cooperatives in China, and we thought to build them up in Fukien, where most of the Philippine Chinese came from and where their families were starving, as usual. Dee C. Chuan's health was not improved by all the new conflicts, and he died a few months after we first talked with him. His last act was to supply the overseas Chinese with money to get industrial cooperatives started in the Communist areas at the most strategic time, the absolute moment of truth. In point of fact, without his support the whole movement might have been strangled and turned into another rotten, sick boondoggle allowed by Chungking only for the purpose of begging foreign money.

His widow, Mrs. Dee C. Chuan, inherited her husband's mantle and wore it well. Though she was an old-fashioned Chinese woman, she continued to give as much support as possible.

It was very important for both Ed and me to have made friends with such Chinese as Dee C. Chuan. We thereby acquired, from direct personal experience, a broad knowledge of the varied factors in Chinese history that we could not otherwise have gained.

We loved Dee C. Chuan and also the other Chinese who went along with his ideas. Another old man was the dean of the overseas Chinese in Baguio: Lo Sin-hing had exactly the same favorable attitude toward our projects as Dee C. Chuan. Lo Sin-hing was an old Sun Yat-sen man on the liberal side, faced with attacks from every faction—as all of us were then in Indusco, including Madame Sun Yat-sen herself; she was under attack from the Communists for sponsoring Indusco instead of solely raising funds directly for their urgent medical needs. Our idea was to get medical self-help cooperatives going instead of depending on foreign aid.

I still remember the expression on the face of Lo Sin-hing in Baguio when he begged me to make a stand-up speech before his Chinese association to explain our projects. I refused, on the basis that I never, never made public speeches, only private ones. He could not believe such an attitude—the Chinese all love to make public talks at the least provocation. So I had to make the speech, through an interpreter. The committee thereupon voted to send $158.66 to our Pioneer Unit for the Communist guerrillas in Anhui. This was a real revolution for the cautious overseas Chinese.

Lo Sin-hing committed suicide not long after this, for various reasons, including the conflicting political problems of overseas Chinese. Such Chinese were men without a country, aliens in alien lands, yet still tied by the umbilical cord to their ancestral kinship groups. In the Philippines they were partners in American business against the Japanese. It was spark to tinder for two young Americans to come along with a real program to save China—and to give jobs to their immense clans of relatives there, endlessly begging for overseas money.

When I think back and wonder why I spent more than ten prime years of my life in keeping the Indusco work alive, without personal recompense, I remember people like Dee C. Chuan and Lo Sin-hing. These men showed what the Chinese were made of, the real raw material. When they got to the top, in command of millions, they did not become Fascists and vicious reactionaries. They were on the side of the *people*. All they needed was to be shown a way to help. Except for such men, Sun Yat-sen would never have been able to keep going. He himself was such a man. Mao Tse-tung and the popular leaders of China were also made of this good raw material, which was not contaminated by evil even in a lifetime of terrible struggle and effort.

When the individual has choices, when all options are open to him, and he chooses good for its own sake and rejects evil, that is a big commentary on the inherent quality of human nature. This is the quintessence of ethics: the cognition of right and wrong when presented with choice. It is usually an expression of spiritual power. Madame Sun Yat-sen was the first important individual of this kind that I knew. Teilhard de Chardin was another. David Yui was in this category. And many, many others . . . Well, not all that many.

Ed and I had a pet project in the back of our minds from the first: trying to raise money to get industrial cooperatives going under Mao Tse-tung, who had written to Ed welcoming them. But we could not tap any left-wing sources. These were the province of Madame Sun Yat-sen's China Defence League, concerned with helping the war effort, medical matters, and so on.

Rewi first "arrived in Yenan on Feb. 12th [1939], with the Indian Medical Unit," he wrote in a letter. "I saw Chairman Mao, as well as officials of the Border Govt. . . . They agreed . . . to have a branch office of the C.I.C. . . . The Sum of one thousand five hundred dollars was consequently left . . . Five caves are being dug and faced with lime. . . ."

Rewi Alley established the Chinese Industrial Cooperatives (C.I.C.) in Yenan, with the personal approval of Mao Tse-tung, who understood their value immediately. Rewi left his adopted son Mike in charge of a sum of $1,500, plus $20,000 loan capital. Within five months, fifteen projects were started.

The first society was the "Yenan Lamp Cooperative." It consisted

of seven members making lamp fuel of vegetable oil, and also man-
ufacturing an improved metal lamp. Cotton- and wool-weaving cooperatives came next, then units making shoes, bedding (in a cave at
Pao-an), and "chemicals" (soap, ink, chalk). At Pao-an a "medical"
cooperative gathered herbal medicines for dysentery, "brain tonic,"
etc., sixteen kinds in all. Yenan also soon had a flour mill, an oil press
(for castor beans), a pottery cooperative, and a transport cooperative.

All these began from scratch and spread throughout the Red
areas. In 1944, Mao Tse-tung wrote a pamphlet *On Cooperatives:* "A
revolution in productivity development has occurred . . . the system-
atic organization of the public and private laborers into cooperatives.
. . . This method can be extended to the various anti-Japanese bases.
. . . It will occupy an important place in the future economic history of
China. . . . This production theory on a mass basis has crushed the
various incorrect thoughts and views of the past."

In June 1939, Andrew T. Roy, a missionary, wrote about the
cooperatives he saw in Yenan "in caves," adding: "I am a pacifist . . .
but there are many things in the Northwest that should send a Christian to his knees."

In Chengtu, Roy and his friend J. Spencer Kennard later started a
Christian fund for sheepskin mitts for the children in Yenan. As soon
as I got a letter from Kennard on January 15, 1940, I sent it on to Polly
Babcock in Manila. She and a YWCA secretary, Anne Guthrie, immediately thought up the "Dear Friends Everywhere Cooperative
School and Workshop" for children in the Northwest Communist
area, and the same month sent over $17,000 to fund it.

This was a time for planting mustard seeds, no matter how stony
the ground. And I knew it. In April 1939, the committee Mrs. E. E.
Crouter and I had started sent about U.S. $200 toward the Interna-
tional Centers planned for the Communist areas, which would put
about thirty Chinese to work in a new cooperative. Natalie Crouter got
the Baguio gold-mine engineers concerned; they could see the value of
production. "One hundred Igorot women in a church group gave 28
pesos to take care of two refugees," Natalie wrote, as she mobilized the
town in tiny amounts, getting ninety-two individual contributions.

Dee C. Chuan and his Philippine Chinese sent $20,000 to start a
machine shop in Anhui. More important, the Philippine Association
for Industrial Cooperatives in Manila, our fund-raising committee,
voted to earmark one fourth of their regular funds for this Communist

unit. A total of over $100,000 had been sent to Rewi to get the Anhui center moving.

Rewi had to make the dangerous trip to the war front in the lower Yangtze Valley; and in July 1939, the first Anhui cooperatives were started. The Number 1 unit made uniforms at the rate of twenty a day. The second unit was for leather goods—belts, knapsacks, revolver holsters, and leather boots. By October 1939, fifteen cooperatives were started, including a printing shop and one for medical supplies.

An important thing was happening. Every peso collected was like a ruby mined. It meant a whole revolution in thinking on the part of these Americans and others, not only about relief work but also in showing goodwill toward the hard-struggling Communists in China. The same people who contributed to Loyalist Spain helped Indusco, but many others helped, too. Natalie Crouter's concern came from reading *Red Star Over China*, as did that of many others.

On January 7, 1941, the Anhui Incident occurred. Chiang Kai-shek's army attacked the civilian units of the Communist New Fourth Army numbering about eight thousand, killed the vice-commander, Han Ying, and made a prisoner of General Yeh Ting. Among the casualties were many of our industrial cooperatives, yet every Baguio peso had been productive—we had shown the way with pilot projects, and the guerrillas could now be on their own.

I had left China by ship a month earlier, in December 1940, but I found the news of the Anhui Incident alarming, if hardly astonishing. Chiang Kai-shek was still more interested in destroying the Reds than in resisting the Japanese occupation. In Chungking our old student friend Miss K'ung P'eng risked her life to get the facts to foreign newspapermen; so did her husband, Ch'iao Kuan-hua (later minister of foreign affairs). In Singapore and Java, our publisher, Hu Yu-tze, carrying along quantities of our two books, became the mentor of patriotic overseas Chinese like Tan Kah-kee, another fabulous self-made millionaire. Tan made a trip to China in 1940 to promote the United Front. The ancestral lands and families of these overseas Chinese (mostly from Fukien and Kwangtung) were being ravaged now by the Japanese occupation, and they wanted resistance, not civil war.

After Ed and I had both left (Ed in February 1941), the Chungking government launched a big propaganda tour of overseas Chinese in the Philippines, Singapore, Java, and elsewhere "to combat the Communist propaganda that had made headway there," they said.

This "Communist" propaganda was being carried out by the top millionaires, bankers, and Chamber of Commerce Chinese in East Asia! But Chungking depended on them for much of its ready cash—which was generally put into use only by those who could first put it into their pockets.

By 1941, Rewi had 1,800 workshops functioning, and hundreds more were springing up in both the Red and non-Red regions. This is a great parable of the mustard seed. Wherever one fell, there did it grow into a field—mostly in the desperate, Japanese-threatened Communist areas, where Indusco was not only ideal but the only possible way to get into production.

In 1944, Rewi was forced out of his post by the reactionaries, but allowed to remain unofficially as field secretary of the American Committee in Aid of Chinese Industrial Cooperatives in New York, where we raised over 3.5 million American dollars for the work by the time we closed down in 1951. (I was vice-chairman then.)

In 1947, the civil war was renewed in China. Our committee split three ways, with two opposite sides trying to destroy Rewi, and others not even aware they were doing so—this, at a time when our Indusco people were being arrested in Sandan by the right-wing elements, and one organizer even buried alive.

For a long time I could hardly write about the Indusco denouement or even think about it. After 1949, all trace of good American influence was being obliterated in China. Rewi was translating T'ang poetry in Peking. I had been struck to earth for daring to challenge the impossible. Indusco seemed a parable of the middle way, all quicksand through a Slough of Despond. I resented the sacrifice of my time, my youth, my health, my own work.

Yet history, like nature, has its own economy, its own balancing of forces in the final accounting. Nothing can be lost, except to awareness. The project had been impossible from the first, yet we had accomplished the impossible. Everything Rewi did was impossible, yet he accomplished it.

Much of the magic was the result of *Red Star Over China*, which garnered so much valuable publicity and made so many converts, while I did the legwork and manual labor involved in managing the difficult political situation and raising funds, and Rewi turned those funds into going concerns in the field. The contradictions were so myriad that Indusco was actually nothing but a meeting point, where the negative became the positive. The name Snow was detested in Chungking, and we had tried to keep our role in the work private; yet nobody else could save the situation. We were blamed for "too much publicity," especially about Rewi—but publicity was essential to starting Indusco, and to saving it.

The gung ho industrial cooperative idea was supported by almost every American in China then, and President Franklin D. Roosevelt and his advisers were sympathetic. But no official American assistance was given, except for pointedly placing Eleanor Roosevelt on the Board of Sponsors in 1940. Later, it was *too* late. The civil war was renewed in 1947.

Already, in 1944, Mao Tse-tung had brought his immense influence to bear in favor of producers' cooperatives, not only as emergency stopgap measures in wartime—he supported those from the first—but in principle to build up village prosperity and get labor power organized at long last.

By 1959, the whole of China had industrial cooperatives in city and country. Then the system was changed to big communes, which owned the industries that gave wages by work points instead of the workers' holding shares. However, these communes were not feasible in the cities, where "collectives" were organized from the grass roots in the neighborhoods, largely by housewives and other women. These collectives were close cousins of our old gung ho cooperatives, though not using the name or our old constitution and by-laws.

When I returned to China in 1972 and 1973, it was very thrilling to see these small industries, including the "backyard furnaces," for which we had once raised money in the Philippines. The gung ho industrial cooperatives had served as the bridge between the preindustrial, ancient village society and economy and the new "commune" concept advocated by Mao Tse-tung. Both land reform and cooperatives may have been necessary to break up the powerful cohesion of the Chinese kinship system of nepotism and local autonomy, to make change possible in the most changeless society on the face of this turbulent earth.

CHAPTER 43

Farewell to Asia

The gung ho friends had been coming and going, but not until 1940 did we all join together for our first, and last, reunion. It was held at the beautiful Worcester Cottage, which we rented in Baguio, with its mountain view and two orchid houses.

Jim Bertram was lecturing to raise money for Madame Sun Yat-sen.

Evans Carlson had resigned his commission and was getting out his book *Twin Stars of China*. He was bursting over with his "ethical indoctrination" concept, a combination of Protestant self-sacrifice and gung ho Rewi Alley-ism, plus Chu Teh-ism for army morale and spirit. During World War II, Evans would put the term *gung ho* into the English language by indoctrinating his Carlson's Raiders in this recondite philosophy. Evans, a disciple of *Red Star Over China* and a special friend of President Roosevelt, became for many people the symbol of the best in American civilization. He was a leader and he had a following.

Rewi Alley had come out of his bouts of malaria and typhoid earned in the line of duty, and was functioning on all twelve cylinders, a one-man revolution in China stirring up fundamental change wherever his sturdy, red-haired legs carried him. He was taking the industrial revolution to interior China for the first time—changing the mode of production to the cooperative system and setting up pilot projects for the future.

Edgar Snow was finishing his fourth book, *The Battle for Asia*, and his silent, self-effacing secretary, Kuo Ta, had come from China to help in this as he had helped with *Red Star Over China*. (In the 1980s, Kuo Ta wrote to me now and then. He was in Peking working on the first English-language newspaper in mainland China since 1949, the *China Daily*, published chiefly for students of English.) Ed was overflowing with a sense of achievement, a celebrity now, and enjoying his life and work, but he was reaching a point of exhaustion from several years of overwork and tension combined with real wartime malnutrition.

Instead of resting, as I had intended to do in the Philippines, I had written two books and made a dent in another, as well as working constantly on the Indusco program. I still weighed only 101 pounds. All during the years since we had left the States, neither of us had eaten any uncooked food, except for fruit that could be peeled, to avoid dysentery. We were starving for vitamins and desperate for total rest.

Our first priority was to escape from the East before Japan made us prisoners of war. Women and children were ordered evacuated late in 1940. It was heartbreaking not to be able to go home by way of Europe, as we had planned since 1932, but Europe had been at war since 1939. Ed could go, as an accredited war correspondent, and the *New York Herald Tribune* offered him a job. Naturally I urged him to take it. I noticed he seemed a little uneasy about my enthusiasm!

In Shanghai in December, I said farewell on shipboard to Ed and J. B. Powell, who was wearing a bulletproof vest but refused to leave that doomed city. Ed was undecided but in good spirits.

"Of course, it's life and death for you to get to Europe," I said. "You'll always regret it if you don't—and so will I."

"I suspect you of preferring to travel with those forty boxes than with your lawful wedded husband," Ed grumbled. "Of course, I can always take the Pan American clipper if I don't go by way of Europe." That was what he secretly wanted: to fly home, even at the fierce price.

The one thing Ed had prized all his life was to be free, not to be tied down. No human being was ever more free than he was, always, with all the advantages of a home and a wife and scarcely any of the drawbacks. He had taken it for granted. Now, as he watched the President liner carrying his wife out of sight on the Whangpoo River, going *home* without him, for the first time in his life Ed began to feel alone.

I had told Ed that I was going to rest all the way across the Pacific, and that when I got to California I was going to take an absolute nutrition and rest cure. He needed one, too, but I was even worse off.

In San Francisco, Pat Tobin, my eighteen-year-old bellhop on the ship, took care of all those forty boxes at the pier and put them in storage for me. (Pat later became a power in the International Longshoreman's Union.) It was Christmastime. I went to Carmel to stay with a friend awhile. A doctor there told me I needed a diet sanitarium, but I found them much too costly.

In Carmel I began to get desperate (and expensive) telephone calls, first from Manila, then from Honolulu: "Something's wrong with me. I'm sick," Ed complained. "I really am. I'm depressed and nervous and I can't make decisions. I don't think I want to go to Europe. I'm worried about you, too. I wonder if you feel neglected—do you?"

"No, I don't, and I wish you'd stop drinking and wasting money on telephone calls. Why don't you send airmail letters instead?"

I did not realize anything was really wrong with him until he began saying, "I'm jumpy. My health has been destroyed. I'm nothing but a big failure. We've wasted all my savings. I'm already homesick for China, and I haven't left yet."

"You're not a failure—you're a big celebrity," I kept reassuring him. "What you need is to come home by air and then get your feet back on the ground again. You have no idea what a great big beautiful country this is. I love every inch of it. Everybody I see is dying to meet you. You'll have a grand time right off."

That was what he wanted—for me to make the decision that he should come home by clipper and give up the trip by way of Europe.

More than one thing was happening. On January 7, 1941, came the Anhui Incident, when some of our civilian Indusco personnel were killed. Chiang Kai-shek was back again in the old civil-war stance—meaningless massacres with no alternatives. In these few months before Pearl Harbor, there was again a living death in Kuomintang China, with only one bright hope anywhere: our industrial cooperatives and Rewi Alley, so valiantly struggling in a totally impossible situation—and succeeding.

It was an old folk adage in China that nothing whatsoever could happen except by force—by guns and killing. No change was possible except by this primitive method. We had been trying to build a united front not for its own sake, but because so many important factors, including American influence, were involved for the future, internationally as well as in China. We had set up a viable program for American policy to support, and we were certain it was *dead right*. We had even printed a petition to President Roosevelt to earmark $50 million in aid to China for the industrial cooperatives—which could easily have changed history.

This petition was burning a hole in my luggage, and both Ed and Evans were "maximum gung ho" about the idea. We needed some well-known Hollywood names, and here I was in California. But though I felt too exhausted to organize a committee, the gung ho mystique takes no account of such personal feelings. Ed and I had no intention of having this project end up in failure, not with a Roosevelt as President.

Ed especially resented all the overwork and responsibility I had assumed beyond reason, common sense, and our pocketbook. We had both gone beyond our capacities, living on natural adrenaline and the momentum of a second wind. Only the intoxication of constant, unexpected success had kept this gung ho team going at high speed. Now the powerful cohesion brought about by isolation in alien lands was broken. We were on opposite sides of the Pacific Ocean. We were truly separated for the first time. We couldn't be separated when we were in Asia; we carried the living tie intact wherever we happened to be. Distance caused it to grow stronger, not weaker, because it thrived on danger and reunion.

Ed's peculiar aberration did not last long. In February 1941, we met at an old hotel in Hollywood on Sunset Boulevard (was it the Garden of Allah?). Ten minutes later, Ed had forgotten all his nightmares and specters. We were off looking at used-car lots, and we put a down payment on a Packard. Every few minutes, it seemed, we carried big packages from the supermarkets to our cottage—everything fresh, everything uncooked. Lettuce! We had not even tasted lettuce for ten years!

Ed found himself a big celebrity in Hollywood, and he enjoyed it. I was the Number 2 celebrity, to my surprise. A photographer, J. A. Piver, asked to photograph me and put the result in his window, since it "looked like Joan Bennett."

Hollywood was the reflection of the whole country then, in its own prime. It was also left-wing anti-Fascist democratic and full of self-help philosophy. We arrived just at the one point when we were most needed—as real-life and also symbolic representatives of whatever it was we stood for. For example, director Lewis Milestone had recently ventured into the Chinese civil war on the side of the "poor people" with *The General Died at Dawn*; Gary Cooper played the American do-gooder against warlords and Madeleine Carroll (one of Ed's favorite stars) was the heroine. Milestone was an admirer of *Red Star Over China*, along with John Ford and others then at their professional peak.

The committee that was organized in Hollywood for the petition to earmark $50 million for Indusco had John Garfield and Lin Yutang as co-chairmen, and some of the best movie people as sponsors. Evans had told the President and Mrs. Roosevelt about our gung ho project, and Eleanor Roosevelt had been a sponsor on the American Committee to Aid Chinese Industrial Cooperatives since 1940.

Donald Ogden Stewart and his wife, Ella Winter, widow of Lincoln Steffens, hailed us with delight; he found my Hollywood organizing hilarious, especially my talks with Sam Goldwyn. We met Irwin Shaw, and other screenwriters who later were victims of McCarthyism for a while. Michael Blankfort loved my book *Song of Ariran*, and later wrote the biography of Evans Carlson called *The Big Yankee*. *Gung Ho!*, the 1943 movie about Evans, with Randolph Scott in perfect casting, was a classic and is still revived.

Ed actually gained thirty pounds in a month—partly at an Arizona dude ranch, where we hid to forget about China and the world long enough to recuperate. The owner of the dude ranch said she had never seen such devotion on the part of a husband.

"I'm going to put both our names on all my books from now on," Ed announced virtuously. "I should have done that from the first." Even if I had nothing to do with them, he said, he would put my name on as co-author. It would be a new kind of authorship: "I'm the writer and you contribute to the content as you always have."

Of course I would not allow such a thing—which he knew. I attributed his overcompensation to drinking too much orange juice!

We found a little 1752 house in Connecticut—just big enough to hide those forty boxes in the basement. I moved an old corncrib to our lot for Ed to use as his private studio. He simply loved it. When I came back from a trip to New York, I found he had bought another one and moved it alongside. Here he wrote three books in between his travels.

We spent time in New York and Washington during the winters. The New Dealers received us with open arms and demanded talks, reports, and more books. We filled a unique niche, as we had in China. We were independent and had never been Communists, of course, and that was exactly what was needed in the years before McCarthy. But that was just what the McCarthyists wanted to destroy—the influence of anyone who had total credibility on the left.

All during World War II, I had constant worries. Ed was usually overseas in the midst of the war, as correspondent for *The Saturday Evening Post*. Evans Carlson was at the front during the Pacific islands campaign (and died in 1947 as the result of his war wounds and stress). All three of my brothers were in uniform, and two died from war-related illness, while the other was a fighter pilot with the Pacific advance squadrons. In China, Rewi was constantly in danger—and in the end some of his gung ho personnel were arrested and some killed. Worst of all, Jim Bertram was a prisoner of war; we knew nothing of him at all until 1945, when the Americans took him off the waterfront in Japan, where he had been treated like a coolie on the docks.

With his objectivity and his ability to compartmentalize, Ed could keep China in his China department, but I was not able to extricate myself until 1951, after the split in the Indusco Committee, on which I was the last vice-chairman. (I revived it in 1981.)

Ed was liberated from the past—not entirely—but more so than I. Not until Ed's death in 1972 and my return visit to China in 1972–1973 was I able to rewrite or even to reread this old manuscript, begun so many years ago. It meant reliving every page, and remembering what little compensation had come my way for all the long years of struggle and sacrifice.

I think of those two young people in their twenties—how brave they were, how little they asked of anyone, even of each other, how much they gave and without even mentioning it, not even to each other. It was an experience worthy of a better ending than the divorce in 1949, yet the end was implicit in it. What is a good play without pathos, without tragedy, without conflict, without the struggle between good and evil?

And the end is not yet. In 1961, Section 601 of the Foreign Assistance Act made cooperatives official United States policy, twenty years after we had tried so hard for this in 1941. Now, not only India but Africa and all pre-industrial nations are beginning to build a bridge to the future. And it is, out of necessity, unlike any bridge ever built before. But the blueprint being used—industrial cooperatives coexisting with Big Industry—is the one Indusco created in China.

Epilogue

In 1978, at the age of seventy-two, I took a film crew to China, with Tim Considine as producer and still photographer, Eric Saarinen as cameraman, and Nelson Stoll as sound man. Almost every day for six weeks I was interviewed by Tim on the Snow experience of the 1930s. All during the 1978 trip, I was surprised and delighted to bridge the generation gap with the crew, who were not only half my age but dyed-in-the-sunshine Californians of the movie world.

I was astounded to find that the young, experienced but exhausted film crew shared my energizing exhilaration on our final project: a visit to Pao-an. It was only the sixth time that foreigners had ever appeared in this remote village of cave dwellers not far from the end of the Great Wall of China. Edgar Snow had been the second foreigner ever in Pao-an. Through his books, Ed had become known in the Northwest as their "Lafayette," and now I was received like a Second Coming, even forty-one years afterward.

In Pao-an we were right at the grass roots of revolution in China, among the real people, the cave dwellings where life was all but Neolithic, yet minds were as advanced as anywhere, wise in the ways of survival at least. Pao-an had already established a Communist party and government before Mao arrived.

As I walked out of Mao Tse-tung's cave into the clear, intoxicating air, my interpreter said, "The widow of a Red Army veteran has asked if she can shake your hand. A veteran and his wife also want to shake your hand and to invite you to have a bowl of tea in their cave house nearby."

I looked across a little ravine and saw the three waiting with welcoming smiles on the hillside. The beautiful white-haired widow had her feet still bound in bandages, and she was wearing old-fashioned cotton peasant pants fastened at the ankle. The grizzled, wrinkled veteran had on his army uniform.

In a flash I felt a line of communication stretching back forty-seven years to the first time I ever saw a woman with bound feet. When

328

I shook hands with the bound-footed widow, we were both aware of the freemasonry engendered. It crossed the Pacific Ocean and had enough tradition to spare for the future—for the special Chinese-American relation that has already been built up with so much bravery, sacrifice, and enterprise over the generations.

In my opinion, capitalism is now and always has been impossible in China. For example, any concept of individualism in the Western sense is incomprehensible to any Chinese, and impossible in a nation of a billion people. That is one reason why it was comparatively so easy for China to move into "socialism," instead of any other system. China moved from the kinship-clan system into another system for group survival, never having known an individualist phase.

China is still "feeling the way," I was told. It is still experimenting and still in transformation, out of necessity if not choice. It could develop into a mixed economy of socialism, but never into the other historical Western systems.

The big question is, just how progressive has China become, especially in the villages? Obviously, development occurs on many different levels and phases. A powerful nation without Western ethics or socialist ethics would confront the rest of the world with difficult problems, especially in the nuclear age. It is very much in the future interest of the rest of the world, and especially of the people of the United States, that China should continue on the road to socialism and its historical high ethics as progressively as possible. There is no alternative—none but the unthinkable.

Among sixty others, I was nominated for the Nobel Prize for Peace in 1981, and renominated in 1982. The nomination was not for any particular achievement, but for the potential that my ideas and world view hold for peace and progress in the world. I have been surprised to find that year by year our gung ho idea is becoming more and more relevant and feasible, notably for the developing nations and most of all because of the urgent need to build a bridge between them and the industrial powers and areas.

In 1972, I visited some of the fifty thousand flourishing industrial cooperatives in India, started in 1942 by Jawaharlal Nehru using my book *China Builds for Democracy* as a textbook. Prime Minister Indira Gandhi told me how favorably disposed she was to them. I considered the writing of *China Builds for Democracy* worthwhile even if only half a dozen people read it—and so they did: President and Mrs. Franklin D. Roosevelt, Nehru and Gandhi (both of whom Ed knew), and the chief people involved in aid to China in the United States and Britain. Only Gandhi refused to support the Indusco idea.

By the 1980s, the destabilization and chaos in emerging countries made our Indusco idea urgent, and desirable diplomatically as well as economically, in such areas as Central America. In 1981 I revived our old American Committee for Industrial Cooperatives. We tried to get Congress to reactivate Section 601 of the Foreign Assistance Act of 1961, which had made cooperatives official United States policy. The Nairobi Conference in 1981 advocated renewable energy projects, but failed to mention the cooperative method of starting such industries, and the Cancun Conference that year ended in total deadlock and failure. This proved that a golden opportunity had opened up for our gung ho Indusco producer cooperatives. Neither the United States nor the Soviet Union could rationally object to this method of industrialization, a compromise least harmful to both systems, co-existing with capitalism, socialism, feudalism, clan-tribalism, or whatever.

In 1982, upon request of some of the cooperative's founders like Rewi Alley, Lu Kuang-mien, and S. T. Meng, the Peking government began to discuss giving permission to revive our Chinese Industrial Cooperatives of the 1938 type. Similar cooperatives had been established since 1979 as part of the government employment program for jobless youth. And in the spring of 1983, that permission was granted.

I am for the Human Achievement, for space exploration, invention, and originality. I am for pushing back the frontiers of knowledge ever so little and have tried to do so myself. I am for healthy organic living and thinking, for the balance of nature, including the human reasoning power. I am for maximum development of the individual, and I know this is possible in the United States, where we have all the resources to build the highest possible type of future civilization.

Like the old Chinese, I worship my ancestors, wear baggy pants, and drink tea.

I love tiger cats, my little 1752 house, Robert Redford, Bruce Jenner, my old IBM typewriter, the *Encyclopedia Britannica*, British movies on public television, fluffy blouses, the nuclear family, the English language as it used to be, trains, the Parthenon, American history (up to 1960), pizza, Coca-Cola, tuna fish sandwiches on rye, Westminster Cathedral, Delphi . . . and Pao-an.

GLOSSARY

AMAH   a female servant

BANNERMAN   a Manchu or Mongol belonging to one of the primary divisions of the Manchu dynasty army, each having a distinctive banner

CHÜN TZǓ   perfect gentleman

COMPRADOR   a Chinese national employed as an agent by, or associated with, a foreign business or diplomatic service, to take charge of Chinese affairs

CUMSHA   a gratuity, or a reward for service

DING HAO   an expression of approval, roughly translatable as "Wow!"

FENG-SHUI   wind-water relationship in geomancy or fortune-telling

GODOWN   warehouse

HAO, HAO TI-HEN   good, very good

HSIAO KUEI   literally "little devil"; the term applied to the boy orderlies of the Red armies

HSIEN   a land division comparable to a county

HSIEH-YI   a style of brushstroke in Chinese art

HUTUNG   lane

K'ANG   a raised sleeping platform of brick

KE-MING   the changing of fate; revolution

LAO PAI HSING   literally "old hundred names" or clans; the common people

LATHI   a policeman's heavy stick (an Indian term)

LATZUCHI   a dish of chicken and peppers

LI   a variable unit of distance, but roughly one third of a mile

MAFOO   groom or animal handler

MAN-T'OU   boiled biscuits

MEI-YU-FADTZE, AIYEH   phrase meaning "no way, ah"

MEX.   literally a Mexican dollar, used to differentiate between the local currency and American dollars or gold

MING   destiny or fate

MO-TENG   modern

P'AI-CHANG   sergeant

PAI K'ERH   a Chinese wine

P'AILOU   an elaborate archway, usually erected to honor someone

PA-KUA   the Eight Principles or diagrams for fortune-telling

P'ENG   awning

PONG   a group of gangsters

SYCEE   silver ingot

TAIPAN   an important merchant, usually head of a foreign business establishment

TAO-TIEH   ogre

TSU   clan

T'U-HAO   evil landlord

TU-LOTSKY-P'AI   Trotskyist

T'U-TI   apprentice

WU WEI   philosophy of Lao Tzu, meaning "do nothing" or "let nature take its course"

YANG-CHÊ, LAI, LAI   ricksha, come, come

YIN-YANG   female-male, a concept of opposites underlying everything in the universe, such as dark-light

KEY TO PINYIN SPELLING

In the first column are the romanized spellings of the Wade-Giles system, as they appear in the book. In the second column are the equivalents in *pinyin*, the system now in use in most Western countries. Where spellings remain the same in both systems (as with most F's, L's, M's, N's, W's), they are not included here. Huang Hua, for instance, remains Huang Hua.

W-G	PINYIN	W-G	PINYIN
cha	zha	jo	ruo
ch'a	cha	juo	ruo
che	zhe	ju	ru
ch'e	che	jun	run
chi	ji	jung	rong
ch'i	qi	ka	ga
chiang	jiang	k'a	ka
ch'iang	qiang	ke, ko	ge
chien	jian	k'e, k'o	ke
ch'ien	qian	ku	gu
chih	zhi	k'u	ku
ch'ih	chi	kuei	gui
cho	zhuo	k'uei	kui
ch'o	chuo	kung	gong
chou	zhou	k'ung	kong
ch'ou	chou	lieh	lie
chu	zhu	lien	lian
ch'u	chu	lo	luo
chung	zhong	lün	lun
ch'ung	chong	lung	long
chü	ju	mieh	mie
ch'ü	qu	mien	mian
erh	er	nieh	nie
hsi	xi	nien	nian
hsieh	xie	nung	nong
hsien	xian	nüeh	nüe
hsü	xu	o	e
hsüeh	xue	pa	ba
i, yi	yi	p'a	pa
jan	ran	pieh	bie
jih	ri	p'ieh	pie

W-G	PINYIN	W-G	PINYIN
pien	bian	ts'e	ce
p'ien	pian	tso	zuo
po	bo	ts'o	cuo
p'o	po	tsou	zou
pu	bu	ts'ou	cou
p'u	pu	tsu	zu
shih	shi	ts'u	cu
so	suo	tsung	zong
ssu, szu	si	ts'ung	cong
ta	da	tu	du
t'a	ta	t'u	tu
tao	dao	tung	dong
t'ao	tau	t'ung	tong
tieh	die	tzu	zi
t'ieh	tie	tz'u	ci
tien	dian	yeh	ye
t'ien	tian	yen	yan
to	duo	yu	you
t'o	tuo	yung	yong
tsa	za	yü	yu
t'sa	ca	yüeh	yue
tse	ze		

Equivalents of some of the well-known names of people and places:

WADE-GILES	PINYIN
Chang Hsueh-liang	Zhang Xueliang
Chou En-lai	Zhou Enlai
Chu Teh	Zhu De
Lin Piao	Lin Biao
Lin Po-chu	Lin Boqu
Liu Shao-chi	Liu Shaoqi
Lu Hsun	Lu Xun
Lu Ting-yi	Lu Dingyi
Mao Tse-tung	Mao Zedong
P'eng Teh-huai	Peng Dehuai
Teng Hsiao-ping	Deng Xiaoping
Yeh Chien-ying	Ye Jianying
Canton, Kwangchow	Guangzhou
Chungking	Chongqing

WADE-GILES	PINYIN
Fukien	Fujian
Hangchow	Hangzhou
Kwangsi	Guangxi
Kwangtung	Guangdong
Nanking	Nanjing
Pao-an	(now called Chitan)
Peking	Beijing
Shansi	Shanxi
Shensi	Shaanxi
Sian	Xi'an
Soochow	Suzhou
Swatow	(now called Shantou)
Tientsin	Tianjin
Tsinan	Jinan
Yangtze River	(now called Changjiang River)
Yenan	Yan'an

Index

337

"Old Peking" (Helen Snow), 154

Oliver, Frank, 160, 161

"On Contradiction" (Mao Tse-tung
    lecture), 269

On Cooperatives (Mao Tse-tung), 318

"On the New Democracy" (Mao Tse-
    tung), 174

Opium, 69

Outline of History (Wells), 75

Ouyang, Captain, 237–238, 242, 243,
    246, 254, 287

P

Pai Chung-hsi, 180–181

Pa-kua, 71, 72

Pao-an, 328, 330

Paramount News, 52

Pater, Alan F., 154n

Paul VI, Pope, 145

Peita University, 167

Peking, 85–97

    Americans in (1933), 95, 97–99

    history of, 89

    Japanese occupation of, 293

    living conditions for foreigners in,
        92–93, 95–97

    servant system in, 107–110, 190

    student movement in, 137, 154–164,
        170–173, 206–207

Peking Student Union, 166, 179

P'eng Teh-huai, 202, 214, 257, 258–
    259

Philippine Association for Industrial
    Cooperatives, 318

Philippines, financial aid for Indusco
    from, 313–317

Ping Hsin, 154

Po I-po, 180

Po Ku, 260

Porter, Lucius, 135

Powell, J. B., 19, 21–22, 29, 31, 32,
    56, 64, 65–66, 68, 162, 171,
    204, 224, 299–300, 323

    Chiang Kai-shek and, 67

industrial cooperatives and, 302–306

Japan and, 64, 148

Pravda, 212

Pre-industrial nations (emerging nations)

    industrial cooperatives and, 330

    Maoism and, 271

President Lincoln, S.S., 19, 20–21, 299

Price, Betty, 136, 141, 176, 185, 217,
    227

Price, Frank, 226

Price, Harry, 135, 136, 141, 185, 217,
    222, 227

Protestantism, failure in China of, 144

Pruitt, Ida, 222, 301

R

Random House, 124

Random Notes on Red China (Edgar
    Snow), 213

Reader's Digest, 123, 302n

Red Army, 240

    Chang Hsueh-liang and, 181, 193,
        210

    Chiang Kai-shek and, 179, 180–181,
        193, 244

        Sian incident, 210, 212, 213–214

    esprit de corps of, 279

    language problem of, 277

    Long March and, 164, 173, 179,
        194, 257

    Mao Tse-tung and, 77

    respect for private property of, 285

    Snow (Edgar) and, 180–183, 184,
        189, 193

        life endangered because of visit to,
            239, 255

        published articles about, 200–203

    Snow (Helen) and, 275–279, 282–
        286

        visits to, 189–196, 231, 232, 234,
            253–264

Red Army Daily, 213

Red Dust (Helen Snow), *see Chinese
    Communists, The* (Helen Snow)

Red Scourge, The (pamphlet), 142